AF334117

Thomas Hoccleve

EXETER MEDIEVAL TEXTS AND STUDIES

Series Editors: Vincent Gillespie and Richard Dance

Founded by M.J. Swanton and later co-edited by Marion Glasscoe

Thomas Hoccleve

Religious Reform, Transnational Poetics, and the Invention of Chaucer

Sebastian J. Langdell

LIVERPOOL UNIVERSITY PRESS

First published 2018 by
Liverpool University Press
4 Cambridge Street
Liverpool
L69 7ZU

British Library Cataloguing-in-Publication data
A British Library CIP record is available

ISBN 978-1-78694-129-9

Typeset by Carnegie Book Production, Lancaster
Printed and bound in Poland by BooksFactory.co.uk

Contents

Abbreviations

EETS	Early English Text Society (1864–)
	O.S. Original Series (1864–)
	E.S. Extra Series (1867–1920)
	S.S. Supplementary Series (1970–)
ELH	*English Literary History*
ELN	*English Language Notes*
f., ff.	folio, folios
LGW	*Legend of Good Women*
MÆ	*Medium Ævum*
NML	*New Medieval Literatures*
RES	*Review of English Studies*
SAC	*Studies in the Age of Chaucer*
YLS	*Yearbook of Langland Studies*

Acknowledgments

First, I would like to thank Vincent Gillespie, who helped launch this project, and who offered expert guidance and support during the years spent writing and revising. I have benefited greatly from his generosity, his ability to suggest new and illuminating directions for my research, his encouragement, and his enduring faith in my work. I also owe a debt of gratitude to David Lawton and Bernard O'Donoghue, who served as early readers of this project, and offered words of encouragement and support at a pivotal phase in its development.

The initial research for this project was funded by an Oxford University Clarendon Fund Scholarship and a St Edmund Hall Humanities Fellowship. I would like to express my deep gratitude to both organizations for their generous support.

Portions of the chapters took shape at academic conferences and seminars, and I am grateful to those audience members and seminar participants who offered suggestions, asked questions, and contributed information to my papers at the International Congress on Medieval Studies at Western Michigan University, Kalamazoo (2011); the Biennial Congress of the New Chaucer Society in Portland, Oregon (2012) and Reykjavik, Iceland (2014); and the Oxford University Medieval English Research Seminar (2012). I am also grateful to the New Chaucer Society Howard Scholarship Fund, St Edmund Hall, and the Oxford English Faculty Meyerstein Research Fund for helping to fund my travel to these conferences.

The following people have also helped to guide my research, and have invigorated this study with valuable insights, comments, and suggestions: Helen Barr, K.P. Clarke, Susanna Fein, Shannon Gayk, Ralph Hanna III, Nicholas Havely, Kathryn Kerby-Fulton, Philip Knox, Robert Meyer-Lee, Jenni Nuttall, Nicholas Perkins, Steven Rozenski, David Rundle, Daniel Wakelin, Nicholas Watson, and David Watt. I am also grateful to the editors of *Medium Ævum* for their assistance in the development of Chapter

1 of this study, which was published in that journal in an earlier form. And I am grateful to the editors and anonymous readers at *New Medieval Literatures* (Boydell & Brewer), who assisted in the development of Chapter 3, which was published in that journal in an earlier form.

I also wish to thank the following libraries for granting me permission to use images from their collections in this study: the British Library in London (Figures 1, 3, 5, 6); the Huntington Library in San Marino, California (Figure 2); and the Bodleian Library in Oxford (Figure 8). I am also grateful to the National Archives (UK), Wiley-Blackwell, and the New Chaucer Society for permission to print Figures 4, 9, and 10, respectively.

I was first introduced to Hoccleve as an undergraduate, studying abroad at St Edmund Hall, Oxford, and reading medieval literature with Jane Griffiths. I thank her heartily for upending my expectations of what the period held – and for introducing me to Hoccleve, Lydgate, Skelton, and others. This book would not exist without her expert teaching, her ability to match content to individual, and her willingness to share her expertise and her avenues of intellectual pursuit.

I am also delighted to thank the editors, series editors, and anonymous readers for the Exeter Medieval Texts and Studies Series at Liverpool University Press. Thank you very much for your commitment to this project, for your generous support, and for guiding this project in its final stages. Thank you in particular to Jenny Howard for her expert advice, responsiveness, and general helpfulness.

I have been deeply fortunate to call Vassar College my academic home as this book has progressed through the stages of publication. I would like to thank my Vassar colleagues for their support and camaraderie during this period – in particular: Mark Amodio, Paul Russell, Paul Kane, Heesok Chang, Ami Kumar, Wendy Graham, Robert DeMaria, Marc Michael Epstein, Shane Slattery-Quintanilla, Chris Raymond, and M Mark. I would also like to thank certain former colleagues from Oxford and Austin, who helped shape this project with their warmth and encouragement: Michael Sprague, Andrew MacDonald, Andrew Stiles, S. Pearl Brilmyer, Dustin Stewart, and Emily Bloom.

Lastly, I would like to thank my wife, Anna, for her loving support, her enthusiasm, and her continual encouragement as this project developed. This is for her. And for the little one, soon to be seen, who may someday read these pages.

Introduction

Thomas Hoccleve has enjoyed renewed critical attention in recent years, and has been read, in turn, as a Lancastrian spokesman,[1] a failed laureate,[2] and a bureaucrat whose interests in creating autobiographical poetry emerge from intense anonymity in the workplace.[3] This study takes a different approach: it situates Thomas Hoccleve as an individual who cultivates, throughout his works, the role of poetic mediator – 'intermediary' in the most virtuous sense, and also in the most explicitly Christian sense – and who uses his poetic works to engage with contemporary religious reform movements and religious debate. The study situates Hoccleve firmly within the context of heresy, orthodox reform, and ecclesiastical controversy – including fervent debate over the role of the Eucharist and religious images, the role and function of priesthood, and the position of laypeople within the church. It positions Hoccleve, furthermore, as a poet less interested in securing earthly

1 Larry Scanlon, 'The King's Two Voices: Narrative and Power in Hoccleve's *Regement of Princes*', in *Literary Practice and Social Change in Britain, 1380–1530*, ed. Lee Patterson (Berkeley: University of California Press, 1990), 216–47; Derek Pearsall, 'Hoccleve's *Regement of Princes*: The Poetics of Royal Self-Representation', *Speculum* 69.2 (1994): 386–410.

2 Robert J. Meyer-Lee, *Poets and Power from Chaucer to Wyatt*, Cambridge Studies in Medieval Literature 61 (Cambridge: Cambridge University Press, 2007); John M. Bowers, 'Thomas Hoccleve and the Politics of Tradition', *Chaucer Review* 36.4 (2002): 352–69. See also John M. Bowers, *Chaucer and Langland: The Antagonistic Tradition* (Notre Dame: University of Notre Dame Press, 2007), 190–202.

3 Ethan Knapp, *The Bureaucratic Muse: Thomas Hoccleve and the Literature of Late Medieval England* (University Park, PA: Pennsylvania State University Press, 2001). While I agree with Knapp that Hoccleve's identity as a civil servant is central to his poetic persona, I do not agree that Hoccleve's approach to quasi-autobiography is motivated primarily by his identity as an anonymous bureaucrat. We will explore the complex interplay between bureaucratic identity, poetic identity, and literary tradition in Chapter 4 of the present study.

fame, and more genuinely interested in creating works that contribute to the spiritual health of English society – from translating the *Ars moriendi* treatise from Henry Suso's *Horologium sapientiae*, to writing devotional poems to the Trinity and the Virgin, to using his poems to contemplate Christ's sacrifice and commenting allusively on ecclesiastical wounds, to indicating possible solutions for such wounds and offering emblems of unity in the face of clear division.[4]

This study benefits from the revitalized critical conversation surrounding the effects on poetry of heresy, the church's response to heresy, and orthodox ecclesiastical reform both at home and abroad in the early fifteenth century. The religious turn in medieval studies of the 1990s has given way to contrasting yet invigorating debates over the effects of Archbishop Arundel's *Constitutions*, the role of the conciliar movement (and the Council of Constance in particular), the purposes and manifestations of ecclesiastical reform in England, and the fate of vernacular religious writing in fifteenth-century England.[5] These debates have led, in turn, to some re-evaluations of

---

4 Hoccleve's focus throughout is on emphasizing the extent of his labor, whether by describing in detail the pains of scribal labor in the *Regiment* (ll. 981–1029) or indicating the toll that translating takes on the body and mind in the *Series* (ll. 2.239–252). Hoccleve puts immense effort into creating his version of Chaucer in the *Regiment*, and he sends his Chaucer in the direction of Virgil ('The steppes of Virgile in poesie / Thow folwedist eek' (ll. 2089–90)). But he does not presume to claim such an august position himself. The identity he attempts to cultivate is one of intermediary and 'maker' of both devotional texts and texts that will serve the common good. We might consider Hoccleve's role, then, more in terms of personal sacrifice than as a bid for renown.

5 On the religious turn in medieval studies, see *Literary History and the Religious Turn*, ed. Bruce Holsinger, *ELN* 44.1 (2006), especially pp. 77–140. James Simpson's extensive work in situating the 'reformist' energies of fifteenth-century literature has been especially influential on refocusing critical interest on fifteenth-century English authors. (See James Simpson, *Reform and Cultural Revolution: The Oxford English Literary History*, II: *1350–1547* (Oxford: Oxford University Press, 2002)). Nicholas Watson's influential article on Archbishop Thomas Arundel's *Provincial Constitutions* (1407–09) sparked an important critical debate surrounding the impact of Arundel's legislation on vernacular writing after 1409. (See Nicholas Watson, 'Censorship and Cultural Change in Late Medieval England: Vernacular Theology, the Oxford Translation Debate and Arundel's Constitutions of 1409', *Speculum* 70 (1995): 822–64; see also Watson's modifications to his conclusions in the above-mentioned study on the religious turn: Nicholas Watson, 'Cultural Changes', *ELH* 44.1 (2006): 127–37.) Recent critical efforts, such as those compiled in *After Arundel: Religious Writing in Fifteenth-Century England*, have sought to explore anew the associations between theological inquiry, vernacular writing, and ecclesiastical doctrine, and to survey the developing understanding of intellectual life in fifteenth-century England. (See

the role that heresy plays in Hoccleve's works – from the relevance of John Badby in the *Regiment of Princes*, to Hoccleve's poetic address to the Lollard knight John Oldcastle, to valences of ecclesiastical rehabilitation alongside narratives of authorial recovery in the *Series*.[6] Critics have also highlighted the way in which Hoccleve entertains both textual and pictorial images in his works, and have discussed Hoccleve's use of image – particularly in his translation of the *Ars moriendi* treatise from Suso's *Horologium* – in the context of religious iconoclasm, the theology of optics, and late medieval debates over the role and function of images in religious worship.[7] While

---

After Arundel: Religious Writing in Fifteenth-Century England, ed. Vincent Gillespie and Kantik Ghosh, Medieval Church Studies 21 (Turnhout: Brepols, 2013).) Other important recent contributions to this ongoing critical dialogue include: Kathryn Kerby-Fulton, *Books Under Suspicion: Censorship and Tolerance of Revelatory Writing in Late Medieval England* (Notre Dame: University of Notre Dame Press, 2006); Vincent Gillespie, 'Vernacular Theology', in *Middle English*, ed. Paul Strohm (Oxford: Oxford University Press, 2007), 401–20; Fiona Somerset, 'Censorship', in *The Production of Books in England 1350–1500*, ed. Alexandra Gillespie and Daniel Wakelin (Cambridge: Cambridge University Press, 2011), 239–58.

6 See, for instance, Andrew Cole, *Literature and Heresy in the Age of Chaucer*, Cambridge Studies in Medieval Literature 71 (Cambridge: Cambridge University Press, 2008), Chapter 5; Vincent Gillespie, 'Chichele's Church: Vernacular Theology in England after Thomas Arundel', in Gillespie and Ghosh, *After Arundel*, 3–42; David Watt, *The Making of Thomas Hoccleve's Series*, Exeter Medieval Texts and Studies (Liverpool: Liverpool University Press, 2013), Chapters 3 and 4. An article of mine ('"What World Is This? How Vndirstande Am I?": A Reappraisal of Poetic Authority in Thomas Hoccleve's *Series*', *MÆ* 78.2 (2009): 281–99) offers a reading of Hoccleve's *Series* in the context of the Council of Constance and societal pressure to appear orthodox. Chapter 1 of the present study constitutes an updated, adapted version of the article in question.

7 Knapp, *Bureaucratic Muse*, 137–46; Simpson, *Reform and Cultural Revolution*, 429–34; Steven Rozenski Jr., '"Your Ensaumple and Your Mirour": Hoccleve's Amplification of the Imagery and Intimacy of Henry Suso's *Ars Moriendi*', *Parergon* 25.2 (2008): 1–16; Shannon Gayk, *Image, Text, and Religious Reform in Fifteenth-Century England*, Cambridge Studies in Medieval Literature 81 (Cambridge: Cambridge University Press, 2010), Chapter 2; James Simpson, *Under the Hammer: Iconoclasm in the Anglo-American Tradition*, Clarendon Lectures in English (Oxford: Oxford University Press, 2010), 78–83. Recent discussions have also highlighted the role of confession, devotional reading, and clerical commentary in Hoccleve's poetic works: Katherine C. Little, *Confession and Resistance: Defining the Self in Late Medieval England* (Notre Dame: University of Notre Dame Press, 2006), 112–28; Jennifer Bryan, *Looking Inward: Devotional Reading and the Private Self in Late Medieval England* (Philadelphia: University of Pennsylvania Press, 2008), Chapter 5; Gillespie, 'Chichele's Church'; Robyn Malo, 'Penitential Discourse in Thomas Hoccleve's *Series*', *SAC* 34

such treatments have been successful in identifying portions of Hoccleve's oeuvre that indicate an interest in theology and ecclesiastical debate, most assessments tend not to read Hoccleve himself as a religious writer, nor do they indicate Hoccleve's sustained interest – *throughout* his career – in ecclesiastical commentary, the devotional applications of vernacular poetry, the role and function of priesthood, the spiritual health of the institutional church, the treatment of laypeople, and the ability of poetry to act as a conduit for prayer, penance, and reflection.[8] Such a reading of Hoccleve brings the writer closer to William Langland, for instance, than to Chaucer. Hoccleve cultivates a role for himself as a mediator, and he indicates the capacity of poetry to fulfill a quasi-religious, intercessory function, such as achieving peace between warring nations or reorienting a wayward reader towards virtue. This is the first full-length study to consider Hoccleve as a religious writer engaged, throughout his career, with the ecclesiastical controversies of his time.

This context proves relevant not only to the content of Hoccleve's poetry – and the manner in which Christianity, selfhood, and sacred rites are inscribed therein – but also to Hoccleve's presentation of his poetic predecessor, Chaucer. There has been a critical tendency to situate the Chaucer–Hoccleve dynamic as one of oedipal anxiety, wherein the son (Hoccleve) cowers before the prowess of a pre-established literary authority (Chaucer).[9] In one of the most influential recent studies on Hoccleve, Ethan

(2012): 277–305. David Lawton discusses medieval voice (including Hoccleve's voice) in the context of Augustine's *Confessions* – and confession more broadly – in 'Public Interiorities', in *A Handbook of Middle English Studies*, ed. Marion Turner (Chichester: Wiley-Blackwell, 2013), 93–107.

8 Two recent articles should be acknowledged here for encouraging re-evaluations of Hoccleve's self-presentation within religious contexts: Jenni Nuttall has suggested in a recent article that Hoccleve be seen as, 'in some parts of his diverse literary career, a clerical commentator'; and Amy Appleford reads Hoccleve as a devotional writer who inhabits, in the *Series*, 'the cultural role of the ascetic'. See Jenni Nuttall, 'Thomas Hoccleve's Poems for Henry V: Anti-Occasional Verse and Ecclesiastical Reform', *Oxford Handbooks Online* (Oxford: Oxford University Press, 2015), 1–23 (14); and Amy Appleford, 'The Sea Ground and the London Street: The Ascetic Self in Julian of Norwich and Thomas Hoccleve', *Chaucer Review* 51.1 (2016), 49–67 (49). See also Amy Appleford, *Learning to Die in London, 1380–1540* (Philadelphia: University of Pennsylvania Press, 2015), 127–36.

9 See, for instance, Seth Lerer, *Chaucer and His Readers: Imagining the Author in Late-Medieval England* (Princeton, NJ: Princeton University Press, 1993); A.C. Spearing, *Medieval to Renaissance in English Poetry* (Cambridge: Cambridge University Press, 1985); A.C. Spearing, 'Renaissance Chaucer and Father Chaucer', *English: The Journal of the English Association* 34 (1985), 1–38.

Knapp has attempted to present a more agential Hoccleve, seen less as cowering before the prowess of Chaucer and more as engaging antagonistically with Chaucer, even going so far as to attempt 'a strategy for poetic usurpation'.[10] His presentation of the Hoccleve–Chaucer relationship is laudable for its ability to call attention to Hoccleve's role not as a passive recipient of literary tradition, but rather as an active, purposeful, and even antagonistic recipient of Chaucerian authority. It also, however, continues to situate the Hoccleve–Chaucer relationship as one in which the literary son draws upon the pre-existing authority of the established poet-father. In Knapp's view, Hoccleve's presentation of Chaucer has primarily literary connotations, and is marked by a self-conscious display of reputational circularity. However complex the 'circuit of authority', Chaucer remains an 'informal laureate' – a 'predecessor whose prominence might legitimate Hoccleve's own efforts'.[11] In this study, I argue that the moral version of Chaucer that emerges in the *Regiment of Princes* is less the result of Hoccleve's anxiety towards a preeminent Chaucer, less a meditation on the complexities of oedipal insurrection and succession, and more the result of Hoccleve's anxiety in the face of an increasingly militant and repressive English church. Hoccleve's Chaucer does not predate the text; rather, it is the product of the text.[12] The intellectually and morally authoritative version of Chaucer that Hoccleve presents in his *Regiment* is not a pre-made artifact, but rather a Hocclevian invention. In manufacturing this version of Chaucer, Hoccleve invents a poetic 'father' figure who might plausibly be seen as acceptable under the heightened scrutiny of the English church.

Hoccleve's positioning of Chaucer in the *Regiment* allows Hoccleve to bridge the realms of church and *poesie*. It allows, therein, the possibility of an English 'literary' tradition capable of navigating the complexities of early fifteenth-century religious life. I approach the question of Hoccleve's role in establishing an English literary tradition not only in the context of religious reform, but also through a transnational literary context. This involves exploring French and Italian literary precedents for Hoccleve's moralization of Chaucer in the *Regiment*, as well as examining the influence and impact of contemporary French poetry on Hoccleve's work: I build on John Burrow's suggestion that Hoccleve draws from Eustache Deschamps

10 Knapp, *Bureaucratic Muse*, 14.

11 Knapp, *Bureaucratic Muse*, 123–24.

12 I respond here to the tendency to treat Chaucerian authority in the *Regiment* as if it is a pre-established fact. See, for instance, Pearsall, 'Hoccleve's *Regement*', 398: '[Chaucer's] already established reputation made him eminently well suited to serve as the father of English poetry.'

in his works, and I interrogate further the dynamics of the French *dit* in Hoccleve's *Series*.[13] I also examine Hoccleve's *Epistle of Cupid* (1402), a translation of Christine de Pizan's *Epistre au dieu d'amours* (1399), and situate the *Epistle* within the context of Chaucer's treatment of Cupid in the *Legend of Good Women*, and within the historical context of Richard II's deposition and Henry IV's accession to the throne at the turn of the fifteenth century. As we will see, ecclesiastical, literary, and transnational threads interweave throughout this study, from Hoccleve's use of Christine's *Epistre* to consider the role of the language of 'vice and virtue' in poetry, to the confluent influences of Deschamps, Chaucer, and the Council of Constance in the *Series*.

In order to demonstrate Hoccleve's role as a poetic 'mediator', I first examine the role of moralization and the language of 'vice and virtue' in Hoccleve's *Series* and his *Epistle of Cupid*. I structure my study in this way in order to indicate that moralizations – and the dynamics of vice and virtue – are constant concerns throughout Hoccleve's work. The *Series* and the *Epistle* prove instructive in this regard because both foreground the polarizing role that the language of vice and virtue plays in poetry. Hoccleve himself gives the precedent for reading these two poems together: in the 'Dialogue' section of the *Series*, the Friend references Hoccleve's *Epistle of Cupid* as a poem that has offended women readers, and this, in turn, leads to a discussion of how Hoccleve might amend his misdeeds through further translation.[14] Readings of the *Epistle*, and of the *Series* and the *Epistle* in tandem, have tended to focus foremost on the question of feminist versus antifeminist critique in the poems, taking their lead from the Friend's presentation of the *Epistle* in the *Series*.[15] While I entertain this aspect of

---

13 Burrow suggests the influence of French poetry on Hoccleve in *Thomas Hoccleve*, Authors of the Middle Ages (Aldershot: Variorum, 1994), 10. He expands his analysis of Hoccleve's debt to his French predecessors in 'Hoccleve and the Middle French Poets', in *The Long Fifteenth Century: Essays for Douglas Gray*, ed. Helen Cooper and Sally Mapstone (Oxford: Clarendon Press, 1997), 35–49. Burrow argues that Hoccleve is 'more Gallic than his master' – 'better understood as, say, an English Deschamps than as a latter-day Chaucer' (38). More recently, A.C. Spearing has argued further for the influence of the French *dit* on Hoccleve's poetry, as a means of exploring the development of a type of writing that predates autobiography, which Spearing calls 'autography'. See A.C. Spearing, *Medieval Autographies: The 'I' of the Text* (Notre Dame: University of Notre Dame Press, 2012).

14 See ll. 2.750–826. I use Roger Ellis's edition of the *Series* throughout this study. See Thomas Hoccleve, *'My Compleinte' and Other Poems*, ed. Roger Ellis, Exeter Medieval Texts and Studies (Exeter: University of Exeter Press, 2001).

15 See John V. Fleming, 'Hoccleve's "Letter of Cupid" and the "Quarrel" over the

each poem's presentation, I focus more specifically on Hoccleve's approach to coded political and ecclesiastical commentary, and on the attempt to counteract poetry's potential ambiguities with simple and straightforward presentations of moral virtue. In Chapter 1, I focus on the role of reading and moralization in the *Series*, specifically in the context of the church's response to heresy in England and at the Council of Constance. Then, in Chapter 2, I approach Hoccleve's response to the language of vice and virtue in Christine de Pizan's *Epistre au dieu d'amours*, and its relevance to the broader political context of regal deposition, accession, and legitimation in the *Epistle*. In Chapter 2, I also examine Anglo-French poetic crosscurrents in the *Epistle* and the *Series*, and raise the question of how poets on either side of the Channel engage with the Hundred Years War and its effects.[16] I suggest a role for Hoccleve as a poetic mediator in this discussion, a role that – I argue – Hoccleve cultivates throughout his works: mediating in the politically tense environment following the violent accession of Henry IV; using his *Regiment* to mediate between England and France, and to position peace between the two nations as a Christian imperative; and using his poem 'To Sir John Oldcastle' as a means of mediating between the institutional church and a heretic-at-large.

Roman de la Rose', *MÆ* 40 (1971); Diane Bornstein, 'Anti-Feminism in Thomas Hoccleve's Translation of Christine de Pizan's *Epistre au dieu d'amours*', *ELN* 19 (1982): 7–14; Thelma S. Fenster and Mary Carpenter Erler, eds., *Poems of Cupid, God of Love: Christine de Pizan's Epistre au dieu d'amours and Dit de la rose, Thomas Hoccleve's The Letter of Cupid: Editions and Translations with George Sewell's Proclamation of Cupid* (Leiden: Brill, 1990); Anna Torti, 'Hoccleve's Attitude Towards Women: "I shoop me do my peyne and diligence / To wynne hir loue by obedience"', in *A Wyf Ther Was: Essays in Honour of Paule Mertens-Fonck*, ed. Juliette Dor (Liège: Université de Liège, 1992), 264–74; Karen A. Winstead, '"I Am Al Othir to Yow Than Yee Weene": Hoccleve, Women, and the *Series*', *Philological Quarterly* 72.2 (1993): 143–55; Roger Ellis, 'Chaucer, Christine de Pisan, and Hoccleve: The "Letter of Cupid"', in *Essays on Thomas Hoccleve*, ed. Catherine Batt, Westfield Publications in Medieval Studies 10 (London: Centre for Medieval and Renaissance Studies, Queen Mary and Westfield College/ Brepols, 1996), 29–54. Ethan Knapp explores the poem in the context of gender and poetic identity in *Bureaucratic Muse*, Chapter 2.

16 The most influential recent study on Chaucer, his contemporaries, and the Hundred Years War has been Ardis Butterfield, *The Familiar Enemy: Chaucer, Language, and Nation in the Hundred Years War* (Oxford: Oxford University Press, 2009). This study, however, does not bring Hoccleve into the conversation surrounding Anglo-French relations at the turn of the fifteenth century, and it touches only intermittently on Christine. My chapter on Hoccleve and Christine aims to bring these two poets into this dialogue, and to situate them further with respect to Deschamps, Chaucer, the Hundred Years War, and the early fifteenth-century ecclesiastical reform movement.

In Chapter 3, I offer a case for Hoccleve's mediating influence in perhaps his greatest contribution to English literary tradition: his presentation of Chaucer. By positioning Chaucer within a conspicuously orthodox religious framework, Hoccleve mediates between the realms of church and *poesie* in the *Regiment*, and offers English vernacular writers an authority who can plausibly be seen, in the eyes of poets and priests alike, as 'the best of any wight'. Hoccleve's transformation of Chaucer into this figure of moral authority is the subject of Chapter 3. I begin by considering Hoccleve's dialogue with the old man in the first section of the *Regiment*, highlighting therein Hoccleve's motivations for creating his moral version of Chaucer. I then explore references to Chaucer prior to the *Regiment*, and indicate the international literary context for re-reading a poetic predecessor in more explicitly Christian terms. In doing so, I enter Hoccleve's achievements into an international context of medieval authorship, moralization, and literary fame.[17]

In Chapter 4, I turn to explore the *Regiment*'s 'Hoccleve' persona in greater depth, in the interest of investigating other English poetic and religious voices that contribute to Hoccleve's self-presentation, and to his presentation of Chaucer in the *Regiment*. This chapter explores the case for Langlandian influence on the *Regiment*, and considers parallels between Hoccleve's writing and the works that comprise the *Piers Plowman* tradition. It also examines the role that Chaucer plays as a figure of exemplary (and explicitly Christian) prudence in the poem, and discusses the connotations of poetic prudence for Hoccleve and his readers during the period in which the poem was being written – 1410–11.

In Chapter 5, I explore further the dialogue between Hocclevian 'endytyng' and the English church by examining the role that the Eucharist plays in Hoccleve's works. I bring the *Regiment* into conversation with not only the *Series*, but also Hoccleve's devotional poems to the Virgin and the Trinity in his autograph 'collected poems' manuscripts.[18] Hoccleve depicts

---

[17] Portions of this argument, concerning Hoccleve's version of Chaucer arising out of England's tense ecclesiastical climate, were introduced in my article, '"What shal I calle thee? What is thy name?": Thomas Hoccleve and the Making of "Chaucer"', *New Medieval Literatures* 16 (2016): 250–76. The version presented in Chapter 3 expands upon the material presented there: it offers a broader discussion of the degree to which Dante – and the Italian humanist tradition more generally – entered into late medieval notions of fame, literary memorializing, and authorship beyond Chaucer. It also offers a broader context for Chaucer's 'textual presence' in Hoccleve's works, an examination of Chaucerian allusion in the *Regiment*, and an evaluation of textual and thematic links between Boethius, *Troilus and Criseyde*, and the *Regiment*.

[18] John Bowers discusses the two manuscripts in question – San Marino, Huntington

the Eucharist in his works either in terms of absence and withholding, or as an instrument used in the fight against heresy. After exploring this context, I examine Hoccleve's presentation of John Badby's Eucharistic heresy and his subsequent execution in the *Regiment*. I read this episode as a counterpoint to Hoccleve's positioning of the body of Christ, throughout the *Regiment* proper, as a mirror for the contemplation of the virtues of mercy, humility, patience, and charity. I argue that Hoccleve responds to Prince Henry's role in Badby's execution by directing the prince's attention to the body of Christ, not in the form of the Eucharist but rather in human form, so that he might contemplate the Christian qualities befitting a just ruler. In the final section of this chapter, I indicate the way in which Hoccleve's presentation of Chaucer in imagistic form participates in these sacramental discourses. This underscores the variety of ways in which Hoccleve uses the Chaucer figure in the *Regiment* – and it highlights the sacramental, political, and literary valences at play in Hoccleve's version of Chaucer.

Our reading of Hoccleve also compels us to reconsider the question of Hocclevian influence. Hoccleve is generally discussed as having little, if any, influence on English literary tradition. Even Ethan Knapp, one of Hoccleve's most supportive critics, offers that, 'unlike Lydgate, [Hoccleve] has no progeny'.[19] In the conclusion to this study, I argue against this claim: first by indicating the way in which Hoccleve's poetry is interpreted

---

Library, MSS HM 744 and 111 – in detail, and in terms of setting the precedent as the first instance of a 'collected poems' in English, in John M. Bowers, 'Hoccleve's Huntington Holographs: The First "Collected Poems" in English', *Fifteenth-Century Studies* 15 (1989): 27–51. These two manuscripts are both written in Hoccleve's own hand. They date to the same period – 1422–26 – as Hoccleve's autograph manuscript of the *Series* (Durham, University Library, MS Cosin V.iii.9), and Hoccleve's *Formulary* (London, British Library, MS Additional 24062), the collection of bureaucratic documents that Hoccleve compiled towards the end of his career in the Office of the Privy Seal. The autograph verse manuscripts are compiled in facsimile in *A Facsimile of the Autograph Verse Manuscripts: Henry E. Huntington Library, San Marino (California), MSS HM 111 and HM 744, University Library, Durham (England), MS Cosin V. III.9*, ed. J.A. Burrow and A.I. Doyle, EETS, S.S.19 (Oxford: Oxford University Press for the Early English Text Society, 2002). On the dating of the autograph verse manuscripts, see pp. xx–xxi of Burrow and Doyle's *Facsimile*. On the dating of Hoccleve's *Formulary*, see Burrow, *Thomas Hoccleve*, 26. Linne Mooney has suggested recently that the copy of the *Regiment* preserved in London, British Library, MS Royal 17 D.xviii is also in Hoccleve's own hand. (See Linne Mooney, 'A Holograph Copy of Thomas Hoccleve's *Regiment of Princes*', *SAC* 33 (2011): 263–96.) However, there is no consensus yet as to whether the manuscript in question is indeed an autograph.

19 Knapp, *Bureaucratic Muse*, 11. John Bowers echoes this argument in *Chaucer and Langland*, 194.

in the fifteenth century; and then by exploring the broader afterlife of Hoccleve's moral version of Chaucer, in both textual and imagistic forms. Because Hoccleve's presentation of Chaucer in the *Regiment* relies in part on Hoccleve's simultaneous self-effacement, it is tempting to see this 'Chaucer' as a pre-established artifact, rather than as Hoccleve's own cultural production. In order to demonstrate the influence that this specific, 'Christianized' version of Chaucer has had on English literary culture, I explore John Lydgate's use of the figure in his *Life of Our Lady*, and Nicholas Brigham's use of the figure during Chaucer's 1556 reburial. I also indicate how the figure continues to be used in present-day academic circles. Our discussion – there, and throughout this study – aims to reopen the question of how 'major' a poet Hoccleve is, what form his influence takes, and what role the poet plays in our still-developing picture of England's vibrant and tumultuous fifteenth century.

Chapter One

'What world is this? How vndirstande am I?': Reading and Moralization in the *Series*

> Aftir þat heruest inned had hise sheues,
> And that the broun sesoun of Mihelmesse
> Was come, and gan the trees robbe of her leues,
> That grene had ben and in lusty freisshenesse,
> And hem into colour of ȝelownesse
> Had died and doun throwen vndirfoote,
> That chaunge sanke into myn herte roote.
>
> (1.1–7)

These lines, which begin Thomas Hoccleve's *Series*, have been described as the opening to Chaucer's *Canterbury Tales* transposed into a minor key.[1] Rather than beginning his poem amid the 'shoures soote' of April, Hoccleve chooses as his starting point the withering leaves of autumn.[2] Chaucer begins his poem eagerly awaiting a pilgrimage, whereas Hoccleve lies in bed 'vexid' by a 'þouȝtful maladie' (1.21). Far from boasting Chaucer's 'ful devout corage' (I.22), Hoccleve bemoans his lack of 'lust' and his 'langour' (1.25–28). By the end of his prologue, he has reversed the tone of Chaucer's opening entirely. He chooses to 'braste oute on þe morwe' not because of,

1 Knapp, *Bureaucratic Muse*, 164.

2 See the 'General Prologue' to the *Canterbury Tales* in *The Riverside Chaucer*, ed. Larry D. Benson, 3rd ed. (Oxford: Oxford University Press, 1987), line 1. All quotations from Chaucer throughout this study are taken from this volume.

but *despite* his surroundings (1.35). And, unlike Chaucer, who gears up for a pilgrimage, Hoccleve sits down and begins to write. This instance of writing despite the bleakness of one's surroundings serves as a fitting introduction to the *Series* – a work that depicts the compromised state of English *poesie* about two decades after Chaucer's death.

Hoccleve was writing the *Series* between 1419 and 1426, a period of considerable unrest for the English nation.[3] In 1422 Henry V died, leaving the English throne to his nine-month-old son. Humphrey, duke of Gloucester, struggled with John, duke of Bedford, for the title of Protector, while England continued its war with France and its ongoing battle against heresy.[4] Fresh in the collective English memory was the Council of Constance (1414–18), which saw attempts by delegates from Italy, France, Spain, Germany, and England to reform the Christian Church in 'head and members', to end the papal schism, and to censure the heterodox views of heretics such as John Wyclif and Jan Hus.[5] As England was 'home' to the Wycliffite heresy, it became a political necessity for Lancastrian spokesmen to stress England's 'return' to a simpler and more orthodox Christian faith in order to differentiate between the strong, reform-minded English nation

3 Hoccleve appears to have begun the *Series* in November 1419 (see Burrow, *Thomas Hoccleve*, 26–27); Burrow dates the original manuscripts of the *Series*, the Durham manuscript and 'the Variant Original', to the period between 1422 and 1426 (see *Thomas Hoccleve's Complaint and Dialogue*, ed. J.A. Burrow, EETS, O.S. 313 (Oxford: Oxford University Press for the Early English Text Society, 1999), x–xi, lxiii; and Burrow and Doyle, *Facsimile*, xx–xxi).

4 K.H. Vickers, *Humphrey Duke of Gloucester* (London: Archibald Constable, 1907), 103–14.

5 C.M.D. Crowder, *Unity, Heresy, and Reform 1378–1460: The Conciliar Response to the Great Schism* (London: Edward Arnold, 1977), 7–14. For an overview of the conciliar movement see J.H. Burns and Thomas M. Izbicki, eds., *Conciliarism and Papalism* (Cambridge: Cambridge University Press, 1997). On the Council of Constance, see John Hine Mundy and Kennerly M. Woody, eds., *The Council of Constance: The Unification of the Church*, Records of Civilization: Sources and Studies 63 (New York: Columbia University Press, 1961); Walter Brandmüller, *Das Konzil von Konstanz, 1414–1418*, 2 vols (Paderborn: Schöningh, 1991); and for the effects of the Council on English religious writing, see Gillespie, 'Chichele's Church'; Alexander Russell, 'Conciliarism and Heresy in England'; and Kantik Ghosh, 'Wyclif, Arundel, and the Long Fifteenth Century'; in *After Arundel*, ed. Gillespie and Ghosh. On Lollard–Hussite exchange and the factors that gave rise to the Great Schism, see Michael Van Dussen, *From England to Bohemia: Heresy and Communication in the Later Middle Ages* (Cambridge: Cambridge University Press, 2012). The 'head and members' analogy was used throughout the Council of Constance to describe the process of reform: see Crowder, *Unity, Heresy, and Reform*, 20, 107.

and weak, heterodox interlopers such as Wyclif.[6] The idea of a 'pure' faith to which one could return was necessary if only to position heterodox views within the opposing camp of the impure. In order to be politically useful, writers such as Hoccleve needed to participate in this game of polarizing people and ideas. In 'To Sir John Oldcastle', we see Hoccleve using the right language for this: he emphasizes the military prowess of the orthodox and the intellectual weaknesses of the heretics; he appeals to authorities such as Justinian and Constantine and thereby links the English Church with a Christian tradition far removed from hazardous, contemporary attempts at theological inquiry.[7]

In the *Series*, however, Hoccleve indicates how this polarization of good and bad, pure and impure, orthodox and heterodox, can compromise the quality and function of poetry produced. Particularly when discussing Hoccleve's poem the *Epistle of Cupid*, Hoccleve's Friend[8] insists on there being only one possible interpretation, and hesitates to entertain any alternative, even though the alternative in question is put forth by none other than the author himself. The moralizations that the Friend tacks onto Hoccleve's translations offer similarly unilateral perspectives. They confirm the orthodoxy of the poems by offering interpretations in Christian terms, but do so by ignoring other possible interpretations. The very fact that these moralizations need to be 'knyt' to the poems suggests that they are, in fact, the official readings. The poems prove useful only insofar as their characters

---

6 There has been a great amount of recent scholarly attention given to the Wycliffite movement. For an extensive overview of the movement, see Anne Hudson, *The Premature Reformation: Wycliffite Texts and Lollard History* (Oxford: Clarendon Press, 1988). See also Rita Copeland, *Pedagogy, Intellectuals, and Dissent in the Later Middle Ages: Lollardy and Ideas of Learning*, Cambridge Studies in Medieval Literature 44 (Cambridge: Cambridge University Press, 2001); Kantik Ghosh, *The Wycliffite Heresy: Authority and the Interpretation of Texts*, Cambridge Studies in Medieval Literature 45 (Cambridge: Cambridge University Press, 2002); Fiona Somerset, Jill C. Havens, and Derrick Pitard, eds., *Lollards and Their Influence in Late Medieval England* (Woodbridge: The Boydell Press, 2003); and Mishtooni Bose and J. Patrick Hornbeck, eds., *Wycliffite Controversies* (Turnhout: Brepols, 2011).

7 See 'To Sir John Oldcastle', in *Hoccleve's Works: The Minor Poems*, ed. Frederick J. Furnivall and I. Gollancz, EETS, E.S. 61 & 73 (London: Oxford University Press for the Early English Text Society, 1892; revised by J. Mitchell and A.I. Doyle, 1970), 8–24 (ll. 185–92, 217–24, and 433–40). All quotations from this poem are taken from this edition. John Lydgate's 'A Defence of Holy Church' provides a good point of comparison. See, 'A Defence of Holy Church', in *The Minor Poems of John Lydgate*, ed. Henry Noble MacCracken, EETS, E.S. 107 (Oxford: Oxford University Press for the Early English Text Society, 1967), 30–35. Both poems date to c. 1415 and focus on the threat of heresy.

8 This individual is called 'freend' throughout the *Series*. He has no proper name.

and plot-points can be made into signifiers for Christian doctrine. Similarly, books are praised for their ability to signify, rather than for literary merits. When the Friend suggests texts for Hoccleve to translate, he speaks of the specific ends to which they will be used. He imagines how well they will serve as possessions – as signs of socio-political status.

This is an attack on poetry's ability to *mean* on a variety of levels, and it is an attack Hoccleve guards himself against fervently. He defends his poems, notes his Friend's errors, and encourages the reader to 'looke in the same book' – to judge the material for himself, instead of relying on society's simplification of the material. How a writer is read, ultimately, determines what authority he has. In the following chapter, I point out the specific ways in which the act of reading is represented in the *Series*, and the political implications of these representations for Hoccleve himself. We will study the Friend's attitude towards reading in the 'Dialogue' and the function of the prose moralizations, before moving on to the politics of book ownership. It should be said that the *Series* is by no means Hoccleve's admission of defeat. On the contrary, in writing a difficult and polyvalent text at a time in which it is more politically advantageous to appear guileless and frank, Hoccleve claims victory over the pressures of his age. Despite the hunt for heretics, and despite the cold wind of political scrutiny, Hoccleve is capable of fashioning a meaningful and multi-faceted text for those readers still interested in reading.

*

We first see literature described in dichromatic terms in the 'Dialogue' section of the *Series*. In the course of deciding which text Hoccleve should translate for Duke Humphrey, the Friend points out that Hoccleve has offended women in the past. 'Thy wordes fille wolde a quarter sak', he says. 'Which thow in whyt depeynted haast with blak' (2.669–70).[9] This rather peculiar metaphor allows the Friend to express literature in terms of white or black, right or wrong. The Friend argues that, were one to put Hoccleve's 'wordes' about women into a sack, Hoccleve would be obliged to paint over the sack's virgin white – the color characteristic of women – and to label it instead with the black mark of error. The Friend suggests that, by writing in praise of women, Hoccleve could potentially remove this former error; he could return the sack to its original white – to its

9 A 'quarter sack' is a 'sack capable of holding a quarter (eight bushels) of grain' – a double sack (see *Selections from Hoccleve*, ed. M.C. Seymour (Oxford: Clarendon Press, 1981), 138; and Ellis, *'My Compleinte'*, 159).

original purity. The Friend's language reflects this dichromatic mentality of error and correction: 'Sumwhat now wryte in honour and preysynge / Of hem', he says. 'So maist thow do *correccioun* / Sumdel of thyn offense and misberynge' (2.673–75; italics mine). Hoccleve's poetry has already been judged and painted 'black' – it has been announced impure, given to error. Hoccleve's only recourse is a return to purity through writing in praise of women.

Until this point, Hoccleve and his Friend have not been discussing any of Hoccleve's poems in particular, and this vagueness proves much to the point. Metaphorically speaking, Hoccleve's words lay jumbled in a sack intended for grain, and Hoccleve himself has been told that these words are impure. Hoccleve listens to his Friend's reproach for about eighty lines before realizing that he is not, in fact, guilty. 'But what haue I agilt?' Hoccleve asks. 'Nat haue I doon why … / Out of wommennes graces slippe or slyde' (2.751–53). He questions what it is exactly that he has done wrong. The Friend offers Hoccleve's much earlier poem the *Epistle of Cupid* (1402) as an example.[10] He describes Hoccleve's enraged women readers as 'swart wrooth' (2.756) – black with rage – and thereby links the *Epistle* with that black sack of Hocclevian error. As the two continue to talk, however, it becomes clear that the Friend has not, in fact, even read the *Epistle*:

> 'The book concludith for hem, is no nay,
> Vertuously, my good freend, dooth it nat?'
> 'Thomas, I noot, for neuere it yit I say.'
> 'No, freend?' 'No, Thomas.' 'Wel trowe I, in fay,
> For had yee red it fully to the ende,
> Yee wolde seyn it is nat as yee wende.'
>
> (2.779–84)

Hoccleve reassures his Friend that, were he to read the text 'to the ende', he would find Hoccleve innocent of the charges leveled against him. But his words fail to reassure the Friend. The stigmatization of Hoccleve's poetry apparently has little to do with the poetry itself, and more to do with an abstraction of the poetry. The Friend can voice only what he has heard from this anonymous population known to us only as 'wommen'. So apparently strong is this public opinion that the Friend has no qualms about delivering a verdict and punishing Hoccleve, his so-called 'friend', without

[10] The *Epistle of Cupid*, Hoccleve's earliest dated poem, is an English adaptation of Christine de Pizan's French poem, *Epistre au dieu d'amours* (1399). This poem will be discussed in much greater detail in the next chapter of the present study.

even having read what Hoccleve has written. Reading the text 'fully' and 'to the ende', as Hoccleve suggests, is out of the question. Popular opinion deems Hoccleve's words black, and so black they remain, at least until he has consented to punishment.

This would all seem quite reminiscent of Chaucer's prologue to *The Legend of Good Women* were it not for the fact that Hoccleve is not in a dream vision, cowering before the God of Love – he is at work in his London home, talking to a visitor.[11] The Friend's misreading of Hoccleve's poetry as offensive does not seem nearly so light-handed as the God of Love's relatively whimsical dismissal of Chaucer's verse. When Chaucer is accused of offending women, he reverts to his usual excuse – he was only following the will of his 'auctour' – before assenting to Alceste's command that he write tales of good women.[12] The danger is never real because the situation is never real: Chaucer is only dreaming. In the *Series*, however, the danger seems eerily present. As Hoccleve puts it, 'Thyng þat or this methoghte game and play / Is ernest now' (2.255–6). When responding to his Friend's reproach, Hoccleve seems shaken, even ungrounded as a result of being so misunderstood. 'What world is this?' he asks. 'How vndirstande am I?' (2.774).[13] These questions resonate, if only because the world of English politics and heretic hunting seems to have overlapped with the private world of Hoccleve's writing. Hoccleve finds himself relinquishing ownership of his poems, or rather attempting to explain his poems to an audience that can only refer to an abstraction of his text, in which nuance is missing and the only relevant question is – pure or impure?

Indeed, the language used in Hoccleve's 'Dialogue' becomes increasingly reminiscent of that used at the Council of Constance. Hoccleve says,

> Looke in the same book. What stikith by?
> Whoso lookith aright therin may see
> Þat they me oghten haue in greet cheertee,
> And elles woot I neuere what is what.
>
> (2.775–78)

Jan Hus finds himself in a similar situation. In an account of his examination at Constance on June 7, 1415, Hus can be seen defending the nuances of his

11 See *The Legend of Good Women* in Benson, *Riverside Chaucer*.

12 See *LGW* G.460–61; 525–45. See also G.340–48.

13 Cf. John Gower, *Confessio amantis*, ed. Russell A. Peck and trans. Andrew Galloway, 3 vols., TEAMS Middle English Texts (Kalamazoo, MI: Medieval Institute Publications, 2000–04), 1, 8.1207.

work before a jury concerned with the broader task of cornering him into a position in which he might be seen, without nuance, as an upholder of impure beliefs. Hus's disciple Peter of Mladoňovice records Hus's qualification of Wyclif's belief that a priest in mortal sin cannot consecrate, nor transubstantiate, nor baptize:

> Et [Hus] limitavit, quia digne talia non facit, sed indigne, cum pro tunc sit indignus minister sacramentorum dei. Et ipsi dixerunt: 'Ille stat simpliciter in libro tuo.' Et ipse respondit: 'Ego volo comburi, si non stat sic, sicut ego limitavi.' Et postea invenerunt illum sic limitate stare in tractatu, capitulo secundo Contra Palecz, in principo.
>
> [[Hus] qualified that he does not do so worthily, but unworthily, for he [the priest] was at the time an unworthy minister of God's sacraments. And they [the council] said: 'It is stated unqualifiedly in your book.' He replied: 'I am willing to be burned if it is not stated as I have qualified it.' Afterward they found it so qualified in the treatise *Contra Paletz* at the beginning of chapter two.][14]

Like Hoccleve, Hus defends the nuances of his works against an inquiring body that wishes to label his writing impure. Like Hoccleve, he exhorts his accusers to engage with his work – to 'look in the same book', and thereby experience the text in its original, multi-faceted state. I do not mean to imply that Hoccleve wanted to associate himself directly with the most notorious heretic still living at the time of the Council of Constance. The point is that, in a time of political and ecclesiastical turmoil, nuance is among the first things to be forgotten. The delicacies of a text come second to identifying the enemy. And, employed as he is in the art of delicately conferring meaning at numerous levels, Hoccleve has as much right as the heretic to rage when his accuser polarizes the subject matter of his poems in the hope of labeling them impure.

That Hoccleve should echo the Council of Constance in his portrayal of the polarization of literature is not altogether surprising. Hoccleve seems to be channeling Constance throughout the *Series*. For example, in the 'Complaint', Hoccleve mentions that 'the substaunce of [his] memorie /

---

[14] Peter of Mladoňovice's account was printed in Václav Novotný, 'Historické spisy Petra z Mladoňovic a jiné zprávy a paměti o M. Janovi Husovi a M. Jeronymovi z Prahy', in *Fontes rerum Bohemicarum*, vol. 8 (Prague: Nákl. N.F. Palackého, 1932), 77; the translation is from *John Hus at the Council of Constance*, trans. Matthew Spinka (New York: Columbia University Press, 1965), 172.

Wente to pleie' but returned 'at Alle Halwemesse' five years before he 'braste oute on þe morwe' to begin the *Series* (1.50–51, 55). If John Burrow's dating of the 'Complaint' is correct, then the date of Hoccleve's figurative return to health would have been November 1, 1414, which – as David Watt points out – was the projected opening date for the Council of Constance.[15] As a clerk of the Privy Seal Office, Hoccleve inevitably came across a large number of communications concerning the proceedings at Constance.[16] By connecting the return of his autobiographical narrator's memory with the opening at Constance, Hoccleve invites the reader to view Constance as a possible intellectual setting for the *Series* – as one of the 'worlds' in which Hoccleve finds himself during his dialogue with a friend. When read this way, it seems more feasible that Hoccleve would be using the language of Constance to express his own reservations concerning the Church's response to heresy and the effect of this response on the production of poetry.[17] The Friend becomes a deputy of sorts, standing in for the major

---

15 David Watt, 'The Thoughtful Maladie: Melancholy and Society in Thomas Hoccleve's *Series*' (Ph.D. diss., University of Oxford, 2004), 195. See also Gillespie, 'Chichele's Church', 39–40; Watt, *Making*, 8–10. The date of Hoccleve's return to health has been disputed. While Burrow fixes the date at November 1, 1414 (*Thomas Hoccleve*, 22), recent scholarship by Linne Mooney suggests that Hoccleve's recovery may have occurred in late 1416. See Linne R. Mooney, 'Some New Light on Thomas Hoccleve', *SAC* 29 (2009): 293–340. Neither dating is conclusive and, as Watt notes, whether the return to health occurred in 1414 or 1416, it would have occurred in the time of Constance (*Making*, 9 n. 33). Also relevant here is Hoccleve's otherwise unacknowledged use of a ballad by Deschamps to describe his recovery, which I discuss in the next chapter.

16 See Van Dussen, *Heresy and Communication*, 111: 'Hoccleve's formulary as well as that of his associate John Prophete (Keeper of the Privy Seal from 1406–15) both contain many of the documents from which we learn about the embassies that passed between England and the Empire in the years preceding the Council of Constance.' Vincent Gillespie also draws attention to an undated poem of Hoccleve's addressed to 'tresnoble roy H. le quint (que dieu pardoint) et au tres honourable conpagnie du Iarter' [the most noble King Henry V (may God pardon him) and to the most honorable company of the Garter], which Gillespie argues was written for the meeting of the Knights of the Garter in 1416, when Emperor Sigismund received the regalia of the order. A main contributing factor to his argument is Hoccleve's apparent allusion to the ongoing ecumenical council at Constance in the lines, 'But ay we truste in yow our p*ro*tectour; / On your constance we awayten alle' (ll. 23–24). See 'Chichele's Church', 38–39. The poem in question is nos. V–VI in *Hoccleve's Works* (pp. 41–43).

17 Given this framework, it is instructive that Hoccleve's illness dates to the exact period at which he wrote his most seemingly 'official' anti-heresy poem, 'To Sir John Oldcastle'. Hoccleve may be drawing attention to the level of anti-heretical zeal in London during that period (the 'wylde woodnesse' of both heresy and its effects on

interrogators at Constance, individuals such as Emperor Sigismund and Pierre d'Ailly of France.

The Friend also aligns himself linguistically with Duke Humphrey, who was swiftly becoming a symbol of orthodox chivalry at home.[18] In the 'Dialogue', Hoccleve describes Humphrey as a foil of sorts, an anti-Hoccleve who writes his autobiography not with a trembling hand, but literally with a 'swerd in steel' (2.583–84).[19] When informing Hoccleve that he will be 'ouersee[ing]' his return to purity, the Friend seems to position himself within Humphrey's camp of chivalric sword-writers by saying, 'Thow fynde me shalt *also* treewe as steel' (2.798; italics mine).[20] To my knowledge, this is the only other use of the word 'steel' in the entirety of the *Series*. If the Friend was trying to scare Hoccleve, it seems to have worked. Hoccleve says, 'Whan he was goon, I in myn herte dredde / Stonde out of wommennes beneuolence' (2.799–800). And perhaps he is right to be scared. This 'Friend' has just visited him to remind him of a debt he owes Humphrey – the man who is, by 1422, in line to be Protector of England – and he has informed Hoccleve that popular opinion deems his writing impure. Hoccleve is evidently not in Chaucer's dream-court of Love. He is far from it.

The final stanzas of the 'Dialogue' indicate how the imposition of the world of politics on the world of poetry can force Hoccleve himself to think in absolutes – in terms of black or white, good or bad. Hoccleve seems to recognize the sinister implications of his Friend's exhortation. He begins to speak in terms of war and peace. He addresses his women

cultural production – to use the phrase put forth in Hoccleve's 'To Henry V and the Knights of the Garter' (line 50)). It is instructive, too, that, even in 'Oldcastle', Hoccleve remains much less militant in his approach, and more willing to compromise, than Lydgate in the contemporary 'Defence of Holy Church' (see especially ll. 85–126 of Lydgate's 'Defence'). I discuss Hoccleve's role with regard to 'Oldcastle' further in the next chapter.

18 In the prologue to *Fall of Princes*, John Lydgate describes Humphrey as a 'verray support, vpholdere and eek guide' to 'hooli chirch' ... 'That in this land no Lollard dar abide'. He is a 'punysshe[r]' of 'all tho that do the chirch wrong' (ll. 400–06). In the 'Dialogue' (ll. 561–616), Hoccleve and the Friend discuss Humphrey's fearsome 'knyghthode'. For the *Fall of Princes*, see John Lydgate, *Fall of Princes*, ed. Henry Bergen, 4 vols, EETS, E.S. 121–24 (London: Oxford University Press for the Early English Text Society, 1924–7). I use this edition for the *Fall of Princes* throughout.

19 'For to reherce or telle in special / Euery act þat his swerd in steel wroot there / And many a place elles...' (2.583–84).

20 The Friend also aligns himself with the *Legend of Good Women*'s figure of Cupid in his use of this phrase: see *LGW*, F.334.

readers, but his language gestures more towards Humphrey – the man for whom he is translating the tale, the man he has portrayed as a symbol of orthodox chivalry. He says he would rather translate a tale for Humphrey 'than open werre / Yee make me, and me putte atte werre' (2.818–19). He must show his allegiance through his craft or – as he says – 'take my way for *fer* into France': that is, the site of England's current war, where he would truly be put to the test as a defender of his country and of his faith (2.823; italics mine). Unlike Hus, who insists on the integrity of his works until the day of his death, Hoccleve eventually bows to the demands of his accuser.[21] He agrees to recognize his poetry as impure and, therefore, to cooperate in the labeling of literature in terms of absolutes – if only to save himself. His deference to authority, however, is far from heartfelt – 'I am al othir to yow than yee weene', he says at the end of the 'Dialogue'. 'By my wrytynge hath it and shal be seene' (2.811–12). In other words, Hoccleve's writing has already absolved him of blame, but, as he is addressing a majority unwilling to read what he has already written, a majority that is willing to discuss only a polarized version of his texts, he will have to try again.

Hoccleve's Friend takes measures to ensure that even Hoccleve's second try will appear adequately one-dimensional. Once Hoccleve has completed his translation of 'The Tale of Jereslaus's Wife', the Friend returns to track his progress. Having looked over Hoccleve's draft of the translation, the Friend notes that 'greet substance [is] aweye' – Hoccleve has forgotten to include the tale's moralization (3.963). According to the Friend, the moralization is one of the most important elements of the tale. 'Of þat tale it is parcel', he says. 'Y seen haue it ofte, and knowe it wel' (3.972–73). The Friend goes home to fetch this integral text and then returns, ordering Hoccleve to affix it to the end of his poem. Hoccleve assents, saying he will 'knyt' the moralization to the translation (3.980). What follows is a one-dimensional reading of 'The Tale of Jereslaus's Wife' using Christian terminology. The text unambiguously positions Hoccleve's translation within the realm of the orthodox. It reduces the colorful characters and events put forth in the tale to vehicles for Christian meaning. The most striking scenes – the empress hanging by her hair from an oak tree, or a 'ship claf / In two' by 'an hidous storm' (3.914–15) – become signifiers for the more popular ecclesiastical issues of the day: the need for penance after sin, the importance of confession, and the potential for 'inobedient flessh' to be tamed (3.988). The emperor becomes Christ, the empress the soul, and the emperor's

21 Spinka, *John Hus*, 229.

sinful brother becomes man. 'Þat is to seyn' serves as a common refrain. The phrase allows people, objects, and actions to be efficiently paired with their equivalent Christian 'meanings':

> ... the wrecchid flessh ... robbith the soule of hir clothes (þat is to seyn, goode vertues) and hir hongith on an ook (þat is to seyn, worldly delyt and delectacioun) by the heeres (þat is to seyn, by wikkid concupiscences and desirs) ...
>
> (3.1010–13)

This reading simplifies the tale by presenting it as a text with one real interpretation. Because the reader is assigned a reading of the poem, he or she no longer needs to seek out alternative readings.

In applying this moralization to Hoccleve's translation of 'The Tale of Jereslaus's Wife', the Friend participates in a specific literary tradition – that of the *Gesta Romanorum*.[22] The term 'Gesta Romanorum' is used to refer to a large corpus of manuscripts that contain stories from a variety of sources, many stories involving the bawdy misadventures of a given Roman emperor. The manuscripts vary with regard to which tales they contain, but the majority of manuscripts agree in one respect – they follow each tale with a moralization. In her study of the *Gesta Romanorum*, Brigitte Weiske argues that these moralizations are the most vital components of the collections; many collections seem to have been arranged based on the thematic connections between the moralizations, and so each moralization enters the tale it follows into a greater system of Christian interpretation.[23] The stories themselves take on secondary importance, in that they are read

---

22 'Gesta Romanorum' is an abbreviated title by which the collections are currently known. Many original manuscripts were disseminated under the more specific title, 'Gesta Romanorum Moralizata' (Sidney J.H. Herrtage, ed., *The Early English Versions of the Gesta Romanorum*, EETS, E.S. 33 (London: Oxford University Press for the Early English Text Society, 1879), xiii). See Herrtage's edition for an introduction to the English version of the *Gesta Romanorum*. For a broader introduction to the *Gesta Romanorum* tradition, see Brigitte Weiske, *Gesta Romanorum*, 2 vols (Tübingen: M. Niemeyer, 1992). For further discussion of Hoccleve's *Series* in the context of the *Gesta Romanorum*, with a focus on literary theory and commentary tradition, see also Eleanor Johnson, *Practicing Literary Theory in the Middle Ages: Ethics and the Mixed Form in Chaucer, Gower, Usk, and Hoccleve* (Chicago, IL: University of Chicago Press, 2013), Chapter 6.

23 See Weiske, *Gesta Romanorum*, I, 129–41. See especially p. 131: 'Die Allegorese bezieht die Texte in ein Deutungssystem ein, in dem jeder einzelne Text zur Demonstration einer die Sammlung als ganze überspannenden Heilslehre dient.'

not for their own sake, but for the sake of the moralization and, indeed, for the sake of the overarching doctrinal focus of the collection. Upon reading Hoccleve's translation, then, the Friend recognizes the tale from his copy of the *Gesta Romanorum*, and he dutifully pairs it with its pre-prepared Christian interpretation. In doing so, he mimics the compilers of the *Gesta Romanorum*: he finds a memorable secular tale and transforms it into a vehicle for Christian meaning.

Hoccleve presents this as an authoritative act on the Friend's part. He reminds us of the Friend's authority by using the verb 'ouersy' to describe his reading process. 'My tale anoon Y fette', Hoccleve says, 'and he it nam / Into his hand and it al *ouersy*' (3.957–58; italics mine). The word 'ouersy' reminds us of the Friend's self-assigned role as overseer of Hoccleve's return to purity – 'I wole it ouersee', the Friend says at the end of the 'Dialogue' (2.796). Whereas Hoccleve uses the verb 'rede' to describe his own reading of texts,[24] he underscores the authoritative position of the Friend by having him 'ouersy' the text. Hoccleve's use of the word conflates the *Middle English Dictionary*'s sense 1(b), 'to read through, peruse', and sense 1(d), 'to inspect in an official capacity'.[25] By reading Hoccleve's translation, the Friend does his duty as a Humphredian deputy: he inspects the tale for possible lapses in orthodoxy. When he subsequently announces that 'greet substance [is] aweye', the Friend is noting a blatant error on Hoccleve's part – Hoccleve has supplied the tale without including its official interpretation.

What the moralization attempts to cure, after all, is the multifaceted nature of the tale. Without the moralization the tale stands alone, and the reader is free to explore its different allusions and various layers of meaning. 'The Tale of Jereslaus's Wife' does lend itself, after all, to some striking readings. In the tale, Hoccleve transforms his ship into a site for prayer (3.657–58), and then destroys it immediately afterwards. In post-Council of Constance England, the ship served as a popular symbol for the Christian Church. We see this metaphor used, for instance, in Lydgate's 'A Defence of Holy Church' (ll. 43–70) and in the moralization to Hoccleve's 'The Tale of Jonathas' (l. 726). One macaronic sermon in Oxford, Bodleian Library, MS Bodley 649 refers to Henry V as a 'maistur mariner' who has successfully steered the ship of the Church to safe waters. In 'The Tale of Jereslaus's Wife', Hoccleve adds to his source the fact that the ship is 'claf in two' – evoking one of the main problems addressed at Constance: the papal

[24] See, for example, 1.314 ('For whan I had a whyle in the book red …') and 2.17 ('And right anoon I redde him my conpleynte').

[25] *Middle English Dictionary Online*, s.v. 'Oversen (v.)', http://quod.lib.umich.edu/m/med/.

schism. By both laying claim to papal power, John XXIII and Benedict XIII threatened to pull the Church-ship in separate directions and thereby cleave it 'in two'.[26] As if to underscore the potential for such parallels to be drawn between the fictional world of the tale and the real world of contemporary politics, Hoccleve adds a series of suggestive passages to his source.[27] He tells the reader, 'This chaunce shoop many a yeer agoon. / That tyme, par cas, was no swich array / As þat in sundry countrees is this day' (3.194–96). Such lines entice the reader to consider the text in a contemporary light.[28] The moralization, however, offers its own obvious interpretation, implicitly overshadowing any other such interpretations.

The notion that such a tale could be presented without an official reading – and thereby left open to be freely interpreted by the reader – shocks the Friend. He 'marvels' that Hoccleve's source text would neglect to supply a moralization:

> 'Was ther noon in the book
> Out of the which þat thow this tale took?'
> 'No, certes, freend, therin ne was ther noon.'
> 'Sikirly, Thomas, therof I meruaille ...'
>
> (3.965–68)

---

26 The macaronic sermon in question is 'Sermo 25' in *A Macaronic Sermon Collection from Late Medieval England: Oxford, MS Bodley 649*, ed. Patrick J. Horner (Toronto: Pontifical Institute of Mediaeval Studies, 2006), 527. Hoccleve's devotional poem 'Ad Spiritum Sanctum' also describes the Holy Spirit as 'seur port' in the time of 'shipbreche', a reference that takes on added significance when we consider it in the context of these representations of the 'church-ship'. (See 'Ad Spiritum Sanctum', in *Hoccleve's Works*, 281–83.) For an earlier use of the metaphor, see John Gower's 'In Praise of Peace': 'Thogh Petres schip as now hath lost his stiere, / It lith in hem that barge forto stiere' (ll. 230–31). (See John Gower, 'In Praise of Peace', in *Chaucerian Apocrypha: A Selection*, ed. Kathleen Forni, TEAMS Middle English Texts Series (Kalamazoo, MI: Medieval Institute Publications, 2005)).

27 Lee Patterson suggests a different, however similarly timely, political reading of the tale: '[The tale] records, among other things, the political and sexual misbehavior of the emperor's brother while "steward" of the empire in his brother's absence. Since Duke Humphrey was at this very time serving as the king's lieutenant in England while Henry was in France, Hoccleve's narrative has an obvious and stunningly tactless political relevance.' See Lee Patterson, 'Beinecke MS 493 and the Survival of Hoccleve's *Series*', in *Old Books, New Learning: Essays on Medieval and Renaissance Books at Yale*, eds. Robert G. Babcock and Lee Patterson (New Haven, CT: Beinecke Rare Book and Manuscript Library, 2001), 80–92 (86).

28 For further examples, see 3.246–66, 385–99, 484–97, and 575–81.

Hoccleve seems to possess the version of the *Gesta Romanorum* that forces no single interpretation upon the reader, and thereby allows the reader to form his own conclusions. He refers to his source as 'the Roman stories' ('the Romayn deedis' (2.820); 'the Romain actes' (3.1)) and, indeed, stories are all his source seems to contain. His copy of the *Gesta Romanorum* – like Cambridge, University Library, MS Kk. 1. 6 – offers the stories without accompanying moralizations.[29] By presenting the tales without their prescriptive readings, manuscripts such as MS Kk. 1.6 maximize referentiality: they allow readers to interpret the tales as they please.[30] The Friend evidently realizes how hazardous free interpretations can be. He touts the more common version of the *Gesta Romanorum*, in which the explanation of a tale in moral terms is at least as important as the tale itself.[31]

The Friend becomes an evangelist, in this sense, spreading the gospel of good orthodox interpretation. He proves so eager to have this reading 'knyt' to Hoccleve's tale that he 'walke[s]' straight home, returns with the

---

[29] MS Kk. 1.6 is by no means the only *Gesta Romanorum* manuscript without moralizations. The following also have no moralizations: München, Bayerische Staatsbibliothek, Clm 3040; Zürich, Zentralbibliothek, MS Car. C 113; Berlin Staatsbibliothek Stiftung Preußischer Kulturbesitz, MS germ.fol. 942; Wien, Österr, Nationalbibliothek, Cod.15325; and Heidelberg, Universitätsbibliothek, Cpg 101. Alternatively, Göttingen, Niedersächs. Staats- und Universitätsbibliothek, 4° Cod. Ms. Theol. 94 is almost completely without moralizations, and the following manuscripts include some stories without moralizations: Dresden, Sächs. Landesbibliothek, Cod. C.398; München, Bayerische Staatsbibliothek, Clm 4721; München, Bayerische Staatsbibliothek, Clm 12730; and München, Bayerische Staatsbibliothek, Cgm 414. I take my information on manuscript contents from Hermann Oesterley, ed., *Gesta Romanorum* (1872; reprint, Hildesheim: G. Olms, 1963), 5–260, which is still the most detailed list in existence, and I have updated the manuscript titles according to Weiske's list in Weiske, *Gesta*, 121–44.

[30] It is possible that such collections would have been used by individuals like Hoccleve who wanted to make use of the tales but not of the accompanying interpretations. Chaucer makes use of a tale similar to 'The Tale of Jereslaus's Wife' (or perhaps the tale itself) in his 'Man of Lawe's Tale'. In his edition of the Middle English *Gesta Romanorum*, Herrtage prints a very similar version of the tale with the subtitle, 'The Story of Constance in Chaucer's "Man of Lawe's Tale"' (311). Ellis points out similarities between Hoccleve's translation and Chaucer's tale in his edition of the *Series*, p. 191. Of course, Chaucer's version includes no moralization. One might say it does not 'require' one.

[31] Glossing Hoccleve's source ('the Romayn deedis' (2.820); 'the Romain actes' (3.1)) as 'the *Gesta Romanorum*' is therefore somewhat problematic. Hoccleve's source is not the *Gesta Romanorum* as we know it. It is not the *Gesta Romanorum Moralizata* – the Roman tales *with their accompanying moralizations*. Hoccleve's source is simply a collection of the tales themselves.

text, reads it out loud to Hoccleve, and even counsels Hoccleve on how to copy the text into the manuscript. Hoccleve tells us, 'to this moralyzynge I me spedde, / In prose wrytynge it *hoomly and pleyn*, / For he conseillid me do so ...' (3.976–78; italics mine). The text of the moralization showcases none of Hoccleve's talents as a metrist or as a 'maker' of mellifluous verse. This new text – this 'greet substance' of the poem – is not a poem at all, but rather a block of prose, 'homely and plain'. In writing the moralization, Hoccleve must learn how to offer only one meaning, instead of a bouquet of redolent and colorful meanings. And, similarly, he must learn how to render prose that is homely and plain.

The Friend is not alone in demanding that verse writers learn to compose thus. In the prologue to his *Fall of Princes*, John Lydgate says that his patron has requested he

> ... writen as I fynde,
> And for no fauour be nat parciall –
> Thus I meene to speke in generall,
> And noon estat syngulerly depraue,
> But the sentence of myn auctour saue.
>
> (I.444–48)

After discussing the 'fressh dite[s]' and 'fressh stories' of Cicero, Petrarch, Dante, Boccaccio, and especially Chaucer,[32] Lydgate declares that he will not be dealing with fresh material in his *Fall of Princes*. 'Off fressh colours I took no maner heede', he says (I.452). By announcing this, he seems to place himself in opposition to every poet he has just named. The *Fall of Princes* will not be 'fressh', he tells us, but derivative. After announcing that 'clerkis in writyng ... With ther colours agreable off hewe, / Make olde thynges for to seeme newe' (I.21, 27–28), Lydgate says he is bereft of colors. He writes 'Hauyng no colours but onli whit and blak' (I.465). His patron, after all, is none other than Duke Humphrey. And, not surprisingly, Humphrey's advice accords with that of the Friend: he exhorts Hoccleve to write 'pleynli' and with deference to authority (I.444–48, 453). Throughout the prologue, Humphrey becomes the 'upholder' not only of 'hooli chirch', but also of a particular school of poetry – a school in which old stories are not enlivened with new color and meaning, but merely translated into English with the simplest palette possible.[33]

---

32 Lydgate repeatedly labels the writings of these individuals 'fressh'. See lines I.244, 246, 256, 262, 352, 358, and 364.

33 This declaration of colorlessness has much to do with Lydgate's subject matter.

We begin to wonder, then, whether the Friend's insistence on including moralizations is less a matter of personal taste and more a reflection of Lancastrian social policy. It is with the moralizations, arguably, that the Friend holds sway over Hoccleve's style and over his ability to convey meaning. When the Friend delivers 'The Tale of Jonathas' from his own version of the *Gesta Romanorum*, noting that he is giving Hoccleve 'the copie verray' of the tale (5.34), Hoccleve feels free to enliven the tale with his own asides and embellishments.[34] He often interjects his own opinions (5.138–47, 246–52, 432–41), emphasizes the element of haste (5.21, 121, 153, 258, 273, 328–29, etc.), and strengthens the thematic connections between this tale, his Suso treatise (5.88–89), the 'Dialogue' (Cf. 5.190 with 2.175; 5.512 with 2.85), and the 'Complaint' (Cf. 5.244–45 with 1.211–12; 5.582 with 1.70; and 5.194–95 with 1.144–45). Hoccleve renders the tale's moralization, however, exactly as he finds it. His moralizations vary little, if at all, from other surviving moralizations of the tales in question.[35] Tampering with the moralization would mean disrupting the 'true message' of the tale. It would mean distorting the block of text that makes the Friend's copy 'verray' – that makes it true, just, and complete. While the Friend cannot stop Hoccleve from infusing his tales with allusions to other texts and to the contemporary socio-political climate, he can use prose moralizations to make Hoccleve's poems *seem* relatively harmless.

It is in his peddling of these orthodox interpretations that the Friend really shows himself to be 'treewe as steel'. We begin to see him as an upholder of a Lancastrian initiative to restore 'normalcy' in post-Council of Constance England. As Vincent Gillespie asserts, the 'blandness' of these prose moralizations is the point. They can be seen as part of the Lancastrian agenda to present England as a nation that has returned at last to a state of constancy and normalcy. Amid the hunt for heretics, 'dullness and predictability are a state to be aspired to'.[36] As a Humphredian

In order to appear harmless Lydgate must put himself forward as one who is merely translating the text and not hinting at more pertinent, contemporary examples of 'the fall of princes'.

34 See Albert E. Hartung, ed., *A Manual of the Writings in Middle English 1050–1500*, Vol. 3 (Hamden, CT: Connecticut Academy of Arts and Sciences, 1972), 751–52; cf. 'The Tale of Jereslaus's Wife' with Herrtage, *Gesta*, 311–19 and, for a Latin version, Oesterley, *Gesta*, 648–57; cf. 'The Tale of Jonathas' with Herrtage, *Gesta*, 180–93 and Oesterley, *Gesta*, 466–69.

35 Cf. Herrtage, *Gesta*, 193–96 and 319–22; and Oesterley, *Gesta*, 653–54 and 469–70.

36 Vincent Gillespie (unpub. lecture, University of Oxford, 2007). In 'Chichele's Church', Gillespie also describes 'that generality, that blandness, and the idealism that

deputy, the Friend supplies Hoccleve with moralizations in order to help his work better reflect this return to normalcy. The moralizations prove that their corresponding tales cooperate with the Lancastrian agenda. They can be seen as marks of approval, not unlike Archbishop Arundel's memorandum to Nicholas Love's *Mirror of the Blessed Life of Jesus Christ*, which confirms the orthodoxy of the text and was compiled with the text in several manuscripts.[37] Unlike Love, however, Hoccleve is not the prior of a charterhouse. Nor is he actively seeking ecclesiastical or political approval. On the contrary, in the *Series* approval is being urged upon him.

That this *Series* 'world' may be accurately mirroring Hoccleve's actual social climate is implied by the way these moralizations are glossed in Oxford, Bodleian Library, MS Selden supra 53, by far the earliest of the five non-autograph *Series* manuscripts. Throughout 'The Tale of Jonathas', the Selden scribe underlines those words that bear the most relevance to the tale's moralization. He pays particular attention to the words 'brooch', 'ryng', and 'clooth' (ff. 136v–137v, 138v–139r, and 146r). These words are then underlined throughout the moralization, perhaps to afford the reader easy access to their 'true' meanings (ff. 146v–147v). This apparently simple scribal gesture proves most illuminating. By underlining in the tale those words that are most relevant to the tale's moralization, the scribe locates the poem's authority in the moralization. He encourages the reader to read the poem in terms of its built-in interpretation and, thereby, to view the poem as relatively monovalent.[38]

This gestures to the way in which books could be made useful in early fifteenth-century England. The poems become all the more valuable for what they seem to be rather than for what they actually are. The Selden

characterizes both the preparatory documents [for the Council of Constance] and the Council's official *acta*' (28).

37 Michael Sargent notes that the memorandum was compiled with the *Mirror*, and placed either before the text or after the treatise on the Eucharist, in 20 of the 42 manuscripts 'not deficient at the appropriate locus'. See Nicholas Love, *The Mirror of the Blessed Life of Jesus Christ: A Full Critical Edition, Based on Cambridge University Library Additional MSS 6578 and 6686 with Introduction, Notes, and Glossary*, ed. Michael G. Sargent (Exeter Medieval Texts and Studies. Exeter: University of Exeter Press, 2005), 36–37. See also *The Idea of the Vernacular*, eds. Jocelyn Wogan-Browne, Nicholas Watson, Andrew Taylor, and Ruth Evans (Exeter: University of Exeter Press, 1999), 252.

38 The scribe glosses 'The Tale of Jereslaus's Wife' in a similar way. He tends to underline names rather than objects throughout the tale, however, probably because the names prove more relevant to the tale's moralization (see ff. 111r–114v; and for the moralization, ff. 116r–116v).

manuscript can therefore be passed from person to person, and even readers as averse to reading as Hoccleve's 'wommen' can tell from a cursory glance that the text is safely positioned within the realm of the orthodox. These moralizations therefore make the poems they interpret arguably more desirable to the politically cautious book owner. The tales travel with their own self-polarizations.

This proves especially necessary because, as the *Series* shows us again and again, the way a book is discussed takes precedence over the actual content of the book. When assembling the *Series*, for example, Hoccleve and his Friend place considerable emphasis on the way tales will be perceived, rather than on the literary merits of the given tales. Particularly when deciding which tale to translate for Duke Humphrey, Hoccleve and his Friend consider texts for their symbolic merit. In the 'Dialogue', Hoccleve mentions that he had thought about translating 'Vegece / Which tretith of the art of chiualrie' (2.561–62). The text to which Hoccleve is referring, Vegetius's *De re militari*, had by the early fifteenth century become a mainstay in aristocratic libraries and an approved marker of orthodox chivalry.[39] The fact that the text was written in the late fourth century and treated much that was irrelevant to the early fifteenth-century knight is part of the point.[40] The text seems to have been touted for what it signified, rather than for what it actually discussed. Hoccleve had used it previously in 'To Sir John Oldcastle' (1415) as a text that would make Oldcastle seem orthodox and chivalric.[41] He places it in contrast to the difficult theological texts that Oldcastle has been reading, and even describes it as a text that can potentially 'correct' Oldcastle's former error:

> Clymbe no more in holy writ so hie!
> Rede the storie of Lancelot de lake,
> Or Vegece of the aart of Chiualrie,
> The seege of Troie or Thebes thee applie
> To thyng þat may to thordre of knight longe!
> To thy correccioun now haaste and hie...
>
> (194–9)

---

39 See R.F. Green, *Poets and Princepleasers: Literature and the English Court in the Late Middle Ages* (Toronto: University of Toronto Press, 1980), 144–45.

40 Ibid.

41 For more information on *De re militari*, see Ruth Nissé, '"Our fadres olde and modres": Gender, Heresy, and Hoccleve's Literary Politics', *SAC* 21 (1999): 291–99. Nissé describes *De re militari* as the epitome of 'a text without thought'. She calls it 'a blunt how-to manual for winning a war with the Roman army' (295).

De re militari had become the epitome of what an upright, orthodox individual should own. It seems perfectly sensible, then, that Hoccleve should align the work with Duke Humphrey. The text serves as an unassailable sign of the Duke's unassailable orthodoxy.

This text, however, does not even seem to be a credible option for Hoccleve's commission. Hoccleve rejects the idea of translating it as soon as he has mentioned it. 'I thoghte han translated Vegece', he says. 'But I see his knyghthode so encrece / þat nothyng my labour sholde edifie …' (2.561–64). Another reason Hoccleve will not be translating Vegetius, perhaps, is because someone else has beaten him to it. In fact, in 1408 both John of Trevisa and John Walton produced English translations for Sir Thomas Berkeley.[42] Furthermore, *De re militari* provided source material for Aegidius's *De regimine principum*, the text on which Hoccleve based much of his *Regiment of Princes*.[43] For Hoccleve, translating *De re militari* would have been tantamount to repeating himself. As in 'To Sir John Oldcastle', then, Hoccleve does not use *De re militari* as a book to be read, but rather as a name-marker that has come to signify 'orthodox chivalry'. In the *Series*, the text is useful because it allows Hoccleve to praise Humphrey as an upholder of English orthodoxy, and because it affords him an easy transition to discussing Humphrey's recent military victories. How masterfully Hoccleve might render *De re militari* in English, or what a pleasure his poetic rendition would be to read, is beside the point.

This issue of how books are 'seen' rather than how they are engaged with affords us a window onto a specific social space in the *Series* – the personal library. The books with which one surrounds oneself become in many ways markers of personal taste and socio-political status. As R.F. Green states in *Poets and Princepleasers*, 'There [was] hardly a single aristocratic library which [did] not contain at least one copy of Vegetius, or, failing that, one of the works by Lull, Bonet, or Christine de Pisan.'[44] Such libraries became social spaces in which visitors might glimpse the interests and even the moral integrity of the book owners. In turn, book owners seem to have been more attentive to how a given book could be described to others. John Paston II offers a good example of this in his description of his copy of *De re militari*. He calls Vegetius's text 'my boke off knyghthod and ther-in … off making off knyghtys, off justys … and

42 Ellis, *'My Compleinte'*, 158.

43 Green, *Poets and Princepleasers*, 144; Nicholas Perkins, *Hoccleve's Regiment of Princes: Counsel and Constraint* (Cambridge: D.S. Brewer, 2001), 89.

44 Ibid. Hoccleve's relationship to Christine de Pizan's writings will be explored in greater depth in Chapters 2 and 3 of the present study.

chalengys, statutys off weer and de Regimi … .'[45] His description does not transcend the obvious; it comes to serve as a simple summary of a relatively innocuous text, a text that – in turn – can potentially confirm Paston's status as an orthodox and chivalric individual.[46] At a time in which Oxford rooms were being searched for the potentially hazardous texts of John Wyclif and Reginald Pecock,[47] an approved text such as *De re militari* could position its owner safely within the camp of orthodoxy. How a text is discussed, therefore, is of the utmost importance. An individual hoping to be seen as unquestionably orthodox would not want to sully his hands with a text that might be read as heterodox, and therefore potentially hazardous to his reputation.

In imagining how Hoccleve's text will be discussed before it has even been written, Hoccleve and the Friend engage in the act of reducing literature to its essential usefulness. When the Friend suggests that Hoccleve write in praise of women, Hoccleve admits that Humphrey would take little interest in such writing. 'What lust or pleisir', he asks, 'shal my lord haue in þat? Noon thynkith me' (2.701–02). The Friend disagrees. He says that the duke will 'shewen' his lady friends 'this book' when they visit him:

> … his lust and his desir
> Is, as it wel sit to his hy degree,
> For his desport and mirthe, in honestee
> With ladyes to haue daliance,
> And this book wole he shewen hem par chance.
>
> (2.703–07)

The book will serve, it seems, as a conversation piece. When in 'dalliance' with his guests, Humphrey might gesture to the freshly bound manuscript

---

45 Ibid., 145.

46 This was evidently of importance to Paston, a gentleman who signed his communications, 'John Paston, Knight', or, more frequently, 'J.P., K.' In 1467 Paston joined the King and Lord Scales for a tournament at Eltham. The following year, he employed William Ebesham as a scribe for his 'Great Book' – a collection of chivalric treatises and other verse and prose texts (Norman Davis, ed., *The Paston Letters and Papers of the Fifteenth Century*, 3 vols, EETS, S.S.22 (Oxford: Oxford University Press for the Early English Text Society, 2004), I, lviii).

47 For more information on Oxford after Wyclif, see J.I. Catto and Ralph Evans, eds., *The History of the University of Oxford Volume II: Late Medieval Oxford* (Oxford: Clarendon Press, 1984), 240–46. For information on the search for Pecock's books, see Wendy Scase, 'Reginald Pecock', in *Authors of the Middle Ages: English Writers of the Late Middle Ages, Volume III*, ed. M.C. Seymour (Aldershot: Variorum, 1996), 114.

on the table and mention how he has just received a fascinating tale written *in praise of women*. The book could potentially reflect the good interests of Humphrey himself and help to situate him as a defender of women.[48] Or, as the Friend suggests, Humphrey might serve as a 'mene' or intermediary for Hoccleve, through whom 'wommen' might forgive Hoccleve for his previous 'offense and misberynge' (2.709, 675). In either case, to be useful the poem would have to be seen as unequivocally written in praise of women. The poem must be capable of being easily described as a positive, rather than negative, text.

That books are being discussed – and even produced – in terms of such abstracts becomes more evident in Hoccleve's prologue to 'The Tale of Jonathas'. As the moralization to 'The Tale of Jereslaus's Wife' serves as a simple answer to a potentially complex text, 'The Tale of Jonathas' is introduced as a simple answer to a complex social problem. The Friend says that his fifteen-year-old son has been cavorting with prostitutes. By translating a tale that highlights the inconstancy of women, the Friend argues, Hoccleve might correct the wayward teenager. In order to explain this idea further to a skeptical Hoccleve, the Friend resorts to his usual dichromatic terminology. He discusses two types of women – 'wikkid wommen' and 'goode wommen' (5.60, 62). The former he describes as 'blakid' – that is, blackened – with 'deshonour' (5.75). Hoccleve's task in writing the poem is to help the Friend's son distinguish between the wicked and the good, the black and the white. Far from announcing the tale as an opportunity for Hoccleve to present a colorful array of diverse meanings, then, the Friend describes it as an opportunity for Hoccleve to depict in black what he has already depicted in white. The Friend admits that this tale is 'nat fer' from the Roman tale Hoccleve translated before (5.29). As he focused on the 'white' before, however, he will now turn to focus on the 'black'. Perhaps unsurprisingly, the moralization to 'The Tale of Jonathas' closely adheres to the Friend's wishes. It equates Jonathas's 'paramour' with 'wrecchid flessh', and presents Jonathas as a 'Cristen man' capable of overcoming the wiles of his (woman) flesh. And as the poem is positioned between Hoccleve's interlinking dialogue with his Friend and the moralization – two texts that declare the seemingly straightforward

48 From 1421 onwards, Humphrey was, after all, attempting to legitimize his relationship with one woman in particular, Jacqueline of Hainault – the woman whom he 'considered his wife'. His requests for a papal annulment of Jacqueline's first marriage were met with scorn by Martin V. See Margaret Harvey, *England, Rome and the Papacy 1417–1464: The Study of a Relationship* (Manchester: Manchester University Press, 1993), 140.

ends to which the poem can be used – it advertises its own simplicity: it touts its monovalence.[49]

As I have said, however, the *Series* by no means signals Hoccleve's admission of defeat. Although Hoccleve agrees to make his tales *seem* as if they can be reduced to mere 'black and white', in actuality he continues to 'make olde thynges for to seeme newe'. As we have seen, the active reader can find in 'The Tale of Jereslaus's Wife' shades of the Council of Constance, the papal schism, and the leadership of Duke Humphrey. Hoccleve's conversational poems – the 'Dialogue' and the interlinking passages in the 'Roman tales' (3.953–80 and 5.1–84) – prove equally valuable. They echo the language of the English heresy hunt, evoke the interrogation halls at Constance, and gesture towards the Lancastrian social agenda that threatens to rob poetry of polyvalence.

Much of Hoccleve's eventual authority, it seems, lies in his ability to preserve his poetry through compilation.[50] While the Friend's moralizations threaten to dull the effects of the tales they interpret, they also help to detract attention from the 'colorful' – and therefore politically hazardous – tales. By compiling the tales with their moralizations (and distancing himself from this act by making the Friend a presiding authority), Hoccleve allows the tales to survive in their original, 'uncensored' states. The tales

---

49 The rubrics that Hoccleve uses for the 'Roman tales' in the autograph manuscript of the *Series* – Durham, University Library, MS Cosin V.iii.9 – underscore the compositional differences between the two tales. Hoccleve introduces the first tale as simply, 'Fabula de quadam Imperatrice Romana' (f. 26v). He passes no moral judgment on the empress and allows the reader to proceed without preconception. By the time he introduces the second tale, however, Hoccleve has been forced to present the tales as moral concepts, rather than as polyvalent stories. His title for the second tale therefore carries with it a moral judgment: he calls it, 'fabula de q*ua*d*a*m muliere mala' (f. 79r).

50 Lee Patterson offers another relevant instance of compilation-for-the-sake-of textual-survival: he argues that Lydgate's 'Dance Macabre' is compiled with the *Series* in all non-autograph manuscripts because the compiler thought it necessary to link the baffling *Series* with a text more suitable to contemporary tastes. According to Patterson, Lydgate's 'unexceptional' and 'conventional' text served as the 'small tail … [that helped] to ensure the survival of the large, rather ill-behaved dog of Hoccleve's *Series*'. See Patterson, 'Survival', 89–90. In this sense, Lydgate's poem comes to serve as a larger, extra-authorial version of the Friend's moralizations – those built-in equivalents that attempt to secure the survival of the texts they follow. Rory Critten offers a consonant argument for the inclusion of Hoccleve's *Gesta* tales and Suso translation in London, British Library, MS Royal 17 D.vi: see Rory G. Critten, '"Her Heed They Caste Awry": The Transmission and Reception of Thomas Hoccleve's Personal Poetry', *RES* 64 (2012): 386–409 (400).

remain available for any readers willing to forge their own interpretations. What Hoccleve seems to be decrying, after all, is not so much a decline in his creative abilities, but rather the dearth of willing and capable readers.

Hoccleve gestures towards this in his *envoi* to the Durham manuscript – the only surviving autograph manuscript of the *Series*. He addresses his *envoi* to Joan Neville, countess of Westmoreland, aunt of Duke Humphrey and Henry V, niece of Chaucer, acquaintance of Margery Kempe, and notable book patron.[51] Hoccleve seems to place Joan in contrast to that group of 'wommen' in the 'Dialogue' who insist on reading his poetry in only one way. He asks Joan to 'receyue' the *Series* 'for hir owne right' and to 'looke thow in *al manere weye*' (5.738–39, italics mine). Here, Hoccleve presents the *Series* as a book that should be interpreted not just in the terms set out by the Friend, but in 'al manere weye'. He welcomes the reader who would use his book not as an indicator of social standing or as a manuscript to be referenced while dallying with suitors, but as a text to be read privately and thoroughly – a text to be used for the reader's 'owne right'.[52]

This *envoi* also allows Hoccleve to position himself in relation to such readers. It avoids the usual confessions of 'unkonnyng' that we find at the end of poems such as *Regiment of Princes* and *Fall of Princes*. In the *Series*, after all, 'unkonnyng' is forced upon Hoccleve. Having made this clear within the body of the text, Hoccleve relinquishes any claim to 'unkonnyng' in his *envoi*. The light touches of humility that he does employ seem to point not to his shortcomings, but to his respect for the astute reader. His use of the phrase 'humble seruant' twice in the *envoi* recalls the earlier instance of the phrase in the 'Dialogue', where Hoccleve uses it to describe his allegiance to Duke Humphrey ('his humble seruant and his man' (2.560)). In the *envoi*, Hoccleve's allegiance has evidently shifted. He

51 See Burrow, *Thomas Hoccleve*, 28; Bowers, 'Politics of Tradition', 356; Burrow, *Complaint and Dialogue*, lv–lvii; and Patterson, 'Survival', 87. For Joan Neville and Margery Kempe, see Barry Windeatt, ed., *The Book of Margery Kempe* (Essex: Longman, 2000), 265. On Joan Neville as a book-owner, see also Carol M. Meale, '"… alle the bokes that I haue of latyn, englisch, and frensch": Laywomen and Their Books in Late Medieval England', in *Women and Literature in Britain, 1150–1500*, ed. Carol M. Meale, 2nd ed. (Cambridge: Cambridge University Press, 1997), 128–58 (140–45).

52 In 1425, Joan's affluent husband Ralph Neville died. It is possible that the Durham manuscript may have been Hoccleve's bereavement gift for the Countess. Part of what she seems to be inheriting, after all, is the scepter of astute, English reading. (For Ralph Neville, see Sidney Lee, ed., *Dictionary of National Biography* (London: Smith, Elder, and Co., 1903), 937.)

prostrates himself not before the 'pure' or the 'orthodox', but rather before the astute English reader. He signs himself over to the reader who is willing to engage seriously with his work – to the reader who is willing to 'look in the same book' and to explore his poems 'in al manere weye'.

Chapter Two

Vice, Virtue, and Poetic Mediation in the *Epistle of Cupid*

In the last chapter, we witnessed the unexpected entrance that Hoccleve's early poem the *Epistle of Cupid* makes into the 'Dialogue' section of the *Series*. When calling Hoccleve to account for his earlier works, the Friend summons to mind not Hoccleve's long poem, the *Regiment of Princes*, but the shorter *Epistle*, written some two decades earlier, in 1402, and translated from Christine de Pizan's *Epistre au dieu d'amours* (1399). In this chapter we will examine the *Epistle* in greater detail, in order to better understand the way in which the *Series* and the *Epistle* operate inter-textually, and to consider Hoccleve's use of both poems to explore matters of political and ecclesiastical division, transnational exchange, literary taste, and specific instances of royal willfulness and betrayal.[1]

Our examination of the *Epistle* will position us to reconsider the role that Hoccleve fashions for himself as a poet. Robert Meyer-Lee has argued that Hoccleve's choice to translate Christine de Pizan's *Epistre au dieu d'amours*, immediately following Henry IV's failed attempt to lure Christine de Pizan into his court, indicates a bid for favor on Hoccleve's part – a bid that, Meyer-Lee argues, Hoccleve mismanages by eschewing the moral

[1] Critical studies of the *Epistle*, and of the *Epistle* and the *Series* in tandem, have tended to focus on questions of gender, feminism, and antifeminism in the poems. See Fleming, 'Hoccleve's "Letter of Cupid"'; Bornstein, 'Anti-Feminism'; Fenster and Erler, *Poems of Cupid*; Torti, 'Hoccleve's Attitude Towards Women'; Winstead, 'I Am Al Othir to Yow Than Yee Weene'; Ellis, 'Chaucer, Christine de Pisan, and Hoccleve'; Knapp, *Bureaucratic Muse*, Chapter 2. I take a different approach in this chapter by focusing on Hoccleve's use, in both poems, of the language of virtue and vice to comment allusively on topical matters of ecclesiastical and political importance.

authority of Christine's original, and redirecting the poem towards a more ambiguous and purposefully 'crafty' presentation.[2] Rather than consider the poem a demonstration of Hoccleve's own poetic cupidity – his lusting after a position of poetic power and renown – I suggest in this chapter that in the *Epistle* Hoccleve takes the first step towards presenting the mediating power of poetry: its potential to mediate between otherwise contentious, even dangerous, social positions through the use of allusive language. Hoccleve cultivates, therein, the role of prudent intermediary, 'middle man' in the most virtuous sense – a role that he will then expand on, as we will see in the coming chapters, when repositioning the figure of Chaucer in the *Regiment of Princes*.

In the first section of this chapter, we will examine Hoccleve's use of the language of vice and virtue in the *Epistle* as a means to coded political commentary. In doing so, we will situate the *Epistle* within a broader English tradition that uses the 'Cupid poem' as a means of allusive commentary on the misuse of royal power. Then, in the second section, we will focus on the relevance of the *Epistle* to the political events unfolding in the years between the writing of Christine's French poem and the writing of Hoccleve's English response: 1399–1402. Finally, in the third section, we will consider the way in which Hoccleve examines the cultural and linguistic 'air-space' between England and France, not only in the *Epistle*, but also throughout his poetic works. This will afford us a clearer impression of how the *Epistle* and the *Series* operate, and how the domains of literary culture and ecclesiastical reform overlap in the first decades of the fifteenth century.

---

2 Meyer-Lee, *Poets and Power*, 94–97. Meyer-Lee writes, 'Hoccleve wasted no time in positioning himself, quite literally, as [Christine's] replacement' (94). Meyer-Lee describes Hoccleve as 'barter[ing] the moral authority of his source for an advertisement of his skills as a crafty usurper of an established text', noting, 'Such craftiness was not at all what Henry IV – as a usurper of a different sort – desired in his court poets' (96–97). John Bowers also discusses Hoccleve's translation as a form of poetic opportunism: 'Hoccleve spotted an opening and quickly attempted to fill it' (358). For Bowers, this proved to be a miscalculation on Hoccleve's part – the Frenchness of Christine's poem was less well suited to 'the new national mood' than 'the robust Englishness of Chaucer's *Canterbury Tales*'. See Bowers, 'Politics of Tradition', 358.

Dispatches from the 'Yle That Clept Is Albioun'

To begin, we might revisit that stanza in the 'Dialogue' in which Thomas engages the Friend in conversation about the *Epistle*, and the Friend reveals his less-than-reliable role as a reader:

> 'The book concludith for hem, is no nay,
> Vertuously, my good freend, dooth it nat?'
> 'Thomas, I noot, for neuere it yit I say.'
> 'No, freend?' 'No, Thomas.' 'Wel trowe I, in fay,
> For had yee red it fully to the ende,
> Yee wolde seyn it is nat as yee wende.'
>
> (2.779–84)

If the Friend had read Hoccleve's *Epistle of Cupid* 'fully to the ende', as Thomas suggests, he would indeed have found that the 'book concludith … vertuously' in its representation of women – *very* virtuously, in fact. Hoccleve ends the *Epistle* with the notion that women serve as vessels of 'vertu' – they are so virtuous that they prove altogether incapable of harboring 'vice' (see ll. 456–62).[3] After discussing the manner in which each of Christ's disciples deserted him and 'wommen forsook him noght' (435–43), the narrator extrapolates that 'in wommen regneth al the constaunce, / And in man al chaunge and variaunce' (447–48). The narrator then carries this polarization of men and women to its extreme by suggesting that women embody virtue and, as such, cannot logically contain vice:

> The more vertu, the lasse is the pryde.
> Vertu so noble is and worthy in kynde,
> Þat vice and shee may nat in feere abyde.
> Shee puttith vice cleene out of mynde.
> Shee fleeth from him, shee leueth him behynde.
> O womman, þat of vertu art hostesse,
> Greet is thyn honur and thy worthynesse.
>
> (456–62)

This passage posits virtue as the polar opposite of vice, and indicates the impossibility of virtue coexisting with vice. It then praises 'womman' by positioning her as 'hostesse' of 'vertu' – which positions her, in turn, as

[3] Throughout this study, I use the edition of Hoccleve's *Epistle of Cupid* in Ellis, *'My Compleinte'*.

incapable of containing 'vice', insofar as virtue 'puttith vice cleene out of mynde'.[4] The polarizing language used here should remind us of the Friend's approach to language in the *Series*: his distinctions between women who are either 'white with virtue' or 'black with sin' and, indeed, his approach to poetry, in which he locates instances of vice and attempts to correct them with textual applications of virtue. In the *Epistle*, such a discussion comes across as parody, insofar as it contradicts what the narrator says elsewhere,[5] and simplifies the difference between the sexes: man embodies change and vice, whereas woman embodies constancy and virtue.

I argued in the last chapter that the Friend's polarized language of 'vice and virtue' affords Hoccleve a means through which to comment allusively on contemporary political and ecclesiastical events – from the actions taken at the Council of Constance to the leadership of Duke Humphrey. As critics have pointed out, a similar dynamic is at play in the *Epistle*: Hoccleve translates his poem from Christine de Pizan's *Epistre au dieu d'amours*, but condenses the poem considerably, with the effect of emphasizing the language of political deceit in the poem, and thereby increasing its relevance to the events that had unfolded in the three-year span between the writing of Christine's poem and the writing of Hoccleve's – the most notable such event being, of course, Henry IV's deposition of Richard II in 1399.[6] Hoccleve's *Epistle* opens some three years after Henry's violent accession to the throne, and in its opening lines it singles out England ('Albioun') as the site of deceitful men: 'passyng alle londes, on this yle / That clept is Albioun … / … ther is croppe and roote of gyle, / So can tho men dissimulen and feyne, / With standyng dropes in his yen tweyne' (15–19).[7]

---

4 See Knapp, *Bureaucratic Muse*, 68–69 for a consonant reading of this passage. Knapp writes, 'The point of this passage is that the best that can be claimed for virtue as a purely formal value is its effectiveness as a policing force, exiling all that is not self-identical outside the bounds of the self' (69).

5 See, for instance, ll. 162–66: 'Of xii apostles oon a traitour was./ The remanaunt yit goode wer and treewe./ Thanne, if it happe men fynden par cas / O womman fals, swich is good for t'escheewe, / And deeme nat þat they been alle vntreewe.'

6 Lee Patterson notes that Hoccleve's decision to use a 'witty parody of the official style that he used in his work as a clerk in the Privy Seal (the king's most intimate government office)' to write a 'poem that dealt on deceit and disloyalty' would 'hardly have amused the king'. See Lee Patterson, '"What Is Me?": Self and Society in the Poetry of Thomas Hoccleve', *SAC* 23 (2001): 437–70 (452–53). See also Meyer-Lee, *Poets and Power*, 97. On Hoccleve's tactics of compression and resequencing in the *Epistle*, see especially Ellis, 'Chaucer, Christine de Pisan, and Hoccleve'.

7 On Richard's deposition, Henry's accession to the throne, and its effects on English literature during the early years of the fifteenth century, see especially Paul Strohm,

The 'gyle' to which the narrator refers here is, ostensibly, the potential that men have to mistreat and slander women. But Hoccleve soon raises the question of masculine deceit more generally, and opens up the question of political betrayal: 'Betrayen men nat remes grete and kynges?' (85). This line has an equivalent in Christine's original, but Hoccleve moves it forward in his presentation, towards the beginning of the poem (it occurs at l. 542 in Christine's poem, and at l. 85 in Hoccleve's), and this has the effect of foregrounding the role of political deceit in the poem. The potential men have to betray 'remes grete and kynges' would have been all too apparent in England in May 1402, after all, and would carry a very different connotation for Hoccleve's contemporary English readership (reading from the 'roote of gyle') than it would have had for Christine's readers in May 1399.[8]

In reading the poem 'fully to the ende', as Thomas suggests, we encounter more lines that use the topic of 'wommen' as a springboard for considering political deceit:

> Malice of wommen, what is it to drede?
> They slee no men, destroien no citees.
> They nat oppressen folk, ne ouerlede,
> Betraye empyres, remes ne duchees,
> Ne men byreue hir landes ne hir mees,
> Folk enpoysone or howses sette on fyre,
> Ne fals contractes maken for noon hyre.
>
> (330–36)[9]

Not only is the subject of betraying realms restated here, the capacity that certain 'men' have for deceit is broadened: they slay other men, destroy

England's Empty Throne: Usurpation and the Language of Legitimation, 1399–1422 (New Haven, CT: Yale University Press, 1998); and Jenni Nuttall, *The Creation of Lancastrian Kingship: Literature, Language and Politics in Late Medieval England*, Cambridge Studies in Medieval Literature 67 (Cambridge: Cambridge University Press, 2007). For an introduction to the events leading to the deposition, see Michael Bennett, *Richard II and the Revolution of 1399* (Stroud: Sutton, 1999). For the documents surrounding the deposition, see Chris Given-Wilson, *Chronicles of the Revolution, 1397–1400: The Reign of Richard II* (Manchester: Manchester University Press, 1993).

8 In the final lines of Christine's and Hoccleve's poems, the poets date their works to May 1399 and May 1402, respectively. See *Epistre* ll. 792–96; and *Epistle* ll. 472–76. I use the edition of Christine's *Epistre* in Fenster and Erler, *Poems of Cupid*.

9 Cf. *Epistre* ll. 641–49. Christine's lines follow from a long discussion of literary and scriptural representations of women, which Hoccleve abbreviates drastically, with the effect of heightening the political relevance of these lines.

cities, oppress people, practice tyranny, steal lands, poison people and set their houses on fire, and draw up false contracts. Focusing on the infallible virtue of 'wommen' allows Hoccleve to simultaneously signal the real vices that certain men do commit. These lines, in tandem with the earlier mention of men betraying realms and kings, prove highly suggestive, given the attempt to legitimate Henry IV's claim to the throne in the first years of the fifteenth century: far from focusing on legitimation and rightful claim to leadership, this poem signals the ability that powerful men have to practice willfulness and deceit – to slay men and steal lands. The ostensible focus on 'wommen', both in the *Epistle* itself and in the Friend's commentary on the *Epistle* in the *Series*, serves, on one level, to deflect attention from the political allegory here. It also suggests a movement, in both poems, from the generalized group of 'wommen', and the generalized language of 'vice and virtue', to more specific – and specifiable – referents in the real world of contemporary London. We can see in Hoccleve's *Epistle*, then, an early version of the trope that Hoccleve will go on to use on a different scale in the *Series*: the use of the language of vice and virtue to comment allusively on matters of contemporary political importance. (For the Friend, the experience of reading the *Epistle* 'fully to the ende' might have been akin to encountering himself in prototype.)

But the *Epistle* also fits into a broader, extra-Hocclevian tradition of English poetry. In using a 'Cupid' poem to comment allusively on the willfulness of royalty, Hoccleve follows in the tradition of Chaucer's *Legend of Good Women* and Sir John Clanvowe's *Book of Cupid*. Cupid's position in the *Legend* has led critics to read the prologue as an allusive commentary on Richard II's rule, and as an indication of Richard freely using what is described in the articles of his deposition as 'the illegal power of his will'.[10] In such a reading, Cupid emerges as a figure through whom the reader can contemplate cupidity and the dangers of exercising 'wilfulhed and tyrannye' (*LGW* G. 355).[11] Lee Patterson offers a persuasive case for

---

10 See Lee Patterson, 'Court Politics and the Invention of Literature: The Case of Sir John Clanvowe', in *Culture and History 1350–1600: Essays on English Communities, Identities, and Writing*, ed. David Aers (London: Harvester Wheatsheaf, 1992), 7–41 (11). See also Margaret Schlauch, 'Chaucer's Doctrine of Kings and Tyrants', *Speculum* 20.2 (1945): 133–56 (155); J.D. Burnley, *Chaucer's Language and the Philosopher's Tradition* (Cambridge: D.S. Brewer, 1979), 11–43. In the *Legend of Good Women*, it is Alceste who draws attention to Cupid's capacity for tyranny: see G.317–431.

11 Intriguingly, Hoccleve introduces his 'Betrayen men nat remes grete' stanza by way of a discussion of Troy being 'betrayed ... thurgh the deceit of man' (l. 82). In the *Legend of Good Women*, Cupid uses Chaucer's portrayal of Criseyde – the central female character in Chaucer's 'Troy' poem – as evidence of Chaucer's violations against

positioning Sir John Clanvowe's *Book of Cupid* within such a tradition of commentary, noting the tyrannical role that Cupid plays in that poem and the adverse effects his willfulness has on his court ('In this court ful selde trouthe avayleth, / So dyuerse and so wilful ys he' (204–05)).[12] Patterson also includes Gower's *Confessio amantis* in this tradition:

> if John Gower's revision of the *Confessio amantis* bespeaks his awareness that Richard is less the benevolent Cupid who presides over his parliament of lovers in Book 8 of the *Confessio* than the tyrant whom he was to excoriate in the *Chronica tripertita*; then surely Clanvowe's wilful Cupid is another commentary on Ricardian kingship.[13]

The *Epistle of Cupid* travels alongside the *Legend of Good Women* and the *Book of Cupid* in Oxford, Bodleian Library, MSS Fairfax 16 and Tanner 346, and as such the reader would have the opportunity to read Hoccleve's manifestation of Cupid alongside those of Clanvowe and Chaucer. Far from offering 'examples of elegant light reading on the subject of love', as Fenster and Erler suggest,[14] manuscripts such as MSS Fairfax 16 and Tanner 346 provide the reader with a context in which to appreciate the respective ways in which poets engage metaphorically with the character of Cupid, and reprise the subject of tyranny and misrule from different perspectives, and in different courts.

---

the laws of Cupid (see G.265–67). The use of Troy in Hoccleve's poem heightens its suggestiveness for contemporary events as, in the medieval period, London was considered to be the civic descendant of Troy, having been founded (as legend had it) by Brutus, a 'refugee Trojan noble'. Gower repeatedly refers to London as 'New Troy' in his works. See Barry Windeatt, ed., *Troilus and Criseyde* (London: Penguin Books, 2003), xix–xx. On textual similarities between the *Legend*, Christine's 'Epistre', and Hoccleve's 'Epistle', see also Ellis, 'Chaucer, Christine de Pisan, and Hoccleve', 38–40; and Ellis, *'My Compleinte'*, 108–11.

12 Patterson, 'Court Politics and the Invention of Literature', 11–13. On Clanvowe, see also K.B. McFarlane, *Lancastrian Kings and Lollard Knights* (Oxford: Clarendon Press, 1972); Paul Strohm, *Social Chaucer* (Cambridge, MA: Harvard University Press, 1994), 42–45, 78–82; Helen Barr, *Socioliterary Practice in Late Medieval England* (Oxford: Oxford University Press, 2001), Chapter 7.

13 Patterson, 'Court Politics and the Invention of Literature', 11. For a contrasting view to Patterson's, see Lynn Staley, 'Gower, Richard II, Henry of Derby, and the Business of Making Culture', *Speculum* 75 (2000): 68–96. On the dynamics of poetic fealty and political commentary during this period, see also R.F. Yeager, 'Chaucer's "To His Purse": Begging, of Begging Off?', *Viator* 36 (2005): 373–414.

14 Fenster and Erler, *Poems of Cupid*, 164.

Hoccleve's poem also indicates the way in which his approach to political commentary in the *Epistle* differs from Chaucer's approach in the *Legend of Good Women*. In the *Epistle*, Hoccleve writes not as a visitor to Cupid's court – as Chaucer does in the *Legend of Good Women* – but rather from the seat of Cupid himself. He follows Christine's conceit in having the poem be delivered as a 'letter patent' from Cupid. This carries with it an added layer of meaning in Hoccleve's presentation, because Hoccleve, as a clerk in the Privy Seal Office, effects the 'will' of the king on a daily basis by writing and disseminating documents on the king's behalf.[15] Insofar as Hoccleve suggests the contemporary political context for 'betrayal of realms', then, he does so not by aligning Cupid with the figure of tyrant, but rather by registering concerns about tyranny and willfulness in the voice of Cupid. Hoccleve, as official letter-writer and poet, is the medium through which this voice manifests itself.

A sense of Hoccleve's identity as poet comes across in the body of the poem. The very stanza in which the narrator raises the issue of men betraying realms simultaneously broaches the question of who can 'shape a remedie' against such instances of betrayal:

> Betrayen men nat remes grete and kynges?
> What wight is þat can shape a remedie
> Ageynes false and hid purposid thynges?
> Who can the craft tho castes to espye,

[15] For an overview of Hoccleve's career in the Privy Seal, see Burrow, *Thomas Hoccleve*. For a wide-ranging consideration of how Hoccleve's poetry interacts with his career as a scribe and bureaucrat, see Knapp, *Bureaucratic Muse*. Sarah Tolmie also considers the relationship between Hoccleve's identity as a professional Privy Seal clerk and his approach to writing in two articles: 'The *Priue Scilence* of Thomas Hoccleve', *SAC* 23 (2001): 281–309; and 'The Professional: Thomas Hoccleve', *SAC* 29 (2007): 341–73. Linne Mooney builds on John Burrow's research into the documents that Hoccleve created as a Privy Seal clerk in 'Some New Light'; and David Watt focuses on Hoccleve's knowledge of book-making and his position within professional networks of scribes and administrators in *Making*, especially Chapters 1 and 2. On the Privy Seal, and Hoccleve's position within it, see also T.F. Tout, 'The English Civil Service in the Fourteenth Century', *Collected Papers*, 3 vols. (Manchester: Manchester University Press, 1934), 3: 191–221; A.L. Brown, 'The Privy Seal Clerks in the Early Fifteenth Century', in *The Study of Medieval Records: Essays in Honour of Kathleen Major*, ed. D.A. Bullough and R.L. Storey (Oxford: Oxford University Press, 1971), 260–81; A. Compton Reeves, 'The World of Thomas Hoccleve', *Fifteenth Century Studies* 2 (1979): 187–99.

But man whos wil ay reedy is t'applie
To thyng þat sovneth into hy falshede?
Wommen, bewaar of mennes sleighte, I rede.

(85–91)

The answer to the question is suggested by another question: who else, Hoccleve says, but those whose 'wil ay reedy is' [will is always ready] to be applied to such matters. The final line of this stanza – 'Wommen, bewaar of mennes sleighte, I rede' – refers momentarily both to the 'sleighte' of those men in line 85 (who betray realms and kings), and to those men of line 89, who use their own will to 'shape a remedie' against misuses of power. In doing so, it also implicitly links the two groups. Both groups are worthy of the reader's wariness. After all, in order to be 'ay reedy' to apply one's will to 'thyng þat sovneth into hy falshede', one must establish one's own, potentially ambiguous, relationship with falsehood. In these three successive questions, Hoccleve approaches something of a self-defining moment for his role as a writer in an English tradition: he positions himself among those who direct their wills against the 'wilfulhed' of tyrants, and among those who venture to 'shape a remedie / Ageynes false and hid purposid thynges'. For Hoccleve this means not positioning himself as a visitor to the court of Cupid, or positioning Cupid as a tyrant, but rather speaking from the voice of Cupid himself: Hoccleve asserts control by manipulating Cupid's voice, and by directing the substance of his address.

The Only Son of Sitheree

If Hoccleve's *Epistle* is a poem that pretends to the placeless place of Cupid's 'air-court' of lovers, but actually roots itself in the royal courts of London, it is also a poem that aspires to timelessness while actually indicating its position in a very specific time period: namely the period between the composition of Christine's *Epistre* and Hoccleve's *Epistle*: 1399–1402. We have already touched on some of the matters that occupied Christine and Hoccleve – and their respective nations – during this three-year span. In 1399, Henry IV claimed the English throne, deposing Richard II and thwarting the steps that Richard had taken towards peace between England and France. In 1396, Richard had married Isabella, the six-year-old daughter of King Charles VI, as a move towards improving relations between the two nations. By 1399, however, Richard had been deposed, and by 1400 he was dead, resulting in a severing of the royal matrimonial tie between England and France. Isabella reportedly refused Henry IV's offer to marry his son – the future Henry V – and the French court insisted on Isabella's return to France.[16]

The period 1399–1402 saw not only the presence in England of this French monarch, but also the exile of Christine de Pizan's own son, Jean de Castel. Jean arrived in England in 1398–99 as a companion for one of the sons of John Montague, earl of Salisbury. Christine had met Montague when he was on a diplomatic mission to France, and she had allowed her son to return to England with Montague. Jean's arrival in England, however, met with the imminent deposition and death of the English king to whom both Christine and Montague were loyal. Montague was beheaded because of his loyalty to Richard II, and Henry IV brought Jean into his court. In the span of a year, Christine found herself in the position of having her son held in the court of another monarch – a monarch she neither trusted nor approved of – and having to conceive a plan to have her son returned to France.[17]

The situation involving Christine's son is notable not only for the way in which it reflects on a more personal level the larger political rupture that had taken place between France and England with Henry IV's accession to the throne (co-reflected in the person of Isabella), but also for the way in which it overlaps and intertwines with questions of literary authority and textual transmission during this three-year period. For example, according to Christine's own account in *L'Avision-Christine* (c. 1405), Montague had originally requested that Jean join him in England because he was impressed by Christine's own poems:

> Et comme ycellui gracieux chevalier amast dittiez et lui meismes fust gracieux ditteur apres ce quil ot veu des miens dittiez tant me fist

---

[16] See J.C. Laidlaw, 'Christine de Pizan, the Earl of Salisbury, and Henry IV', *French Studies* 36.2 (1982): 129–43; Charity Cannon Willard, *Christine de Pizan: Her Life and Works* (New York: Persea Books, 1984), 41–42, 164–65.

[17] Christine recounts these events in her *L'Avision-Christine* (c. 1405). See Christine de Pizan, *Lavision-Christine*, ed. Mary Louis Towner (Washington, D.C.: Catholic University of America, 1932). This work is translated in *The Vision of Christine de Pizan*, trans. Glenda McLeod and Charity Cannon Willard (Cambridge: D.S. Brewer, 2005, repr. 2012). I cite from these editions for the French and English texts, respectively, throughout this study. For a detailed discussion of Christine, her son, and Henry IV, and an examination of dates, see Laidlaw, 'Christine de Pizan'. See also P.G.C. Campbell, 'Christine de Pisan en Angleterre', *Revue de littérature comparée* 5 (1925): 659–70; Willard, *Christine de Pizan*, 42–43, 164–66; Paul Strohm, *Hochon's Arrow: The Social Imagination of Fourteenth-Century Texts* (Princeton, NJ: Princeton University Press, 1992), 91–92; Meyer-Lee, *Poets and Power*, 61–64.

> prier que ie consenti tout le feisse ie envis que lainsnie de mes fils assez abille et bien chantant enfant de laage de .xiii. ans alast avec lui ou pays dangleterre pour estre avec un sien filz aucques de laage
>
> [And as this gracious knight loved poems and was himself a courteous poet, after what he had seen, some of my poems, he begged me through various important people so that I agreed – albeit unwillingly – that the older of my sons, a very clever and a good singer of thirteen years of age, might go with him to England to be a companion to one of his own sons of the same age][18]

Christine goes on in her *Avision* to note that Jean himself had a propensity for poetic writing – 'on ne trouveroit ne rethorique et poetique language naturelment a lui propice gaires plus abte / et plus soubtil que il est avec le bel entendement et autre bonne intiquative que il a'.[19] Indeed, Jean would go on to serve as a royal secretary in France, and to take part in the French literary debate of 1424 over Alain Chartier's *Belle dame sans merci*.[20] The implication is that Jean was already beginning to be known as a literary person, by way of his mother, as early as 1399. Importing Jean to England becomes, for Montague, a means of importing some part of Christine's own literary renown: Jean was, after all, one of Christine's most important 'makings' – a living, breathing person to whom Christine had transferred her knowledge of grammar, rhetoric, and poetic language.

Even after Jean made his way to England, Christine apparently made efforts to continue her son's literary education. Her poem *Epistre Othea* takes the form of an epistle from the goddess Othea to the fifteen-year-old Hector of Troy, in which Christine uses a series of verse vignettes with accompanying prose glosses and moralizations to calibrate the sensibilities of the fifteen-year-old.[21] *Othea* has been discussed as having been written

---

18 Towner, *Lavision*, 165; McLeod and Willard, *Vision*, 106.

19 Towner, *Lavision*, 174. 'One would not find in grammar or rhetoric and poetic language, to which he is naturally inclined, a person more capable and subtle than he is with his fine comprehension and other good mental qualities' (McLeod and Willard, *Vision*, 115).

20 Willard, *Christine de Pizan*, 202.

21 Christine de Pizan, *Epistre Othea*, ed. Gabriella Parussa (Geneva: Librarie Droz, 1999). The *Epistre Othea* was translated into English three times during the fifteenth and sixteenth centuries – the first of these translations having been by Stephen Scrope (c. 1396–1472), stepson and ward of Sir John Fastolf (1380–1459), most likely in the first years of the 1440s. See Stephen Scrope, *The Epistle of Othea*, ed. Curt F. Buhler, EETS, O.S. 264 (Oxford: Oxford University Press for the Early English Text Society,

for, and sent to, Christine's own fifteen-year-old son, Jean, during the years 1400–1, while he was still living in England. Laidlaw notes that Jean would have been fifteen in 1400 or 1401, 'a date which is entirely possible for the *Epistre Othea*', and that a manuscript of the poem may well have been sent to him while he was in England.[22] Read in this context, the *Othea* operates on one level as Christine's attempt to continue fulfilling her parental role as guide and teacher even when separated from her son.

The *Epistre Othea* is also notable, however, for the way in which it serves as a negotiating tool in Christine's dealings with Henry. After having claimed the throne and claimed Christine's son, Henry IV summoned Christine to join him (and Jean) in his court. Christine recounts her attempts to secure the return of her son from Henry in her *Avision*. She describes using her books as a means of feigning interest in Henry's offer to have her join him in his court, and as a means of having her son returned to her in France.[23] As J.C. Laidlaw notes, one extant copy of the *Epistre Othea* includes a dedication which appears to be not for Charles VI, as was originally thought, but rather for Henry IV.[24] The *Epistre Othea*, then, may have served not only as a moral guide for her transplanted son, but also as an instrument that Christine used to secure Henry IV's goodwill, so that she might eventually achieve the return of her son – '[je] dissimulay

1970), xii, xxi. On the popularity of the *Epistre Othea* and other works by Christine in England in the second half of the fifteenth century, see Jennifer Summit, *Lost Property: The Woman Writer and English Literary History, 1380–1589* (Chicago, IL: University of Chicago Press, 2000), 61–107; Stephanie Downes, 'A "Frenche booke called the Pistill of Othea": Christine de Pizan's French in England', in *Language and Culture in Medieval Britain: The French of England c.1100–c.1500*, ed. Jocelyn Wogan-Browne et al. (York: York Medieval Press, 2009), 457–68.

22 'If that work was intended for him, it must have been sent to him in England. Indeed, the [manuscript] rubric states that the work was *sent* and the point is made twice more in the associated gloss.' See Laidlaw, 'Christine de Pizan', 138.

23 'et a brief parler tant fis a grant peine / *et de mes livres me cousta* / que congie ot mon dit filx de me venir querir par de ca pour mener la qui encore ny vois' (Towner, *Lavision*, 166; italics mine). 'To be brief, I did so much with great effort and by means of my books that I obtained leave for my said son to come and fetch me to take me to a place I have yet to see' (McLeod and Willard, *Vision*, 107). I explore this remark in greater depth below.

24 Laidlaw, 'Christine de Pizan', 137–40. The manuscript in which this dedication appears – London, British Library, Harley 219 – very likely descends from the manuscript that Christine sent to Henry IV. See Downes, 'Christine de Pizan's French in England', 461–62. Cf. Meyer-Lee, *Poets and Power*, 62.

tant que mon filx peusse avoir / disant grant mercis / et que bien a son commandement estoye'.[25]

Hoccleve's question in his *Epistle* – 'Betrayen men nat remes grete and kynges?' – has relevance, then, not only for Henry IV's deposition of Richard II, but also for the nuances of Christine's day-to-day life during the three-year period in question. The year 1399 launched a sequence of events that saw Christine mired in the very subjects that Hoccleve echoes throughout the *Epistle*: the slaying of men, the betrayal of realms, the overexertion of a powerful man's will, and the oppression of those who are less powerful. This raises the question of how Hoccleve came into possession of a copy of Christine's *Epistre*, and the extent to which he was aware of the negotiations between the king and Christine. It is possible that Hoccleve, as a Privy Seal clerk in Westminster with connections to the likes of Chaucer (who was still alive until 1400), had access to information about Jean de Castel and his place in Henry's court.[26] By the first years of the fifteenth century, Christine also had a celebrity that transcended French borders: in her *Avision*, she notes that her works had already given her a reputation in foreign courts – in part because they were sent abroad 'par autres comme de chose nouvelle venue de sentement de femme'.[27] We have seen that Christine communicated directly with Henry, but it is likely that the novelty surrounding Christine's place as a woman clerk also manifested itself in England independently of her communications with Henry. The very fact that Hoccleve was able to translate Christine's *Epistre* within three years of its being written indicates the remarkable ability her works had to cross borders quickly at this time.

By the time Hoccleve had written the *Epistle* in May 1402, however, the situation involving Christine and Jean had grown very complicated. Jean returned to France either in late 1401, or, more likely, in the first half of 1402.[28] This dating is based in large part on Christine's *Autre Ballade*, XXII, in which 'Christine recommends her son Jean de Castel, newly returned from England, to the Duke of Orleans'.[29] The *ballade* is included

25 Towner, *Lavision*, 165–66. 'I concealed my feelings until I might have my son, expressing my thanks profusely and saying that I was fully at his [Henry IV's] command' (McLeod and Willard, *Vision*, 107).

26 Given Hoccleve's role as a royal scribe, a maker of verse, and a reader of French poetry, and given the young Jean's literary talents, Hoccleve may have even had reason to encounter the young Frenchman personally.

27 Towner, *Lavision*, 166; 'by others as a novelty arising from the judgment of a woman' (McLeod and Willard, *Vision*, 107).

28 Laidlaw, 'Christine de Pizan', 133–34.

29 Ibid., 130.

in Christine's 'Book', the first 'collected manuscript of her works', which was completed on June 23, 1402 – making that date the *terminus ad quem* for Jean's return to France.[30] If we accept Hoccleve's completion date for the *Epistle* of May 1402 (ll. 472–76), then he would have been composing the poem at the very time in which Jean had been granted leave to join his mother in France. However, this was by no means a straightforward affair. Christine recounts the turn of events with an enigmatic turn of phrase: 'et a brief parler tant fis a grant peine / et de mes livres me cousta / que congie ot mon dit filx de me venir querir par de ca pour mener la qui encore ny vois.'[31] It would appear that Christine asked Henry to allow Jean to return to France so that he might escort her back to England. Christine follows this comment with 'et ainsi reffusay leschoitte de ycelle fortune pour moy et pour lui pource que ie ne puis croire que fin de desloyal viengne a bon terme.'[32] Refusing this 'bequest of Fortune' connects with refusing the return trip to England, and therefore refusing a future in Henry IV's court. Christine also remarks that she feared her son would wish to return to England, due to the high rank he held there. Was Hoccleve writing his poem, then, at the very time in which Christine and Jean's return to England was being anticipated? Or just as Jean was leaving London? In either case, Hoccleve's choice to foreground the language of upheaval and political deceit in his own *Epistle* has very timely political implications. Hoccleve's poem would hardly assist in the king's initiative to ensure that Christine returned to England.

Any reading of the *Epistle* that takes into account Jean de Castel's situation must remain exploratory, as we do not know the extent to which Hoccleve was privy to the events unfolding between Christine and Henry IV at the turn of the fifteenth century. We can, however, note one particular change that Hoccleve makes to Christine's poem, and its relevance to our discussion: Christine opens her poem by describing Cupid as 'Filz de Venus, la deesse poissant' (4). Hoccleve, by contrast, writes: 'Cupido … Of goddesse Sitheree sone oonly' (1, 5). Rather than render Cupid as the son

[30] On French single-author codices (the precedents for Hoccleve's own 'collected poems' manuscripts – San Marino, Huntington Library, MSS HM 744 and 111), see Sylvia Huot, *From Song to Book: The Poetics of Writing in Old French Lyrics and Lyrical Narrative Poetry* (Ithaca, NY: Cornell University Press, 1987), especially Chapter 7.

[31] Towner, *Lavision*, 166. 'To be brief, I did so much with great effort and by means of my books that I obtained leave for my said son to come and fetch me to take me to a place I have yet to see' (McLeod and Willard, *Vision*, 107).

[32] Towner, *Lavision*, 166; 'and so I refused this bequest of Fortune for me and for him because I cannot believe a traitor might come to a good end' (McLeod and Willard, *Vision*, 107).

of Venus, Hoccleve calls Cupid the 'sone oonly' of Venus/Cythera.[33] Cupid was traditionally known to have a brother: as depicted in the *Roman de la Rose*, for example, 'the god of Love ... is the son of Venus and brother to Jocus, called Deduit in French'.[34] Hoccleve's decision to depict Cupid as the only son of Venus proves suggestive, because it was during the period 1399–1402 that Christine experienced the death of her younger son, leaving Jean as her only living son. On describing Jean's return from England, Christine says, 'or fus ioyeuse de veoir cil que ie amoye *comme mort / le meust seul filz laissie* et .iii. ans sans lui oz este'.[35] By 1402, Jean had become the 'sone oonly' of Christine de Pizan. Positioning Cupid in these terms can serve then, on one level, as a means of orienting the subject matter of the poem towards Jean's own personal situation.

Read in the light of Christine's relationship with her son, and Henry's attempt to come between them, the following stanza also takes on new meaning:

> A wikkid tree good fruyt may noon foorth brynge,
> For swich the fruyt is as þat is the tree.
> Take heede of whom thow took thy begynnynge.
> Lat thy modir be mirour vnto thee.
> Honure hire if thow wilt honurid be.
> Despyse thow nat hir in no maneere,
> Lest þat therthurgh thy wikkidnesse appeere.
>
> (176–82)

This stanza follows on from the suggestion that 'euery man' should feel tenderly towards women because every man is born of a woman. The lines in which Hoccleve invites his reader to regard his mother as a mirror ('Lat thy modir be mirour vnto thee. / Honure hire if thow wilt honurid be.') are original to Hoccleve's poem. The address noticeably shifts here from referring to 'euery man' in the third person, to addressing the reader

---

33 Hoccleve's choice to use 'Sitheree' rather than 'Venus' has a precedent in *Troilus and Criseyde*, where Chaucer refers to Venus as 'Citheria' (see III.1254–55: 'O Love, O Charite! / Thi moder ek, Citheria the swete ...'). Cf. Dante, *Purgatorio*, 27.95; and *Knight's Tale* I.2215–16 ('Unto the blisful Citherea benigne – / I mene Venus, honurable and digne ...'). Cythera was the place where, according to legend, Venus 'arose from the sea' (see Windeatt, *Troilus and Criseyde*, 412).

34 Fleming, 'Letter of Cupid', 35.

35 Towner, *Lavision*, 166; italics mine. 'Now I was delighted to see this one whom I loved, for Death had left him my only son and I had been three years without him' (McLeod and Willard, *Vision*, 107).

directly, in the singular second person. Such a presentation raises the question of whether Hoccleve has a specific 'son' in mind in this address. Again, Jean's own situation proves relevant. In the *Avision*, Christine notes how well Jean was treated when in England, and indicates that his return to France may have presented an unwelcome change of course not only for Henry IV, but also for Jean himself:

> Or fus ioyeuse de veoir cil que ie amoye comme mort / le meust seul filz laissie et .iii. ans sans lui oz este / mais crue fu la charge de ma deppense non a moy aysiee / Car ie doubtay que le grant estat / ou quel estoit par de la lui donnast vouloir de retourner comme enfant es quieulx consideracion nest grande volentiers se tiennent ad ce que aux yeulx et a leur aise meilleur leur semble. Si lui quis maistre grant et poissant qui de sa grace le retint.
>
> [Now I was delighted to see this one whom I loved, for Death had left him my only son and I had been three years without him. But the financial burden increased and was not easy for me. Because I feared that the high rank he had held over there might make him wish to return (as children, whose powers of observation are not very great, are prone to be attracted to what seems better and more comfortable to them). So I sought for him a great and powerful master, who might graciously retain him.][36]

Jean had spent three formative years among very influential members of the English nobility. John Montague's son of Jean's age – the boy that Jean originally came to England to accompany – went on to become the 'military genius of Henry V's armies'.[37] Jean's other peers in London would have included the future Henry V and the future Duke Humphrey. On returning to Paris, Jean had nowhere near so eminent a peer group. Instead, his mother scrambled to find a patron for him, and complained of the financial drain he presented. A young man in such a situation might benefit from being reminded to 'take heede of whom thow took thy begynnynge' – particularly if he was considering returning to Henry's court in England.[38]

Such resonances do not prove that Hoccleve was using his *Epistle* to comment on the situation unfolding between Jean, Christine, and Henry,

---

36 Towner, *Lavision*, 166; McLeod and Willard, *Vision*, 107.

37 Willard, *Christine de Pizan*, 165.

38 We might also note here the narrator's stated intention for the *Epistle*, which is to give women 'corage of perseuerance' (l. 454).

but they do, nevertheless, raise this as a possibility. After all, the *Epistle* would not have been the only instance of Hoccleve using an 'open letter' to address a timely personal problem with broader political implications. In 1415, Hoccleve used his poem 'To Sir John Oldcastle' to address the Lollard knight John Oldcastle, and to encourage him to recant his heretical views and return to 'Crystes feith'. There, too, Hoccleve advises the addressee to consider the example of 'fadres olde & modres'. Hoccleve writes: 'Our fadres olde & modres lyued wel, / And taghte hir children as hem self taght were / Of holy chirche ... Our fadres medled no thyng of swich gere: / þat oghte been a good mirour to vs' (ll. 153–55, 159–60). 'Fadres olde & modres' refers here in the first instance to ancestors or forefathers. As in the *Epistle*, these figures are presented as a 'mirour', and as a means of guiding the subject away from inappropriate behavior – in Oldcastle's case, away from the 'wikkidnesse' of heresy.

Our reading of the *Epistle* here indicates not a bid for poetic renown on Hoccleve's part – as Robert Meyer-Lee has suggested – but rather a self-presentation as a poetic mediator, as an individual capable of calling attention to – and even helping to ameliorate – contemporary conflicts. This remains the case whether Hoccleve refers in the *Epistle* to the specific situation unfolding between Christine, Jean, and Henry, or more generally to Henry's violent accession to the throne at the turn of the fifteenth century. This is an approach we see Hoccleve taking throughout his works. In his reading of Hoccleve's 'To Sir John Oldcastle', Andrew Cole notes the way Hoccleve intercedes in the altercation between Oldcastle and Archbishop Arundel, serving in some respects as an alternate version of Arundel – an alternate authority who can meet Oldcastle halfway.[39] Insofar as Hoccleve presents himself as a mediator in the altercation between Oldcastle and Arundel, he aims to use poetry as a space in which to form a bridge between two otherwise contentious or disunited subjects. This is the same Hoccleve who directs his *Regiment of Princes* towards the ultimate section on 'Peace', and towards the suggestion that Henry V marry a member of

39 Cole argues that 'Hoccleve greatly expands the opportunities for mercy that were reported to have been extended to Oldcastle and even goes so far as to substitute himself for the orthodox authority of Archbishop Arundel so as to offer what Arundel would not and could not – counsel in the virtue of mercy suitable to an aristocrat. ... In rewriting official discourses into exemplary narratives on the virtues, and in offering those narratives as outright alternatives to such discourses, Hoccleve endeavors to imagine possibilities that were shut down in the real time of history and only notionally present in the widely publicized, received versions of the events.' See Cole, *Literature and Heresy*, 105.

the French royalty in order to achieve a symbolic marriage between England and France.[40] Notably, too, in both 'Oldcastle' and the *Regiment*, Hoccleve evolves this role as mediator within a religious framework: in 'Oldcastle' Hoccleve attempts to persuade the addressee to return to 'Crystes feith', whereas in the *Regiment* he presents peace between England and France as a Christian imperative. In the *Epistle*, we see Hoccleve taking his first step towards a self-presentation as a poetic mediator – and towards situating poetic mediation as a virtuous pursuit in itself.[41]

Written in the Air

Hoccleve closes his *Epistle* with the conceit that the entire letter was 'writen in th'eir' (472), and it is useful to read the *Epistle* as, on one level, an evaluation of the shared 'airspace' between England and France. Recent scholarship has underscored the extent to which the boundary between

[40] See ll. 5384–429. This is a suggestion he ventriloquizes, no less, through the voice of another 'auctrice' – the visionary Bridget of Sweden. On Henry V's own portrayal as a peacemaker in the Church during this period, see Gillespie, 'Chichele's Church', 29–30. Henry V also discusses the virtue of peace in his founding charter for the Brigittine Monastery of Syon, for which see George James Aungier, *The History and Antiquities of Syon Monastery, the Parish of Isleworth, and the Chapelry of Hounslow, Compiled from Public Records, Ancient Manuscripts, Etc* (London: Nichols, 1840), 25–30. See also Neil Beckett, 'St Bridget, Henry V and Syon Abbey', in *Studies in St Birgitta and the Brigittine Order*, ed. James Hogg, *Analecta Cartusiana* 35.19 (1993): 125–50. For Hoccleve's use of the word 'auctrice' (a word that he coins, in reference to the Wife of Bath), see *Series* 2.694. For the Chaucerian precedent of citing the Wife of Bath as an authority, see 'Lenvoy de Chaucer a Bukton', ll. 29–30 (in Benson, *Riverside Chaucer*, 655–56); and cf. *CT* III.1, IV.1685–7.

[41] While the *Epistle* implicitly questions the use of the categories of 'vice and virtue' to describe groups of people, it also invites its readers to study 'holy writ' and to consider the role of Christ's female companions in the Gospels (see ll. 435–48). The religious context of the *Epistle* would have been amplified for a reader of San Marino, Huntington Library, MS HM 744 – one of Hoccleve's 'collected poems' manuscripts – in which the *Epistle* follows four poems of Marian devotion. The piece immediately preceding the *Epistle* depicts a monk who clothes the Virgin Mary by singing the 'Ave Maria', and that poem ends by compelling the reader to say 'hir psalteer'. The *Epistle*, by comparison, directs its readers to the Gospels, and indicates the one woman who *can* plausibly be called the 'hostesse' of all virtue – Christ's mother. Even the explicit command to honor one's mother ('Honure hire if thow wilt honurid be') communicates with the reader by revoicing the fourth commandment. While all men may not be devoid of virtue, and all women devoid of vice, men and women alike can pursue Christian virtue to the best of their abilities and thereby eschew 'wikkidnesse'.

late medieval English and French culture – as well as the geographical boundary between the respective nations – was constantly shifting, clashing in warfare, but also in dialogic and often antagonistic approaches to intellectual and literary pursuit.[42] Hoccleve's very work environment at the Office of the Privy Seal underscores this dynamic: the majority of the documents that Hoccleve drafted as a Privy Seal clerk would have been in French (of the 885 documents that comprise Hoccleve's *Formulary*, 704 are in French, with the remainder in Latin).[43] And in the final years of Henry V's reign, while the king was engaged on the continent, the Privy Seal had two sections: one in Westminster, and the other across the Channel in Calais.[44] While we do not have records of Hoccleve personally traveling to the continent, it is possible that he did, and his underclerk John Welde certainly did: Welde was rewarded, in May 1418, for his labours 'during the last three years both at Calais and in the kingdom of England'.[45] Ethan Knapp points out, too, that 'Christine and the various participants in the *Querelle* all were in contact with the French civil service, and it is quite likely that the esprit de corps among English clerks … extended internationally and had a significant component of shared cultural interests, even extending to common literary debates.'[46] We do not have documents that betray mutual respect or admiration between Hoccleve and his French counterparts – as we do in Deschamps's *ballade* to Chaucer, in which

---

42 For recent examples, see David Wallace, *Premodern Places: Calais to Surinam, Chaucer to Aphra Behn* (Oxford: Wiley-Blackwell, 2006), Chapter 1; Butterfield, *Familiar Enemy*; Jocelyn Wogan-Browne, Carolyn Colette, Maryanne Kowaleski, Linne Mooney, Ad Putter, and David Trotter, eds., *Language and Culture in Medieval Britain: The French of England c. 1100–c.1500* (York: York Medieval Press, 2009); Keith Busby and Christopher Kleinhenz, eds., *Medieval Multilingualism: The Francophone World and Its Neighbours*, Medieval Texts and Cultures of Northern Europe 20 (Turnhout: Brepols, 2010).

43 Burrow, 'Middle French Poets', 35. Hoccleve's *Formulary* – London, British Library, MS Additional 24062 – is edited in E.J.Y. Bentley, 'The Formulary of Thomas Hoccleve' (Ph.D. diss., Emory University, 1965).

44 Burrow, *Thomas Hoccleve*, 7; Brown 'Privy Seal Clerks', 262, 265; Burrow, 'Middle French Poets', 35–36.

45 Burrow, 'Middle French Poets', 35–36; Furnivall and Gollancz, *Hoccleve's Works*, lxii, n. 5. See also Brown, 'Privy Seal Clerks', 262.

46 Knapp, *Bureaucratic Muse*, 55. Knapp suggests 'the existence of a bureaucratic equivalent to the close cultural links between English, French, and Italian aristocracies that Gervase Mathew outlined under the rubric of "international court culture," some bureaucratic coterie crossing national boundaries'. See Gervase Mathew, *The Court of Richard II* (London: John Murray, 1968). See also Elisabeth Salter, 'Chaucer and Internationalism', *SAC* 2 (1980): 71–79.

Deschamps calls Chaucer 'grant translateur' and praises him for translating the *Roman de la Rose*[47] – but we do see in Hoccleve's poetry an avid interest in, and a propensity for, engaging with contemporary French poetry.[48]

This interest in French poetry is evident not only in the *Epistle*, after all, but throughout Hoccleve's poetry. Hoccleve's 'Complaint of the Virgin' is a translation of a portion of Guillaume de Deguileville's *Pelerinage de l'Ame* (c. 1358), and Hoccleve's translation was integrated into the full Middle English translation of Deguileville's work in ten manuscripts.[49] Hoccleve's short poem for Robert Chichele is also a French translation: the poem turns from a *chanson d'aventure* opening to an explicitly devotional focus, with prayers to Christ and the Virgin.[50] And, as John Burrow and A.C. Spearing have noted, the very format of the *Series* – in which a series of poetic texts arises spontaneously out of a conversation between two people – appears to be rooted foremost in the French *dit*, as employed by poets such as Guillaume de Machaut. The influence of the *dit* explains some of the more

---

47 This is 'Ballade 285' in Deschamps's *Œuvres complètes*. See *Œuvres complètes de Eustache Deschamps*, ed. Auguste Queux de Saint-Hilaire and Gaston Raynaud, 11 vols (Paris: Firmin Didot, 1878–1903).

48 This interest is carried out not only through allusion and specific instances of textual translation, but also through Hoccleve's self-presentation as a writer, and, for instance, through his impulse to create manuscripts of his collected poems – an act unprecedented in England, but for which Hoccleve had clear precedents in France: both Machaut and Christine created 'collected poems' manuscripts in the decades before Hoccleve undertook the production of his collections. On these precedents, see Huot, *From Song to Book*, Chapter 7. On the influence of French poetry on Hoccleve's self-presentation as author, see Spearing, *Medieval Autographies*, Chapters 5 and 6.

49 Burrow and Doyle, *Facsimile*, xii; Burrow, *Thomas Hoccleve*, 24. Hoccleve's translation is item 1 in MS HM 111, and is edited in Ellis, *'My Compleinte'*, 53–60. The colophon in MS HM 111 identifies the recipient of this poem as 'ma dame de Hereford' (f. 7v). The Lady of Hereford in question is Joan Bohun, sister of Thomas Arundel (1353–1414), who served as bishop of Ely, archbishop of York and archbishop of Canterbury. Hereford was also the first wife of Henry IV and the grandmother of Henry V. (See Burrow, *Thomas Hoccleve*, 24; A.I. Doyle, *The Vernon Manuscript: A Facsimile of Bodleian Library, Oxford, MS. Eng.poet. A.1* (Cambridge: Brewer, 1987), 16; Watt, *Making*, 40.) Hoccleve's poem was integrated into the full English translation of Deguileville's *Pelerinage de l'Ame*. As such, it has an analogue in Chaucer's 'ABC', which 'was incorporated into the English version of its source, Deguileville's *Pelerinage de Vie Humaine*'. See Burrow, *Thomas Hoccleve*, 24.

50 Burrow, *Thomas Hoccleve*, 25; Ellis, *'My Compleinte'*, 87. This poem is item 19 in MS HM 111; and is edited in Ellis, *'My Compleinte'*, 82–86. It, too, is dedicated to the sibling of an archbishop: Robert Chichele was the brother of Henry Chichele, who succeeded Thomas Arundel as archbishop of Canterbury, and served in that position from 1414 to 1443. On Henry Chichele's tenure, see Gillespie, 'Chichele's Church'.

unorthodox features of the *Series*, including the foregrounding of Hoccleve's authorial 'je' and the way in which the *Series* evolves in a montage-like way, presenting in the course of an ongoing dialogue 'choses qui existent, ou qui peuvent existent par ailleurs, anterieurement'.[51] Hoccleve uses this form to collect his poetic texts in the *Series*, while also giving his collection an overall unity by framing it as the result of an ongoing dialogue with a friend. His use of the *dit* form proves exceptional because the characters comment not only on the Hocclevian texts within the sequence, but also on Hocclevian texts that exist beyond the sequence, such as the *Epistle*. Furthermore, Hoccleve's poem takes the *dit* form – which was used primarily for love poetry, as in Machaut's *Voir Dit* – and uses it instead to touch on anything but romantic love: mental illness and recovery, warfare, the need to respond to public opinion, and the role of moralization in poetry.

I would like to suggest that even the manner in which Hoccleve portrays his return to health in the 'Complaint' might take its cue from a French poem – in this case, a petitionary *ballade* written by Eustache Deschamps.[52] In the *ballade*, Deschamps complains that he has been suffering from a 'maladie' for five years, but hopes to be 'tous sains' ('entirely cured' / 'all sane') come 'Toussains' (All Saints' Day). Here is the opening stanza:

> J'ay par cinq ans esté en maladie,
> Dont mire nul ne m'a voulu guerir,
> De pou d'argent, ou maint homme mendie;
> Or ay trouvé qui m'a fait l'uis ouvrir
> De surgien pour mes plaies garir,
> Li quelz m'a dit que je seray tous sains;
> Mais il me fault endurer et soufrir
> Le mal que j'ay jusqu'après la Toussains.

---

[51] Jacqueline Cerquiglini, 'Le clerc et l'écriture: le *voir dit* de Guillaume de Machaut et la définition du *dit*', in *Literatur in der Gesellschaft des Spätmittelalters*, ed. Hans Ulrich Gumbrecht (Heidelberg: C. Winter, 1980), 44. This essay offers an introduction to the *dit*, and a discussion of its distinguishing features. On the *dit*, and subjectivity in French and English poetry, see also Sarah Kay, *Subjectivity in Troubadour Poetry*, Cambridge Studies in French (Cambridge: Cambridge University Press, 1990); Michael Zink, *The Invention of Literary Subjectivity*, trans. David Sices (Baltimore, MD: Johns Hopkins University Press, 1999); Burrow, 'Middle French Poets'; Spearing, *Medieval Autographies*.

[52] The *ballade* in question is no. 902 in Deschamps's *Œuvres complètes*. Burrow discusses this *ballade* in 'Middle French Poets', 45–48, but compares it there with Hoccleve's *Male Regle*, rather than the *Series*. The English translation is from Burrow, 'Middle French Poets', 47.

> [For five years I have been suffering from a disease which no doctor has wished to cure – lack of money, from which many a man suffers; but now I have found someone who has opened for me the door to a surgeon who can cure my wounds; and he has said that I will be completely cured, but I must wait and endure the illness that I have until after All Saints' Day.]

This is, to be sure, a playful complaint concerning the narrator's lack of money. But a reader of Hoccleve's 'Complaint' will immediately recognize the resonances: the poet suffering from a 'maladie', which (both poets say) will be cured on All Saints' Day (see 'Complaint', l. 55). Even the period of 'five years' stands out in both – in Deschamps, it is the length of his illness; in Hoccleve, it is the length of time he has been cured (l. 56). It would seem that Hoccleve seized on Deschamps's poem – with its premise of becoming 'tous sains' on 'Toussains' – and adapted it.[53] He begins his *Series* in 'the broun sesoun of Mihelmesse' (2), bringing in that reversal of the *Canterbury Tales*'s spirited spring, and expands on Deschamps's figurative illness to comment on what would appear to be an actual illness. The poem then takes a devotional turn: the 'surgeon' capable of curing the poet's wounds becomes God himself, whom Hoccleve likens to a doctor (see 2.85–91), and Hoccleve positions his recovery, on All Saints' Day, as evidence of 'Goddes visitacioun' (1.382).

In the last chapter, I read Hoccleve's personal recovery in the light of the simultaneous recovery of the Christian Church on a local English level, as well as on an international level, at the Council of Constance. In internalizing a broader process of reform and recovery in his own person, Hoccleve can also be seen to follow a Deschampian *modus operandi*: Ardis Butterfield has shown how Deschamps uses his poetic persona – and his name – to reflect the after-effects of international conflict in his poetry. In *ballade* no. 835, for instance, Deschamps develops his personal identity as a means of signaling the impact that the Hundred Years War has had on his 'terre' – his land:

> Eustace fu appellé dès enfans;
> Or sui tous ars, s'est mon nom remué:
> J'aray desor a nom Brulé des Champs....
>
> Las! ma terre est destruitte et ruyneuse,
> Je suis desert, destruit et desolé ...

53 Given this context, it is also helpful to consider that the Michaelmas installment of Hoccleve's annuity was not paid in 1414. He found himself in quite the same position, financially, as Deschamps's narrator (Burrow, *Thomas Hoccleve*, 22).

[Eustace is what I have been called since my childhood;
Now I am completely burned, my name is changed;
I will have from now on the name Burned of the Fields….

Alas! My land is destroyed and ruined,
I am ravaged, destroyed, and desolate…]

(lines 6–8, 17–18)

This presentation binds the name of the poet to the 'terre' with which he identifies. His own sense of being 'desert, destruit et desolé' arises from the land having been likewise destroyed. The poet takes on the name, therefore, of 'Brulé des Champs [Deschamps]' – indicating in his very person the debilitating effects of English violence, and the ability of this individual to survive and create.[54] Hoccleve can be seen to follow in the footsteps of his French predecessor in the *Series*, by embodying international strife in his own poetic persona, and by using his historical person as both an emblem of strife and a model for recovery and resilience.

The 'transnational', 'ecclesiastical', 'political', and 'poetic' threads interweave almost seamlessly in these aspects of Hoccleve's life and work: the *Series* uses French poetics – both in its adaptation of the *dit* form, and (as I argue here) also in its adaptation of Deschamps – in part to speak to the ongoing nature of the war between England and France, and to reflect the military deeds of Duke Humphrey in places such as Cherbourg and Rouen. In the case of the French *ballade* translated by Hoccleve and addressed to Robert Chichele, it is equally important to remember that Hoccleve's recipient for that poem is none other than the brother of Archbishop Henry Chichele. Vincent Gillespie discusses this poem in the light of the ecclesiastical issues discussed at Constance – and Hoccleve's prayer therein that God 'Graunte pardoun of our stynkyng errour' (l. 152) – and Robert Chichele's identity as the brother of the leader of the English Church proves of utmost importance in this context: it is at Constance that the English Church's 'stynkyng errour' was being engaged, examined, and 'corrected'. Even the fact that Hoccleve was associated with a transnational Privy Seal during his lifetime has very real political implications: the section of the Privy Seal stationed across the Channel existed there because of Henry V's extended presence in France during his reign; and Henry V was

[54] See Butterfield, *Familiar Enemy*, 136–37. I use Butterfield's translation here. Butterfield argues that 'Eustace rises from the ashes of English devastation to become a latter-day poetic master' (137). She also notes that his very surname, 'Deschamps,' may have been invented in this poem, and in another poem, as a result of this wordplay.

there, of course, in large part owing to his ongoing military campaign on the continent. A large number of the documents that passed Hoccleve's desk in the Privy Seal also facilitated warfare: they arranged for the transportation and maintenance of soldiers, and remunerated subjects for holding castles during sieges – much as a number of Privy Seal documents pertained to England's role at the Council of Constance.[55] It is in this context that Hoccleve's *Epistle of Cupid* resurfaces in the *Series*, and it is in this context that the divisive language of virtue and vice, pure and impure, white and black, resurfaces.

In bringing the *Epistle* to the forefront of his 'Dialogue', Hoccleve seems to signal not only a particular poem, but indeed a particular discourse and – with it – a particular polarizing framework. This is evident, as I showed in the previous chapter, in the *Gesta Romanorum* tales and their conspicuously displayed moralizations. It is evident, too, in the Friend's simplified approach to texts and meaning, and in the suggestion that Hoccleve translate Vegetius's *De re militari* for Duke Humphrey – that text which Ruth Nissé calls 'a blunt how-to manual for winning a war with the Roman army'.[56] While we cannot say for certain how much of Christine's poetry Hoccleve had read beyond the *Epistre*, it is instructive to consider how these emblematic texts constellate around an approach to vernacular writing that is noticeably 'Christinian'. One of the closest contemporary analogues for Hoccleve's *Gesta Romanorum* tales would have been Christine's *Epistre Othea*: Christine presents the work as a letter from Othea, the goddess of wisdom, to the fifteen-year-old Hector of Troy; it consists of 100 verse vignettes given in Othea's voice, accompanied by prose glosses and moralizations given in Christine's voice.[57] The work indicates a similar relationship

---

[55] On Constance and the Privy Seal, see Van Dussen, *Heresy and Communication*, 111. Several of the documents that Hoccleve created at the Privy Seal pertain to the funding and facilitation of warfare: see the documents listed in 'Appendix B' to Mooney, 'Some New Light', 322–40. In light of Hoccleve's call for peace at the close of the *Regiment*, we might question whether Hoccleve was at odds with his role as a facilitator of warfare. In the *Series*, after all, Thomas draws a distinction between England as a site of productive translation ('Englishing') and France as a site of warfare (2.204–40; 566–616). Then, at the end of the 'Dialogue', Hoccleve presents translation as a means of remaining in England, rather than being forced to France (and, thus, to war; see 2.820–26). We will explore the *Regiment*'s call for peace in greater detail in Chapters 3 and 5.

[56] Nissé, '"Our fadres olde and modres"', 295.

[57] We might remember here that the Friend positions the second *Gesta* tale in the *Series* as a text to be used in calibrating the moral sensibilities of his 'sone … [of] xv yeer of age' (5.23), much as the *Epistre Othea* is presented as a text for the fifteen-year-old Hector of Troy – and likely, in reality, intended for the fifteen-year-old Jean de Castel.

between verse and prose to Hoccleve's *Gesta Romanorum* tales: it provides moral meaning, in the form of succeeding prose passages, to explain each verse passage. Hoccleve's suggestion earlier in the 'Dialogue' that he could translate Vegetius's *De re militari* also proves relevant to Christine: another of Christine's texts from the early years of the fifteenth century – *Le livre des fais d'armes et de chevalerie* (c. 1404) – draws on *De re militari* and, judging from Thomas's dialogue with the Friend, would have been exactly the type of text that Humphrey would have enjoyed reading.[58] In positioning *De re militari* and the *Gesta* tales as *the* works that reflect Humphrey's literary taste in the *Series*, Hoccleve indicates texts that reflect a given literary taste which accords with Christine's own approach to writing in the early fifteenth century – and he does so by referring simultaneously to that poem in his own corpus which is a translation of one of Christine's works, the *Epistle of Cupid*.[59]

---

58 On the popularity of Christine's *Fais d'armes* in England, and its role in defining masculinity and chivalry, see Dominique T. Hoche, *The Reception of Christine de Pizan's Fais d'Armes in Fifteenth-Century England: Chivalric Self-Fashioning* (New York: Edwin Mellen Press, 2007). See also Summit, *Lost Property*, 71–81. One adaptation of the *Fais d'armes* survives in London, British Library, MS Royal 15 E VI – a manuscript intended for Margaret of Anjou upon her marriage to Henry VI in 1445. Another copy of the *Fais d'armes* was written by a French scribe in London in 1434 (in British Library, MS Harley 4605). See Downes, 'Christine de Pizan's French in England', 459–60.

59 Lydgate also draws from the *Epistre Othea* in his *Troy Book* (c. 1412–20): he departs from his source text when recounting the death of Hector, and draws instead on Christine's moralized reading of the episode from the *Epistre Othea*. See C. David Benson, 'Prudence, Othea and Lydgate's Death of Hector', *The American Benedictine Review* 26 (1975): 115–23; and Benson, *The History of Troy in Middle English Literature: Guido delle Colonne's 'Historia Destructionis Troiae' in Medieval England* (Woodbridge: D.S. Brewer, 1980), 124–29. See also Meyer-Lee, *Poets and Power*, 64–65. Stephanie Downes notes that 'English translations of the *Othea* suggest its reception chiefly as a manual of chivalry in the fifteenth century.' Downes also notes that French manuscripts of *Othea* circulated among English audiences in even greater number than English translations. London, British Library, MS Harley 219 was made in England; British Library, MS Royal 14 E II was made 'before 1483 for Edward IV'; British Library, MS Harley 4431 'was purchased by John of Lancaster, duke of Bedford, in 1425'; and Oxford, Bodleian Library, MS Laud misc. 570 was made for John Fastolf in 1450. Bedford's manuscript had originally been presented to the queen of France, Isabeau of Bavaria, around 1413. MS Harley 219 (mid-15th c.) provides an especially intriguing point of comparison with respect to Hoccleve's works: not only does it include the version of *Othea* that appears to descend directly from that given to Henry IV, but it also includes tales from the *Gesta Romanorum* (in Latin) and a French copy of the pseudo-Aristotelian *Secret des secrets* (the *Secreta Secretorum*, which is one of Hoccleve's three named source texts for the *Regiment*). The epistolary form of the *Secret*

In responding to the polarizing language of vice and virtue in the *Epistle*, after all, Hoccleve is also responding – whether explicitly or implicitly – to Christine's rhetorical approach in the *Epistre au dieu d'amours*. As we have seen, Hoccleve's portrayal of women as 'hostesses' of virtue, who are incapable of containing vice, comes across as parody because it oversimplifies the differences between the sexes. Ethan Knapp underscores the shortcomings of this poetic approach, and the manner in which it indicates the nature of Hoccleve's response to Christine: 'as long as virtue is defined through its power to eliminate the complexities we saw defined above as hypocrisy, these images of pious simplicity risk leading in a rhetorical circle back to the misogynist stereotypes they were meant to oppose'.[60] Given the broader political context of our discussion here, the foregrounding of the polarizing language of vice and virtue in Hoccleve's *Epistle* also has deeper, and more topical, implications. As we have seen, Hoccleve uses his *Epistle* to evoke the actions of Henry IV and their effects in both England and France, much as he uses his *Series* to broach the topic of heresy, and to echo the measures taken against heretics both at home by Duke Humphrey, and at the Council of Constance by representatives of the European nations. Hoccleve's polarizing language in both poems allows him to gesture towards a specific discourse – us versus them, good versus bad, pure versus impure – and its effects not only on literature, but also on the daily lives of individual subjects.

To illustrate this in the context of Christine's *milieu*, we can consider the figure of Jean Gerson, the French scholar, poet, and Chancellor of the University of Paris. Gerson took part in Christine de Pizan's epistolary debate – the *Querelle de la Rose* – against Jean de Montreuil, Pierre Col, and Gontier Col from 1401 to 1402.[61] Gerson's contributions to the *Querelle* – in

des secrets complements the epistolary form of the *Othea*, much as the moralizations attached to the *Gesta* tales complement the glosses and allegories accompanying the verse passages in *Othea*. See Downes, 'Christine de Pizan's French in England', 467, 457–59, 461–63.

[60] Knapp, *Bureaucratic Muse*, 69.

[61] Christine McWebb's anthology, *Debating the Roman de la Rose*, offers an excellent overview of the *Querelle de la Rose*, and collects letters that comprised the *Querelle*, as well as treatises, sermons, and poems that fit into the broader context of the debate. On one level, Christine's *Epistre au dieu d'amours* served as a prelude to the *Querelle*, in that it presented her response to misogyny in French poetic tradition. The *Querelle* focused on the questionable morality of the *Rose*, the use of obscene expressions in the poem, the degree to which an author should be blamed for the immoral content of his work, and whether immoral texts provoke immoral behavior. See Christine McWebb, ed., *Debating the Roman de la Rose: A Critical Anthology* (London: Routledge, 2007).

the form of letters, sermons, and a treatise – indicate the way in which the literary debate also became a theological debate: in responding to the *Roman de la Rose*, Gerson draws on his identity as an ecclesiastical as well as literary authority.[62] He imagines Jean de Meun returning from the dead so that he might confess, submit, and repent: 'je tiens en bonne foy que ynellement, volentiers et de cuer il confesseroit son erreur, demanderoit pardon, crieroit mercy et paieroit l'amende' [I am very confident that without further ado, voluntarily and sincerely, he would confess his error and ask for forgiveness, cry for mercy and pay his repentance].[63] He accuses the *Rose* of quashing the moral sensibilities of the young; and he suggests that those who produce and publish literature such as the *Rose* should destroy their texts (with the help of their confessors) and seek penance.[64] Christine, likewise, uses the *Querelle* to position the defenders of the *Rose* as a 'mauvaise secte' [bad sect] that grows like a weed, and should be eliminated; and she distinguishes between members of that sect ('qui veulent malicieusement vivre' [who wish to live sinfully]), and the opponents of the *Rose* ('qui veulent bien et simplement vivre' [who wish to live well and simply]).[65] Christine bolsters her offensive by aligning it with Gerson's religious authority: 'et comme dit le bon preudomme qui composa la playdoire dessusdicte: «Pleust a Dieu que tele *Rose* n'eust oncques esté plantée ou jardin de Crestianté!»' [As the good

See also Alastair J. Minnis, *Magister Amoris: The Roman de la Rose and Vernacular Hermeneutics* (Oxford: Oxford University Press, 2001).

62 Jean Gerson succeeded his mentor Pierre d'Ailly as Chancellor of the University of Paris in 1395. He was a decidedly influential theologian and reformist, and would become one of the most prominent actors in the early fifteenth-century ecclesiastical reform movement. On Gerson, see Brian Patrick McGuire, *Jean Gerson and the Last Medieval Reformation* (University Park, PA: Pennsylvania State University Press, 2005); *A Companion to Jean Gerson*, ed. Brian Patrick McGuire (Leiden: Brill, 2006); and Daniel Hobbins, *Authorship and Publicity Before Print: Jean Gerson and the Transformation of Late Medieval Learning* (Philadelphia: University of Pennsylvania Press, 2009). At the close of the Council of Constance, and while in exile from France, Gerson wrote his *De consolatione theologiae*, a work based on Boethius's *Consolation of Philosophy*. On this work, see Mark S. Burrows, *Jean Gerson and 'De consolatione theologie' (1418): The Consolation of a Biblical and Reforming Theology for a Disordered Age*, Beiträge zur historischen Theologie 78 (Tübingen: Mohr, 1991).

63 From Jean Gerson's treatise against the *Roman de la Rose*, dated May 18, 1402: McWebb, *Debating the Roman*, 280–81.

64 See Gerson's treatise against the *Rose* in McWebb, *Debating the Roman*, 272–305. See also Gerson's sermons from December 1402 to March 1403 in this anthology (pp. 364–71). See especially pp. 364–65 for the suggestion that owners of impure books such as the *Rose* should be forced by their confessors to destroy them and seek penance.

65 McWebb, *Debating the Roman*, 182–84.

nobleman stated, who composed the above-mentioned complaint, 'Would that it had pleased God for this *Rose* never to have been planted in the garden of Christendom!']

A decade after the *Querelle*, from 1414 to 1418, Gerson applied his energies at the Council of Constance, where the focus of the debate was not the *Roman de la Rose*, but rather the theological treatises of John Wyclif and Jan Hus, and where the stakes for disagreeing with institutional definitions were raised considerably: as we saw in the last chapter, Jan Hus was executed at Constance for his beliefs.[66] Gerson's movement mirrors a transition that Hoccleve evokes throughout the *Series*: a transition from literary exchange and debate, to the use of the same interpretive skills on the world stage to identify and punish heresy – another act, albeit with much harsher consequences, rooted in a totalizing and authoritative understanding of 'virtue' and 'vice'.

This context proves especially relevant to Hoccleve's work because it is at Constance that Gerson misinterprets Hus's texts and uses his misinterpretation as ammunition in accusing Hus of his 'pernicious errors' – which calls to mind the Friend's approach in the *Series*. As Matthew Spinka points out, Gerson conflated Hus's views with Wyclif's, claiming that Hus's 'most pernicious error' was the 'assertion that the foreknown man in mortal sin does not have dominion or jurisdiction over the Christian community' – this is a claim that Wyclif did make, and Hus did not. Gerson demanded that Hus's errors be eradicated 'by fire and sword'. Hus makes his suspicion of Gerson known during his interrogation at Constance in June 1415, while simultaneously differentiating himself from Wyclif and his teachings.[67]

In the *Series*, Hoccleve also appears to enact the process that Christine and Gerson prescribe for literary repentance in the *Querelle*: admitting the 'error' of his past poetry, submitting himself to a process of quasi-religious repentance and reform, and doing so under the guidance of an approved intermediary. But he does so, notably, by alluding to those early champions of the *Roman de la Rose*: Chaucer and Deschamps. While it is possible that Hoccleve had read the *Querelle* epistles by the time he wrote the *Series*, it is equally possible that such an intellectual climate had reached England in its own forms during the first two decades of the fifteenth century – as an aspect, for instance, of the political and ecclesiastical climate that we explored in Chapter 1. It is also possible, given that Hoccleve was writing the *Series* in the years following the Council of Constance, that he had been

66 Gerson had already condemned a selection of Hus's opinions before setting out for Constance. See Crowder, *Unity, Heresy, and Reform*, 90.

67 See Spinka, *John Hus*, 163–81 (171–72).

apprised of Gerson's approach at Constance. As Daniel Hobbins has shown, Gerson seized the opportunity at Constance to disseminate his works, past and present, and to build his fame internationally.[68] The English bishops who served as delegates at Constance would certainly have come into first-hand contact with Gerson's approaches to orthodox reform. Vincent Gillespie notes that 'surviving copies of the *acta* of Konstanz made by, or for, Englishmen often contain copies of the two great reform treatises of Pierre d'Ailly and the works of that other French reformer Jean Gerson'.[69] In any case, we see in the *Series* the imprint of transnational politics, the effects of ecclesiastical reform, and the impact of both on an international literary tradition extending from Jean de Meun through Deschamps and Chaucer.

Tracking the movements of Gerson and Christine also offers us a new light in which to read the *Epistle* and 'Oldcastle', and a new way to comprehend Hoccleve's role as a mediator. Hoccleve betrays an awareness of the heightened stakes in these texts – the implications for so-called heretics, as well as the impact of starkly weaponized language on an emergent English literary tradition. Hoccleve's mediatory stance indicates a reactionary poetics, and a need to locate middle ground as tensions rise.

As we approach the next chapter, we transition from considering Hoccleve's meditation on the limitations of the language of 'virtue' and 'vice' in the *Epistle* and the *Series*, to examining the way in which the figure of Chaucer is itself 'moralized' in Hoccleve's *Regiment*. As we will see, this repositioning of Chaucer does not limit the potentials for narrative complexity in Hoccleve's poem, nor does it limit his ability to convey meaning. Rather, it paradoxically allows Hoccleve to operate more autonomously in the face of institutional pressure. It is to that subject – and Hoccleve's role as a mediator in bringing that version of Chaucer to light – that we now turn.

---

68 Hobbins notes, 'The Council of Constance benefited Gerson, then, not just because intellectuals flocked there and many wanted to read and to copy his works, but because it introduced those works into regions that were producing three times as many manuscripts as France was. His works found new audiences and spread to new readers, beginning the transition to a massive market.' Constance presented Gerson with an opportunity, and Hobbins indicates how readily Gerson seized it: he distributed old works, published nine sermons, and wrote 'no fewer than twenty-eight original compositions'. See Hobbins, *Authorship and Publicity*, 194; cf. 162.

69 The library at Syon also included reformist writings by d'Ailly and Gerson. See Gillespie, 'Chichele's Church', 12, n. 21 and 25–26; and on the *acta* of Constance, see C.M.D. Crowder, 'Constance *Acta* in English Libraries', in *Das Konzil von Konstanz; Beiträge zu seiner Geschichte und Theologie*, ed. A. Franzen and W. Müller (Freiburg: Herder, 1964), 477–517.

Chapter Three

'What shal I calle thee? What is thy name?': Hoccleve, Chaucer, and the Architectonics of Fame

'What shal I calle thee, what is thy name?'
'Hoccleve, fadir myn, men clepen me.'
'Hoccleve, sone?' 'Ywis, fadir, that same.'
'Sone, I have herd or this men speke of thee;
Thow were aqweyntid with Chaucer, pardee –
God have his soule, best of any wight!
Sone, I wole holde thee that I have hight.'

(1863–69)

The stanza in which Hoccleve first names himself in the *Regiment of Princes* is notable not only for the way in which Hoccleve associates himself with Chaucer, but also for the way in which the mention of Chaucer brings with it an immediate commendation and blessing. This stanza not only aligns Hoccleve with Chaucer; it conspicuously affirms Chaucer's good standing in the eyes of a figure who has thus far aligned himself with the institutional church, and who has shown a distinct interest in validating Hoccleve's own religious orthodoxy: the old man.[1] Line 1868 – 'God have

1 For the old man's self-alignment with the church, see *Regiment*, ll. 351–71. For his interest in confirming Hoccleve's own orthodoxy, see ll. 372–85. This character has variously been referred to as 'the beggar' (following Furnivall's sidenotes), 'the almsman', and 'the old man' in Hoccleve scholarship. I refer to him as 'the old man' to refrain from assigning him an official role as beggar or almsman. As we shall see, the vagueness of the old man's identity serves the variety of ends to which Hoccleve uses him in the

his soule, best of any wight!' – has the air of an off-hand comment, but it speaks well to Hoccleve's main objectives for Chaucer in the *Regiment*: to align Chaucer clearly with orthodox Christianity to an unprecedented extent, to marry Chaucer's image with the idea of vernacular literary pursuit, and to apotheosize Chaucer – to put him forth within the social life of the poem as literally 'best of any wight'. The nature of Chaucer's transformation into the 'best of any wight' in the *Regiment* will be the subject of this chapter.

*

The narrative conceit that Hoccleve uses in the first section of the *Regiment*, which he later reprises in his *Series*, appears to have its roots in Chaucer's prologue to the *Legend of Good Women*. There, Chaucer is called upon by the God of Love to defend his works and, implicitly, to explain his way of life as a maker of verse.[2] In the *Series*, Hoccleve is quite similarly called upon to defend both his prior works and his reasons for writing the *Series* itself,[3] but in the *Regiment* Hoccleve's approach is more personal: the old man who engages Hoccleve in conversation is more interested in examining the details of Hoccleve's person. Hoccleve's position as a writer of verse who was 'acquainted' with Chaucer is revealed later in the dialogue; what is immediately important to the old man is whether Hoccleve aligns himself with heretics such as John Badby and, for instance, whether he pursued marriage for 'clennesse' (and therefore orthodox Christian reasons) or 'muk' (and therefore worldly reasons).[4] Moreover, these questions are being leveled at Hoccleve not in Chaucer's timeless dream-court of 'Love', but instead in

poem. His role as a conspicuously orthodox figure, however, is paramount and clearly foregrounded in the *Regiment*. Derek Pearsall has suggested the possibility that this character may be a Carmelite friar, noting the reference to the old man being found daily at the 'Carmes messe', the Carmelite refectory (*Regiment*, l.2007). His alignment with the Carmelite refectory is telling because, as Pearsall notes, 'the Carmelites were particularly fierce in their attacks on Lollardy'. Among the most notable Carmelites of the period were Stephen Patringdon, who became Henry V's confessor when he ascended the throne, and Thomas Netter, who was a staunch opponent of Lollardy, and who also later became the king's confessor. Pearsall concludes cautiously: 'He does not say he is a Carmelite friar, but whether he is or not the deliberate association of the father confessor figure of the poem with the strictest upholders of anti-Lollard orthodoxy is striking.' See Pearsall, 'Hoccleve's *Regement*', 407.

2 See G.234–545.

3 See especially *Series* 2.750–826. See also Chapter 1.

4 See ll. 1555–61.

the very specific environs of London circa 1410–11.[5] The accusations come not from the mythic God of Love, but from a man who aligns himself conspicuously and strongly with the institutional church, and who takes a special, even unsettling, interest in Hoccleve's person.

In Chaucer's poetry, 'Love' can take 'Holy Church' as a referent, much as 'the religion of love' that we find in *Troilus and Criseyde* can navigate a space both within and beyond the confines of institutional Christianity – a space that allows for playful reflection on prayer and the dynamics of religious belief. Hence Chaucer's narrator can address himself to the disciples of Love, rather than the disciples of Christ. He can speak of characters as having been 'converted' by Love, and he can refer to devotees of Love as following a religious 'order' ('In feith, youre ordre is ruled in good wise!' (I.336; see also, for instance, I.988–1001)).[6] Such techniques allow Chaucer to create a separate, pseudo-religious space within his poems, a space within which his characters can pray and philosophize without seeming to impinge on the domain of the institutional Christian church. Pandarus can call out to God in a moment of revelation – '"Immortal god," quod he, "that mayst nought deyen"' – but then quickly clarify that he worships in a separate space than the one occupied on any given Sunday by the reader – '"*Cupide I mene*, of this mayst glorifie ..."' (III.185–86; italics mine). The religion of Love is a safe house of sorts for the maker of verse; it is cautious even as it is playful. So, Chaucer can kneel and 'defend' his works before the God of Love, and he can buoy his defense with the good humor of one who is not, in the end, altogether afraid of the repercussions.

In the *Regiment*, we see Hoccleve attempting to insinuate himself into this 'order of Love' – this order apart – without much success. The old man's questions to Hoccleve focus overwhelmingly on how the poet conceives of himself in relation to the doctrines of the organized church. Hoccleve's responses act as an attempt to define his poetic exemption – his credentials as an individual who thinks not along lines of 'heterodox' and 'orthodox', 'religious' and 'worldly', but rather within that ambiguous and playful other-place presided over by 'Love'. So, for instance, when the old man asks Hoccleve what his 'motyf' was in getting married, he offers Hoccleve two options: either one marries 'to gete children lawfully, / And in clennesse to lede thy lyf', or one marries for 'lust or muk' (1557–59). Hoccleve's answer

---

[5] On the dating of the *Regiment*, see Burrow, *Thomas Hoccleve*, 18; Perkins, *Hoccleve's Regiment*, 1.

[6] See *Troilus and Criseyde* in Benson, *Riverside Chaucer*. For an overview of this dynamic, see Jenni Nuttall, *Troilus and Criseyde: A Reader's Guide* (Cambridge: Cambridge University Press, 2012), 32–33.

conspicuously falls outside the two-dimensional framework that the old man has introduced: 'Fadir, nothyng wole I it qweynte make; / Oonly for love I chees hir to my make' (1560–61). A Chaucerian reader may well notice the connotation of 'love' here as a separate space, a space in which the poet reserves a right to fiction, a space that represents the poet's special status as one who spends his time in a world apart from the world of heresy and executions. The old man refers to Hoccleve as existing within an 'order of wedlock' (1478), and our minds may well travel to Chaucer's 'order of love'. But for the old man this 'order' is only conceivable in terms of the institutional church:

> The ordres of preesthode and wedlok
> Been bothe vertuous, withouten fable;
> But undirstonde wel, the holy yok
> Of preesthode is, as it is resonable
> That it so be, the more commendable
>
> (1478–82)

In the old man's eyes, the 'order of wedlock' is not a playful means of operating outside the two-dimensional strictures promulgated by the church; it is instead a status to be understood – and understood '*well*' – as operating within the structure of the hierarchical church and, importantly, beneath the more 'commendable' order of priesthood. The order of 'love' here fails to operate as a distancing tactic for the poet; instead, it only further entangles Hoccleve in the old man's snare. Hoccleve can claim to be among those who follow no rules but 'oonly ... love', but this only leads to more specific questions from the old man, and to more hortatory sermons on the dangers of lust and 'muk'.[7]

In the first section of the *Regiment*, then, we see a given poetic discourse having to reckon with an overtly religious discourse. This manifests itself in a rhetorical dissonance: Hoccleve fights back against the old man's approach in an attempt to preserve his separate imaginative and social space. This conversation culminates, at last, in Hoccleve's sporadic three-stanza paean to Chaucer and Gower, in which the Chaucerian reader might recognize the influence, for instance, of Chaucer's *Book of the Duchess*. Hoccleve's 'What eiled deeth? Allas, why wolde he sle the?' (1967) carries with it an undertone of the Black Knight's 'Allas, deth, what ayleth the, / That thou noldest have taken me ...' (*BD* 481–82), placing Hoccleve momentarily in

7 See ll. 1562–772.

the shoes of Chaucer's chief mourner (see *BD* 597). The old man may be familiar with Chaucer's name, but he does not appear to be a reader of Chaucer's poems, and so he fails to read Hoccleve's speech allusively, and finds it instead laughable: after his paean has ended, Hoccleve says, 'Fadir, yee may lawhe at my lewde speeche, / If that yow list' (1982–83). This underscores the dissonance between the 'language' spoken by Hoccleve (and Chaucer) and that spoken by the old man. This old man appears here as a precursor to the Friend we see in Hoccleve's *Series*, a philistine of sorts who fails to read Hoccleve's texts fully, and nevertheless insists on his readings as *authoritative* readings.[8]

What we encounter in the first section of the *Regiment*, then, is an environment in which the poet is called upon to define himself in relation to orthodox Christianity. We note that this is a request for self-defense that is forced upon the poet from outside, and which the poet does his best to evade during the course of their itinerant conversation. The usual Chaucerian sidestepping tactics no longer work, however. That third place of 'love' no longer betokens an artistic sphere in which the poet can play the blame game while escaping any real accountability. In Hoccleve, 'love' leads only to more serious and more seriously dogmatic questions. In order to wrest himself free from the old man in the *Regiment*, then, Hoccleve orchestrates a virtuosic 'hand-off' in which the old man transfers control of Hoccleve to the hands of a reverently recast 'Chaucer'. In order to accomplish this, Hoccleve reconstructs the figure of Chaucer so that he can exist credibly, in the mouths of poet and preacher alike, as the 'best of any wight'. This feat has a strong parallel beyond Chaucer's own works, in that great vision of Dante's, wherein Virgil recognizes the limits of his ability to guide Dante at the summit of Purgatorio, and must relinquish him to the care of Beatrice.[9] (We might remember here that it is at this 'guide-exchange' point in Dante's poem that the poet can finally name himself, just as Hoccleve's first self-naming coincides with Chaucer's first 'appearance' in the poem; see *Purg.* 30.55.) Of course, whereas the shade of Beatrice leads Dante to the beatific vision of the *Paradiso*, the spirit of Chaucer leads Hoccleve, foremost, to the beatific vision of Chaucer – that vivid illumination of the poet at the end of Hoccleve's poem, in which we see Chaucer *facie ad faciem*.[10] Whereas Dante undertakes

[8] For a detailed reading of the Friend's role in the *Series*, see Chapter 1.

[9] See *Purgatorio* 30. All references to the *Commedia* refer to Allen Mandelbaum's edition of the poem, which prints both the Italian text and English translation: *The Divine Comedy of Dante Alighieri: A Verse Translation*, trans. Allen Mandelbaum, 3 vols. (Berkeley: University of California Press, 1980).

[10] The illumination in question is preserved on fol. 88r of London, British Library,

a pilgrimage to God and his saints, Hoccleve undertakes a pilgrimage to Chaucer as a textual *place* – a place where Chaucer serves as a metonym for the possibility of English *poesie*; as a historical person; and, most importantly, as a go-between, a means through which poets such as Hoccleve can still practice a degree of artistic autonomy in the face of institutional pressure.

We will now explore earlier textual references to Chaucer – in order to indicate how Hoccleve's Chaucer differs from preceding representations of the poet – before moving on to position Hoccleve's Chaucer within a broader, international context of medieval authorship and literary fame. We focus throughout on defining the 'architectonics' – the fundamental structure and design – that Hoccleve uses to assemble his 'Christianized' version of Chaucer in the *Regiment*.

Towards Father Chaucer

Much criticism has focused on Hoccleve's 'anxiety of influence' over his relationship with Chaucer.[11] It is tempting, after all, to read Hoccleve's positioning of Chaucer as a literary 'father' in Freudian terms, and to posit Chaucer as a 'strong poet' who needs to be dealt with before Hoccleve can write. It is important to remember, however, how early it is for Hoccleve to be claiming the eminent positions for Chaucer that he does. In Hoccleve's hands, Chaucer becomes 'firste fyndere of our fair langage', 'mirour of fructuous entendement', 'best of any wight', and 'universel fadir in science'. Hoccleve writes in 1410, only ten years after Chaucer had died. While the first decade of the century had seen the creation of some deluxe manuscripts of Chaucer's works, there is no evidence that Chaucer enjoyed widespread literary celebrity in England, let alone outside the country, by 1410.[12] As we

MS Harley 4866. See ll. 4992–5005 for Hoccleve's presentation of the image in the *Regiment*.

11 See Spearing, *Medieval to Renaissance*; and Lerer, *Chaucer and His Readers*. See also Spearing, 'Renaissance Chaucer'. Julia Boffey speaks of the 'anxiety of influence' that has been 'signalled as a feature of post-Chaucerian writing' by such critics. See Julia Boffey, ed., *Fifteenth-Century English Dream Visions: An Anthology* (Oxford: Oxford University Press, 2003), 9.

12 Paul Strohm notes that, 'Evidence of manuscript circulation and public reference suggests that Chaucer was relatively little known throughout most of his career, except among a circle of courtly civil servants and London intelligentsia' (Strohm, *Hochon's Arrow*, 92). This picture appears to have changed only gradually after Chaucer's death in 1400. Two deluxe manuscripts of the *Canterbury Tales* were compiled in the first decade after Chaucer's death, and both would have been complete by 1405. To my knowledge, however, no evidence exists from the period before the *Regiment* that

shall see, in Hoccleve's hands Chaucer completes a transformation from a regional love poet to a universal authority with moral credentials.

Poetic representations of Chaucer that date from the poet's own lifetime tend to refer to Chaucer in relation to that poetic realm of 'love'. In his ballad to Chaucer, for instance, Eustache Deschamps calls Chaucer 'd'amours mondains Dieux en Albie' [the god of earthly love in Albion] (c. 1385).[13] Deschamps refers in his ballad to Chaucer's translation of the *Roman de la Rose*, and he seizes upon the name of the book to develop a matrix of agricultural metaphors – metaphors that serve as counterpoint to his wordplay on Chaucer's native land, 'Angleterre':

> Tu es d'amours mondains Dieux en Albie;
> Et de la Rose, en la terre Angelique,
> Qui d'Angela saxonne, est puis flourie
> Angleterre, d'elle ce nom s'applique
> Le derrenier en l'ethimologique;
> En bon anglès le livre translatas;
> Et un vergier ou du plant demandas
> De ceuls qui font pour eulx auctorisier,
> A ja longtemps que tu edifias
> Grant translateur, noble Geffroy Chaucier.

> [You are the god of earthly love in Albion; and in the Angelic land (which from the Saxon lady Angela has flowered into Angleland – from her this name is now applied as the last in the series of names) you translate the Book of the Rose; and long since you have set up an orchard, for which you have asked plants of those who make in order to be authorities; great translator, noble Geoffrey Chaucer.]
> (lines 12–21)

Having established the root of Chaucer's fame here – his translation of the *Rose* – Deschamps goes on to offer trimmings from his own 'plant', which

---

positions Chaucer as a literary celebrity in terms that match those used by Hoccleve in his poem. On the dating of the two earliest manuscripts of the *Canterbury Tales*, see Kathleen Scott, 'An Hours and Psalter by Two Ellesmere Illuminators', in *The Ellesmere Chaucer: Essays in Interpretation*, ed. Martin Stevens and Daniel Woodward (San Marino, CA: Huntington Library, 1997), 87–119 (106).

13 Deschamps's poem for Chaucer, Ballade 285, is included in McWebb, *Debating the Roman*, 46–47. I use McWebb's edition for the original French and the English translation.

he hopes Chaucer will 'cultivate' through translation. Insofar as Chaucer wields power as the 'god of earthly love in Albion', Deschamps proposes he use that power to translate his own verse, and thereby extend Deschamps's own renown in England. But while Chaucer could potentially enlarge Deschamps's international renown, Chaucer's own authority is presented as specifically localized in England and in English: he is a 'Dieux en Albie', and his literary fame is based on his having translated this well-known French poem into English – his role as 'grant translateur'.

In more local, London-based references to Chaucer from the period, the poet also appears within the context of Love, albeit as a servant or disciple.[14] Thomas Usk refers to Chaucer, without naming him, in his *Testament of Love*, written c. 1385–86 – making the reference contemporaneous with Deschamps's ballad.[15] The work is based loosely on Boethius's *Consolation of Philosophy*, with Usk's personified Love taking the place of Boethius's Lady Philosophy. At one point in Love's conversation with Usk, Love refers to Chaucer as 'myne owne trewe servaunt the noble philosophical poete in Englissh whiche evermore hym besyeth and travayleth right sore my name to encrease' (III.559–61). Love goes on to refer to Chaucer's 'Boke of Troylus' and to advise Usk with material drawn from Chaucer's poem.[16] Similarly, in Gower's *Confessio Amantis* (c. 1387–90), Venus sends greetings to Chaucer, referring to him as 'mi disciple and mi poete':

---

[14] The most extensive (but by no means entirely accurate) survey of references to Chaucer is still Caroline Spurgeon, *Five Hundred Years of Chaucer Criticism and Allusion, 1357–1900*, 3 vols (Cambridge: Cambridge University Press, 1925). This has been supplemented by James D. Johnson, 'Identifying Chaucer Allusions, 1953–1980: An Annotated Bibliography', *Chaucer Review* 19 (1984), 62–86. I do not entertain Lydgate in the following survey of English references to Chaucer before the *Regiment* because none of Lydgate's overt references to his poetic predecessor can reliably and definitively be dated to the period before 1410. Pearsall warns against the tendency to date Lydgate's undated love-poems, such as *Flower of Courtesy* and *Complaint of the Black Knight*, by default to the earliest years of his career. He dates Lydgate's two early longer works to the years after the *Regiment*: the *Troy Book*, c. 1412–20, and *Life of Our Lady*, c. 1415–22. See Derek Pearsall, *John Lydgate (1371–1449): A Bio-Bibliography* (Victoria, B.C.: University of Victoria, 1997), 14, 50.

[15] For the dating of this work, see Paul Strohm, 'Politics and Poetics: Usk and Chaucer in the 1380s', in Patterson, *Literary Practice and Social Change*, 83–112 (97–98 n. 18). See also R. Allen Shoaf's introduction to the *Testament*, in Thomas Usk, *The Testament of Love*, ed. R. Allen Shoaf, TEAMS Middle English Texts (Kalamazoo, MI: Medieval Institute Publications, 1998). All quotations from the *Testament of Love* come from this edition.

[16] See III.563–74.

> And gret wel Chaucer whan ye mete,
> *As mi disciple and mi poete*:
> For in the floures of his youthe
> In sondri wise, as he wel couthe,
> *Of ditees and of songes glade,*
> *The whiche he for mi sake made,*
> The lond fulfild is overal:
> Wherof to him in special
> Above alle othre I am most holde.
> For thi now in hise daies olde
> Thou schalt him telle this message,
> *That he upon his latere age,*
> *To sette an ende of alle his werk,*
> *As he which is myn owne clerk,*
> *Do make his testament of love,*
> *As thou hast do thi schrifte above,*
> *So that mi court it mai recorde.*
>
> (*CA* Prologue, first recension, lines 2941–57; italics mine)[17]

As with Usk's Love, Gower's Venus commends Chaucer for the work he has created in her service (those 'ditees and … songes glade, / The whiche he for mi sake made'). Here, Chaucer gains a reputation as, simultaneously, 'poete', 'disciple', and 'clerk' of love; and Venus requests that Chaucer spend his old age making a 'testament of love' for Venus's court to 'recorde'.

After Chaucer's death, however, such an affiliation with Love and its referents abates. In Henry Scogan's 'Moral Balade', Chaucer assumes a more authoritative role: he is referred to throughout as 'maistir Chaucier' and in one instance as 'noble poete of Brettayne' (ll. 65, 98, and 126).[18] Scogan uses Chaucer to underscore the moral lesson of his ballad – namely, that an individual receives his worth not through what he inherits from his father, but rather through what he cultivates in his own person during his lifetime. Here, the Chaucer who writes 'ditees' and 'songes glade' in the service of Venus, or who spends his days in the service of a personified Love, gives way to a Chaucer who is remembered for what he can teach the reader/listener about personal virtue. Scogan's ballad reproduces a version

---

17 For Gower's reference to Chaucer, see Peck's note to line 2940 of the Prologue in his edition of the *Confessio Amantis*.

18 The 'Moral Balade' is collected in Forni, *Chaucerian Apocrypha*. All quotations from Scogan's poem refer to this edition.

of Chaucer's short poem 'Gentilesse',[19] and the ballad as a whole serves to frame and explicate Chaucer's piece. This ballad, written c. 1406–07 and – if Shirley's colophon for the poem is to be believed – delivered before the sons of Henry IV at a dinner sponsored by Lewis John, reframes Chaucer not as a servant of love but rather as a moral advisor.[20]

Chaucer has a more ambivalent presence in the prologue to John Walton's English translation of Boethius's *Consolation of Philosophy*. Walton's preface dates to c. 1410 – that is, the exact time at which Hoccleve was writing his *Regiment* – and it bears striking similarities to Hoccleve's paeans to Chaucer in the *Regiment*: Chaucer is referred to as the 'floure of rethoryk' (cf. Hoccleve's 'flour of eloquence'), and appears in tandem with Gower, much as he does at the end of the first section of the *Regiment*.[21] After establishing Chaucer as 'floure of rethoryk / In Englisshe tong and excellent poete', and after declaring his own inability to write like Chaucer or Gower (2, st. 5), Walton distances himself from his predecessors by declaring his distaste for 'olde poysees derk':

Noght liketh me to labour ne to muse
Upon þese olde poysees derk,
For Cristes feyth suche þing[es] schulde refuse;
Witnes upon Ierom þe holy clerk.
Hit schulde not ben a Cristen mannes werk
Tho false goddes names to renewe,
For he þat hath resayued Cristes merk,
If he do so to Crist he is vntrewe.

(2–3; st. 6)

This stanza reveals a remarkable tension between poetry and Christianity – and, more specifically, between 'Tho false goddes' of pagan poetry and 'Cristes feyth'. As we have seen, such pagan gods not only factor into the poetry of Chaucer and Gower, they also enter into matrices of inter-poetic address, from Deschamps calling Chaucer a 'god of earthly love' to Gower

19 See ll. 105–25.

20 The heading in question appears in Oxford, Bodleian Library, MS Ashmole 59, fol. 25r: 'Here foloweþe nexst a moral balade to my lord þe prince, to my lord of Clarence, to my lord of Bedford, and to my lord of Gloucestre by Henry Scogan at a souper of feorþe merchande in the Vyntre in London, at þe hous of Lowys Johan.'

21 John Walton, *Boethius: De Consolatione Philosophiae*, ed. Mark Science, EETS, O.S. 170 (London: Oxford University Press for the Early English Text Society, 1927). For the dating of Walton's translation, see p. xliv of this edition.

addressing Chaucer through the classical goddess Venus. Walton's preface positions the author quite firmly in the camp of the Christian, in opposition to those who would 'renewe' the names of pagan gods and, in doing so, prove themselves 'untrewe' to Christ.

As Walton continues, his language focuses more intently on Cupid and Venus as examples of the pagan gods that he will avoid when writing. It is unnecessary, Walton says ('it ne nedeþ noght at all'), to summon Cupid to mind or to ask Venus to act as our guide:

> Of þo þat Crist in heuene blisse schal
> Suche manere werkys scholde ben set on side;
> For certainly it nedeþ noght at all
> To whette now þe dartes of cupide,
> Ne for to bidde þat venus be oure gyde
> So þat we may oure foule lustes wynne,
> Onaunter lest þe same on us betide
> As dede þe same venus for hire synne.
>
> (3; st. 7)

Writing that entertains the pagan pantheon emerges as not only un-Christian, but also patently sinful. Walton's mention of Cupid not only brings to mind the God of Love before whom Chaucer cowers in the prologue to the *Legend of Good Women*; it also reminds us of that 'immortal god' to whom Pandarus prays in *Troilus*. The evocation of Venus as a 'gyde', on the other hand, calls to mind the proem to Book III of *Troilus*, in which Chaucer's narrator praises Venus, goddess of love, and asks for her assistance as he embarks on the third book of the poem – the book in which Troilus and Criseyde will finally consummate their love. Chaucer's narrator positions himself in that proem as 'clerc' (i.e., scribe) to 'hem that serven the [Venus]' (III.40–41), offering the precedent for Gower's reference to Chaucer as Venus's 'owne clerk' in the *Confessio*. Walton quite emphatically turns away from this authorial self-presentation in his prologue to the *Consolation*, exempting himself from a school of poetry that would employ pagan gods, even playfully, and positioning himself – and his 'werkys' – in more unambiguously Christian territory.

Walton writes, then, in the curious stance of a poet hoping simultaneously to honor his predecessors and to differentiate himself from them entirely. Walton's words of praise for his predecessors give way not to a demonstration of the ways in which he will develop their poetic tradition, but rather to a demonstration of how he differs from them – and especially from Chaucer:

And certayn I haue tasted wonder lyte
As of the welles of calliope
No wonder þough I sympilly endite,
Yit will I not vnto Tessiphone
Ne to Allecto ne to Megare
Beseychyn after craft of eloquence,
But pray þat god of hys benignite
My spirit enspire wiþ hys influence

(3; st. 8)

Walton's declaration that he will not 'Beseychyn after craft of eloquence' unto 'Tessiphone / Ne to Allecto ne to Megare' arrives as if in direct response to the opening stanzas of *Troilus*, where Chaucer's narrator prays to Tisiphone to assist him in the writing of his poem.[22] Walton says that he will invoke neither Tisiphone nor the other two Furies, Allecto and Megare. Instead, he will pray only to God to inspire his spirit 'wiþ hys influence'. The ability to 'sympilly endite' – as Walton claims to do – emerges here as not so much a gesture of deference to eminent poetic predecessors, but rather a means of distinguishing Walton from these predecessors and indicating the key ways in which his poetry departs from that of Chaucer and Gower. Walton foreshadows Hoccleve's character of the Friend in the *Series*, who champions the Christian moralization to 'The Tale of Jereslaus's Wife', and advises Hoccleve to write 'hoomly and pleyn' (3.977). Walton's 'simple' writing collaborates with his conspicuously Christian approach to inspiration, content, and composition.

We have no way of knowing whether Hoccleve had read Walton's prologue while writing his *Regiment*, but it is striking to read Walton's text alongside Hoccleve's. Both texts acknowledge Chaucer and Gower side by side, and in highly complimentary terms. Both also, however, betray a pressure to be seen as religiously orthodox; and both fashion a response to this pressure that conspicuously involves the figure of Chaucer. Walton's solution is to praise Chaucer for his rhetorical skill in English ('floure of rethoryk / In Englisshe tong and excellent poete') but to distance himself from Chaucer in terms of the content of his poetry – and, specifically, to draw a clear line between the pagan figures that Chaucer entertains in his poetry and the monotheistic God with which Walton concerns himself. Such an approach abandons Chaucer to a pagan past – it acknowledges Chaucer's rhetorical excellence, but then moves on to a simpler, more

[22] See I.6–14.

virtuous present. By contrast, Hoccleve's approach admits Chaucer into this virtuous, Christian present. It assigns a role to Chaucer as a virtuous author, and it confirms this role by verifying Chaucer's good standing in the eyes of Hoccleve's conspicuously devout interlocutor. The first section of Hoccleve's poem builds towards this moment of affirmation, much as the second section of the *Regiment* culminates in an imagistic representation of a devout Chaucer wearing a black robe and holding a rosary. One of Hoccleve's accomplishments here is to present Chaucer as if he has always enjoyed the reputation that he enjoys in the *Regiment.* As we have seen, however, none of the prior poetic representations of Chaucer take this approach.

In many ways, the phrases that Walton, Gower, and Usk use to praise Chaucer more closely recall Chaucer's own lines of praise for his predecessors – we hear, for instance, of 'venus clerk Ovid' (1417) in the *House of Fame.* Dante is 'the wise poete of Florence' and 'the grete poete of Ytaille' ('Wife of Bath's Tale', 1125; 'Monk's Tale', 3650). Petrarch is 'my maister Petrak', and also 'the lauriat poete ... whos rethorike sweete / Enlumyned al Ytaille of poetrie' ('Monk's Tale', 2325; 'Clerk's Tale', 31–33). Chaucer's influence can be seen in the *Regiment,* as well, of course – Hoccleve refers to Chaucer as 'maistir' and, as with Petrarch's poetry in Italy, Chaucer's 'ornat endytyng' in England is 'to al this land enlumnynyng' (*RP* 1973–74). But the degree to which Hoccleve recreates Chaucer in a more conspicuously moral and Christian framework proves unprecedented in the English poetic tradition.

This act has firm precedents on the continent, however, in the 'Christianization' of classical authors such as Virgil, and in the *moralitas* tradition that attached Christian meaning to classical narratives, as in the case of the *Ovid moralisé* and the *Gesta Romanorum* collections.[23] We will examine this tradition in greater detail in order to better situate Hoccleve's rendition of Chaucer in the *Regiment,* but first we will take stock of how Chaucer appears in Hoccleve's poem, not only as a named and illustrated authority, but also on an allusive, textual level. We will examine how Hoccleve's use of Chaucer's own poetic language shapes the very poem that brings this new Chaucer-figure into being.

---

[23] For a discussion of the role of moralization in the medieval period, including the treatment of Virgil, the *Ovid moralisé,* and the *Gesta Romanorum,* see J.B. O'Donoghue, 'Medieval Moralizations and Literary Virtues', in *Sentences for Alan Ward,* ed. D.M. Reeks (Southampton: Bosphoros Books, 1988), 3–20. On the *Gesta Romanorum* tradition more specifically, see Weiske, *Gesta Romanorum*; Herrtage, *Gesta.* See also our discussion in Chapter 1 of the present study.

Chaucer's Textual Presence

The extent to which Hoccleve alludes to Chaucer's works in his poetry has been a matter of serious debate in Hoccleve Studies. Jerome Mitchell, John Bowers, and John Burrow find little by way of Chaucerian echoes in Hoccleve's verse; and, while they note the role that the figure of Chaucer plays in Hoccleve's works, they present Hoccleve's use of Chaucerian language as lacking.[24] Nicholas Perkins has refuted this position in a recent article by offering a series of specific echoes, parallels, and allusions to Chaucer's poetry – and particularly to *Troilus and Criseyde* – in the *Regiment*.[25] Perkins uses these comparisons to propose a different relationship between Chaucer and Hoccleve: he reads the *Regiment* as an instance of Hoccleve 'conversing' with the dead, and suggests Chaucer's 'spectral' presence in the narrative, drawing upon Derrida's *Spectres de Marx*. Perkins focuses on passages of conversation 'in which an older man attempts to counsel and teach a younger one' – a scenario, Perkins says, 'that mirrors the relationship between the two poets'.[26] Such passages not only exhibit Hoccleve's skill at conveying the spontaneity and rhythms of real conversation after a Chaucerian manner; they also indicate how Hoccleve engages with the dynamics of Boethian consolation in the conversational format.

This last point is a particularly tangled one, especially given the account of the old man and Hoccleve that I have detailed above: as we have seen, the old man's attempts at advice and consolation fail to help Hoccleve resolve the real problems that plague him – problems concerning how to live a virtuous, married life, and how to be remunerated for the work he does. On

---

24 Mitchell finds 'very few direct allusions to Chaucer in Hoccleve's verse and almost no indisputable Chaucerian echoes in his diction and phraseology' (Jerome Mitchell, *Thomas Hoccleve: A Study in Early Fifteenth-Century English Poetic* (Urbana: University of Illinois Press, 1968), 122). John Burrow notes formal debts to Chaucer, but describes an overall dearth of 'verbal echoes' (J.A. Burrow, 'Hoccleve and Chaucer', in *Chaucer Traditions: Studies in Honour of Derek Brewer*, ed. Ruth Morse and Barry Windeatt (Cambridge: Cambridge University Press, 1990), 54–61 (59)). John Bowers states that the '*Regiment of Princes* is composed in Chaucerian verse-form, but the overall work entirely lacks the Chaucerian characteristics that became most dearly prized' (Bowers, 'Politics of Tradition', 361). Elsewhere, Bowers comments: 'Although he collaborated on the Trinity *Confessio Amantis* with the professional textwriter Adam Pinkhurst who copied Hengwrt and Ellesmere, Hoccleve himself shows surprisingly little direct knowledge of Chaucer's poetry.' See *Chaucer and Langland*, 192.

25 Nicholas Perkins, 'Haunted Hoccleve? *The Regiment of Princes*, the Troilean Intertext, and Conversations with the Dead', *Chaucer Review* 43.2 (2008): 103–39.

26 Ibid., 104.

the occasions when the old man presents what he hopes will be a solution to a given problem, Hoccleve often clarifies that he has already thought of such solutions and they have failed to work. For instance, when the old man advises Hoccleve to request that his annuity be paid through the department of the Chancery, Hoccleve assures him (twice) that this is not possible (see ll. 1870–97). It is precisely this suggestion, however – and precisely Hoccleve's avid dismissal of it – that leads to the old man's eventual suggestion that Hoccleve write Prince Henry a 'goodly tale or two', which, in turn, affords Hoccleve the opportunity to write the *Regiment* proper. The old man so often misses the mark, and he proves much less authoritative and helpful than Boethius's Lady Philosophy, but Hoccleve also emphasizes a positive side to his interlocutor – his capacity for 'good wil'. In responding to the old man's suggestion that Hoccleve's payment be issued from the department of the Chancery, for instance, Hoccleve says,

> Fadir, as sikir as that I stande heere,
> Whethir that I be symple or argh or bold,
> Swich an eschange gete I noon to yeere;
> Do as I can with that I have in hold;
> For as for that, my confort is but cold.
> But wel I fynde your good wil alway
> Redy to me in what yee can and may.
>
> (1891–97)

Hoccleve insists that the *specific* advice that the old man has given him will not work – 'swich an eschange' will prove fruitless. Nonetheless, the old man exhibits 'good wil' – he offers Hoccleve 'what [he] can and may', and for this Hoccleve proves grateful.

Insofar as Hoccleve presents a Boethian relationship here, it is only Boethian insofar as Troilus's monologue at *Troilus* IV.946–1085 is Boethian. Troilus's monologue on predestination draws heavily upon the *Consolation of Philosophy*, but stops short of offering Lady Philosophy's ultimate insight that free will and God's predeterminism are not mutually exclusive, because God sees all time in an eternal present 'without causing or presupposing events'.[27] In rendering the episode thus, Chaucer allows the reader to consider the limits of Troilus's knowledge – we weigh how much Troilus knows without the help of an exemplary guide such as the personification of Philosophy. The old man–Hoccleve dynamic likewise calls to mind the

27 Nuttall, *Troilus and Criseyde*, 132; see Boethius, *Consolation of Philosophy*, trans. V. Watts, rev. ed. (London: Penguin, 1999), V.4–6.

Boethian paradigm of an authoritative guide serving to lift the subject from despair to hope; but, as with *Troilus*, the eminently authoritative Lady Philosophy is missing, and no eye-opening revelations occur.

The old man does prove successful, however, in rousing Hoccleve from a state of despondency to a state of activity. And, tellingly, Hoccleve marks moments of action and 'awakening' in his dialogue with Chaucerian – and specifically Troilean – allusion. At the moment in which the old man encourages Hoccleve to pick up his pen and write, for instance, we note echoes of Book V of *Troilus*, in which Pandarus encourages Troilus to do the same, and with very similar language:

> 'Althogh thow seye that thow in Latyn
> Ne in Frensshe neithir canst but smal endyte,
> In Englissh tonge canstow wel afyn.'
> 'Fadir, therof can I eek but a lyte.'
> 'Yee, straw! Let be! Thy penne take and wryte
> As thow canst …'
>
> (*RP* 1870–75)

> 'How myghte I than don,' quod Troilus,
> 'To knowe of this, yee, were it nevere so lite?'
> 'Now seystow wisly,' quod this Pandarus;
> 'My red is this: syn thow kanst wel endite,
> That hastily a lettre thow hire write'
>
> (*TC* V.1289–93)

Perkins notes the *lite/endite/write* rhyme at work in both of these passages.[28] The Chaucerian voice in the old man is deepened soon after the given passage in the *Regiment*, as the old man chides Hoccleve, saying, 'Assaye, assaye, thow symple hertid goost! / What grace is shapen thee thow nat ne woost' (1889–90). The old man cheers Hoccleve on in explicitly Chaucerian terms: Chaucer frequently uses the term 'assaye' in his poetry, often serving to encourage active reading and experience, and the term is linked with similar exhortations to 'read with *avisement*'.[29] The 'grace' that 'shapes' Hoccleve would refer, of course, in the first instance to divine

28 Perkins, 'Haunted Hoccleve', 107.

29 Vincent Gillespie, 'Lunatics, Lovers, and Poets: Compact Imaginations in Chaucer and Medieval Literary Theory', in *Shakespeare: Between the Middle Ages and Modernism: From Translator's Art to Academic Discourse*, ed. Martin Procházka and Jan Cermák (Prague: Charles University, 2008), 11–39 (18).

grace: the old man is encouraging Hoccleve to have faith that the events in his life will have a more positive outcome than he expects. But this phrase – 'What grace is shapen thee thow nat ne woost' – coupled as it is with the repetition of 'Assaye' and the echo of Pandarus's negotiations with Troilus, points up the extent to which Hoccleve shapes a dialogue that is recognizably Chaucerian, and uses Chaucerian allusion to punctuate moments of purposefulness and action.

Another example occurs in the first lines of Hoccleve's conversation with the old man, early on in the *Regiment*:

> He stirte unto me and seide, 'Sleepstow, man?
> Awake!' and gan me shake wondir faste,
> And with a sigh I answerde atte laste:
>
> 'A, who is there?' 'I,' quod this olde greye,
> 'Am heer,' and he me tolde the manere
> How he spak to me, as yee herde me seye.
> 'O man,' quod I, 'for Crystes love deere,
> If that thow wilt aght doon at my prayeere,
> As go thy way, talke to me no more;
> Thy wordes alle annoyen me ful sore.
>
> 'Voide fro me, me list no conpaignie.
> Encresse nat my greef, I have ynow.'
> 'My sone, hast thow good lust thy sorwe drye
> And mayst releeved be? What man art thow?'
>
> (131–44)

As with the last passage we considered, here the old man calls to mind the voice of Pandarus: the old man's 'Sleepstow, man? / Awake!' echoes Pandarus's 'Awake! … / What! Slombrestow as in a litargie?' in the first book of *Troilus* (I.729–30). Pandarus proceeds to shake Troilus to rouse him ('And with that word he gan hym for to shake' (I.869)), much as the old man shakes Hoccleve. Even the words with which Hoccleve dismisses the old man recall the words with which Troilus dismisses Pandarus (see I.571–74, I.750–54).[30] This excerpt from the *Regiment* also recalls the beginning of the *Book of the Duchess* (ll. 178–86), in which Juno's messenger awakens the god of sleep ('Awake anoon! … Awake!' (179, 181)), and the messenger answers

30 Perkins notes this parallel with *Troilus* at 'Haunted Hoccleve', 105–06.

Morpheus's 'Who clepeth ther?' with 'Hyt am I' (cf. the old man's 'I … / Am heer'). And Hoccleve's passage ends, of course, with the very same words that the host uses to greet Chaucer himself in the *Canterbury Tales*: 'What man artow?' (see *CT* VII.695–97). In the *Canterbury Tales*, these words serve to rouse the Chaucer-pilgrim from silence, and they lead to Chaucer delivering his own tales. These particular allusions in the *Regiment* prove instructive not only insofar as they are Chaucerian or conversational, but also because of the *nature* of their use in Chaucer's works: they spring from moments of awakening and positive action in Chaucer's texts; and they, in turn, shape a moment in which Hoccleve is literally shaken awake. They also speak – through a Chaucerian lexis – to the old man's function in the *Regiment*: while he cannot provide metaphysical solutions after the model of Lady Philosophy, he can, Pandarus-like, rouse the subject from a state of inactivity and sloth.

We have already seen the role that *Troilus* plays in poetic representations of Chaucer before Hoccleve's *Regiment*: Usk summons Chaucer to mind not by naming him, but by naming the 'Boke of Troylus'; and Gower greets Chaucer, through Venus, in decidedly Troilean terms – as the 'clerk' in the service of Venus that we meet first in the proem to Book III of *Troilus*. John Walton does not name *Troilus* explicitly, but his references to Cupid, Venus, and Tisiphone give the impression that in distancing himself from Chaucer, he also distances himself from the pagan subject matter of *Troilus*, and the pagan figures that Chaucer entertains therein. By contrast, Hoccleve's *Regiment* does not name *Troilus* explicitly, but rather uses Troilean allusion to shape the dialogue in which we will eventually be introduced to Chaucer-the-literary-celebrity. Whereas Perkins suggests that the conversational nature of these passages bespeak Hoccleve's attempt to establish a 'conversational' relationship with Chaucer, I suggest that these passages form a pivotal aspect of Hoccleve's presentation of Chaucer-the-author in the *Regiment*. That is, alongside the episodes in the *Regiment* wherein Chaucer is either named or depicted in the form of an image, these allusions indicate how Chaucerian poetics can be put to use in a contemporary, Christian context. They enact a response to readers who might locate in poems such as *Troilus and Criseyde* an undue concern with the 'false goddes' of classical literature, and they indicate how Chaucerian poetics can operate in contemporary, Christian London. Hoccleve does this, however, by retaining a Chaucerian approach – an approach that does not presume to convey absolute authority, but rather accepts the flawed nature of human interactions. In both passages that we entertained above, Hoccleve recalls the figure of Pandarus in order to indicate, in the old man, a figure who is not particularly exemplary or helpful, but who nevertheless displays 'good wil'.[31] Although the old man ultimately fails to find specific solutions to Hoccleve's specific problems, he nonetheless succeeds in rousing Hoccleve from inactivity and encouraging him to write. In this respect, he codifies an approach to poetry that is characteristically Chaucerian – even Troilean: like Troilus in Book IV, Hoccleve experiences no moment of ultimate revelation in his itinerant dialogue with the old man. What he receives instead is the conversation itself, the substance of which affirms the fallible and complicated nature of each interlocutor's life, and inspires the Hoccleve-narrator to take on the more productive task of writing the *Regiment* proper. The final lines of the first section of the *Regiment* mark the 'unveiling' of Hoccleve's reverently recast Chaucer. What we receive on the way to this iteration of Chaucer is a conversation infused with Chaucerian allusion that highlights the possibility of 'good wil' even where ideal solutions are markedly absent.

In what follows, we will explore in greater depth the international literary context for the moral version of Chaucer that Hoccleve imagines in the *Regiment* and, in doing so, we will also situate Hoccleve's narrative in the context of other itinerant dialogues, both Chaucerian and extra-Chaucerian, that consider the process of memorializing one's poetic predecessor, the vicissitudes of literary fame, and the role of consolation.

Making a Moral Chaucer

The process of recreating a literary predecessor in a more conspicuously Christian light is by no means original to Hoccleve's poem. As mentioned above, literary collections such as the *Ovid moralisé* and the *Gesta Romanorum* focused on repurposing classical narratives as Christian doctrine. Not only were Ovid's stories 'moralized', Virgil himself underwent reinterpretation during the medieval period as a Christian prophet: his Fourth Eclogue came to be interpreted as a prophecy for Christ's birth, positioning Virgil himself as a pre-Christian prophet.[32] Dante dramatizes this in *Purgatorio* 22, where the Roman poet Statius credits his own conversion to Christianity to his reading of Virgil:

> Facesti come quei che va di notte,
> che porta il lume dietro e sé non giova,
> ma dopo sé fa le persone dotte,

[31] On the importance of 'good will' and benevolence in the *Regiment*, see also Tolmie, '*Priue Scilence*', 306–09.

[32] Karla Taylor, 'A Text and Its Afterlife: Dante and Chaucer', *Comparative Literature* 35.1 (1983): 1–20 (3).

quando dicesti: 'Secol si rinova;
torna giustizia e primo tempo umano,
e progenïe scende da ciel nova.'

Per te poeta fui, per te cristiano

[You did as he who goes by night and carries
the lamp behind him – he is of no help
to his own self but teaches those who follow –

when you declared: 'The ages are renewed;
justice and man's first time on earth return;
from Heaven a new progeny descends.'

Through you I was a poet and, through you,
a Christian]

(*Purg.* 22.67–73)

Here, Virgil is cast not only as the means through which Statius learned to write poetry, but also as the means through which Statius became a Christian. The pre-Christian poetry of Virgil is therefore reinterpreted, through the eyes of Dante's Statius, as not only exemplary but capable of moving a non-Christian individual to conversion.

Statius's meeting with (and reading of) Virgil takes place during the course of an itinerant conversation of another kind – Dante and Virgil's progress through purgatory on their way to earthly paradise. The biblical story of Emmaus comes into play here. Dante begins *Purgatorio* 21 thus:

Ed ecco, sì come ne scrive Luca
che Cristo apparve a' due ch'erano in via,
giù surto fuor de la sepulcral buca,

ci apparve un'ombra, e dietro a noi venìa,
dal piè guardando la turba che giace;
né ci addemmo di lei, sì parlò pria,

dicendo: 'O frati miei, Dio vi dea pace.'

[And here – even as Luke records for us
that Christ, new-risen from his burial cave,
appeared to two along his way – a shade

appeared; and he advanced behind our backs
while we were careful not to trample on
the outstretched crowd. We did not notice him

until he had addressed us with: 'God give
you, o my brothers, peace!']

(*Purg.* 21.7–14)

The Emmaus narrative in Luke depicts two disciples being approached by the newly risen Christ (disguised as a pilgrim) on the road between Jerusalem and Emmaus. Central to the story is the 'slowness of heart' of the disciples in question, and their initial inability both to recognize Christ and to read Old Testament scripture in the new way – that is, with a view to its significance as Christian prophecy. In the course of their walk, the disguised Christ starts at 'Moses and all the prophets', and 'expound[s] to them in all the scriptures, the things that were concerning him' (Lk. 24:27). This walk constitutes, in other words, the original instance of the type of Christian reading that Statius performs on Virgil's Fourth Eclogue in the *Commedia*. Christ reinterprets the Old Testament scriptures for the two disciples in order to clarify the precise way in which the scriptures prophesy His coming. As Statius is converted through his Christian 'reading' of Virgil, the two disciples en route to Emmaus are converted by Christ's own reading of the Old Testament scriptures: Luke tells us that they return to Jerusalem, where they find the other disciples and report their renewed faith (Lk. 24:33–35). Herein lies, then, not only the beginning of the Christian hermeneutic tradition, but also the beginning of the gospel tradition – the 'spreading' of Christ's words and deeds by written and spoken record.

In *Purgatorio*, however, the dynamic introduced by the Emmaus allusion enters into the broader framework of trading names and attributing literary fame in the *Commedia*. Statius appears here in the place of the disguised Christ – as a shade 'advancing' behind Virgil and Dante's 'backs'. During the course of their conversation, Statius's identity is revealed – he moves from anonymity into being named and remembered by Dante. Dante furthers this dynamic of delayed recognition – as initiated in the Emmaus narrative – by having Statius not recognize Virgil until much later in their conversation. In one of the more comic sequences in the *Commedia*, Statius praises Virgil at length before Virgil allows Dante to reveal his true identity (*Purg.* 21.100–36). This allows Dante to illustrate the dynamics of fame: praising Virgil gives Statius an opportunity to participate in Virgil's renown, and this meeting between two of Dante's poetic predecessors tightens the web of literary celebrity into which Dante will introduce himself in the *Commedia*. The poets cooperate in a reciprocal cycle of identification and praise, and Dante uses his poem to introduce his own place in this network of literary affiliation.

This scene finds a stark contrast in that work which has been read as Chaucer's extended response to Dante's *Commedia*: the *House of Fame*.[33] After a sequence in which Lady Fame capriciously assigns worldly afterlives to petitioners for fame, Geffrey is approached by a stranger – who advances at his back – and asks him immediately for his name:

> With that y gan aboute wende,
> For oon that stood ryght at my bak,
> Me thoughte, goodly to me spak,
> And seyde, 'Frend, what is thy name?
> Artow come hider to han fame?'
> 'Nay, for sothe, frend,' quod y;
> 'I cam noght hyder, graunt mercy,
> For no such cause, by my hed!
> Sufficeth me, as I were ded,
> That no wight have my name in honde.
> I wot myself best how y stonde;
> For what I drye, or what I thynke,
> I wil myselven al hyt drynke'
>
> (III.1868–80)

Geffrey's unwillingness to offer his name here comes hand in hand with his unwillingness to be seen courting fame. In contrast to the poets we meet in *Purgatorio*, Chaucer makes a display of *not* revealing his name – after all, he says, he would prefer that 'no wight have [his] name in honde'. His refusal to play the 'name game' – to name oneself and ask for a name in return – brings the reciprocal cycle of naming and 'faming' to an abrupt stop. In refusing both to offer his name and to ask the stranger's name

[33] On Chaucer's use of the *Commedia* in the *House of Fame*, see, for instance, Piero Boitani, 'What Dante Meant to Chaucer', in *Chaucer and the Italian Trecento*, ed. Piero Boitani (Cambridge: Cambridge University Press, 1983), 73–90; Howard Schless, *Chaucer and Dante: A Revaluation* (Norman, OK: Pilgrim Books, 1984), 29–76; Piero Boitani, *Chaucer and the Imaginary World of Fame* (Cambridge: D.S. Brewer, 1984), 73–90; Steve Ellis, 'Chaucer, Dante, and Damnation', *Chaucer Review* 22.4 (1988), 282–94; Helen Cooper, 'The Four Last Things in Dante and Chaucer: Ugolino in the House of Rumour', *New Medieval Literatures* 3 (1999), 39–66; Glenn A. Steinberg, 'Chaucer in the Field of Cultural Production: Humanism, Dante, and the "House of Fame"', *Chaucer Review* 35.2 (2000), 182–203.

in return, Chaucer would appear to excuse himself from the process that Virgil, Statius, and Dante demonstrate in the *Commedia*.

The encounter has implications not only for Chaucer's poetic self-image, but also for his relationship with a dominant Italian humanistic poetic tradition. Vincent Gillespie argues that Chaucer's rejection of the naming process here serves as an implicit rejection of the laureation process, 'and of the legitimate glory accruing to the poet in the humanist model of literary production and to the humanist ideal of the poet as a *vir bonus dicendi peritus*'.[34] Far from aspiring to the 'named ranks' of Dante or, for that matter, Petrarch – who was crowned laureate in April 1341[35] – Chaucer makes a conspicuous display of withholding his name. For Karla Taylor, Chaucer's use of Dantean allusion in *Troilus and Criseyde* also points up the lack of control that a given poet has over the reception and use of his poem: 'Chaucer demonstrates the vanity of such human wishes [i.e., the hope of securing the afterlife of one's poem] by reading the *Commedia* in a manner Dante did not intend, using Dante's own words to present a vision of the world quite opposed to the *Commedia*'s idealistic, eschatological vision'.[36] The same is true of the *House of Fame*: indeed, the moment in which Geffrey withholds his name betrays his ambivalence – his terror even – over what happens when his name and his works make their way out of his keeping and into the world. But Chaucer's poem also seems to acknowledge that Fame will assign or withhold celebrity as she pleases: refusing to offer one's name does not necessarily change that. Only 150 lines before Geffrey's exchange with the stranger, we witness a group of writers who fall before Fame and ask her to 'hide her [their] goode werkes ek' – those writers who 'seyden they yeven noght a lek / For fame ne for such renoun; / For they for contemplacioun / And Goddes love hadde ywrought, / Ne of fame wolde they nought' (1707–12). This seemingly noble demand does little to sway Fame: in fact, it only sharpens her resolve to spread their fame far and wide. Fame calls them 'wood' for not desiring fame, and orders Eolus to spread their 'werk' – 'That al the world may of hyt here' (1720–21). Those who hope to avoid fame altogether, it would seem, receive it tenfold.

When Hoccleve's interlocutor in the *Regiment* poses the same question that Chaucer receives in the *House of Fame* – 'What is thy name?' – Hoccleve himself enters into this well-established cycle of reciprocal

34 Vincent Gillespie, 'Authorship', in *A Handbook of Middle English Studies*, ed. Marion Turner (Chichester: Wiley-Blackwell, 2013), 137–54 (151).

35 Ibid., 146.

36 Taylor, 'Text and Its Afterlife', 19–20.

naming. He records his own name not once but twice (once in the voice of the old man), and he immediately links his fame with that of Chaucer:

> 'What shal I calle thee, what is thy name?'
> 'Hoccleve, fadir myn, men clepen me.'
> 'Hoccleve, sone?' 'Ywis, fadir, that same.'
> 'Sone, I have herd or this men speke of thee;
> Thow were aqweyntid with Chaucer, pardee –
> God have his soule, best of any wight!'
>
> (1863–68)

This exchange, which happens almost 1,900 lines into Hoccleve's conversation with the old man, also allows for a moment of delayed recognition, not unlike those experienced in both Dante's *Purgatorio* (between Statius and Virgil) and Luke's Emmaus narrative (between the disciples and Christ). Here, the old man says that he has 'herd or this men speke of thee' [heard men speak of you before this], and he knows the name 'Hoccleve' because of Hoccleve's acquaintance with Chaucer. His commendation of Chaucer, as I have suggested, serves doubly as a seal of approval. Here, Hoccleve presents Chaucer not just as *vir bonus* but, indeed, as *vir maximus* – and, as with the *vir bonus* model of authorship, Chaucer's renown proceeds from his credibility as a moral authority.[37]

Our sense of this moral authority is enhanced by the terms that the old man uses to describe the work that Hoccleve should undertake, as a writer and acquaintance of Chaucer, when writing a piece for Prince Henry. The old man begins by suggesting that Hoccleve 'Wryte to him [Henry] a goodly tale or two, / On which he may desporten him by nyght' (1902–03). The old man says that the tales should be 'fressh and gay', and indicates that Hoccleve should 'wryte on lustyly' – descriptors that would indicate that Hoccleve might write something in the vein of those spirited (and often bawdy) stories that comprise the *Canterbury Tales* (1905–06). After a brief exposition on the dangers of false flattery (ll. 1912–46), however, the old man grows more specific:

> Wryte him nothyng that sowneth into vice.
> Kythe thy love in mateere of sadnesse.
> Looke if thow fynde canst any tretice
> Growndid on his estates holsumnesse.
>
> (1947–50)

[37] Gillespie, 'Authorship', 140–41.

These lines counter-balance the old man's initial request – 'fressh' and 'gay' stories give way here to 'mateere of sadnesse [seriousness]'; and multiple 'goodly tales' give way to a single 'tretice / Growndid on his estates holsumnesse'. The movement between lively and fresh stories and a more sober treatise recalls the same movement that we experience in the *Canterbury Tales* – the progression through a variety of goodly tales, culminating at last in the Parson's more sober contribution – 'this litel tretys', as Chaucer calls it in his *Retractions* (X.1081). The old man's warning against writing material that 'sowneth into vice' also calls the *Retractions* to mind – in the division of literature into categories of vice and virtue, wherein Chaucer's 'translacions and enditynges of worldly vanitees' (X.1085) are set against his 'bookes of legendes of seintes, and omelies, and moralitee, and devocioun' (X.1088). The phrase 'sowneth into vice' in Hoccleve's text has a specific counterpart in Chaucer's *Retractions*: when listing his 'enditynges of worldly vanitees', Chaucer mentions 'the tales of Caunterbury, thilke that *sownen into synne*' (X.1086). In directing Hoccleve in what to write, the old man cooperates in the labeling of literature in terms of vice and virtue: he guides Hoccleve towards material that espouses 'holsumnesse' and eschews 'vice'.

If we can imagine Hoccleve communicating with a spectral Chaucer of sorts in this first section of the *Regiment*, then, it is more specifically the Chaucer of the *Retractions* – the version of Chaucer who would readily sort his texts into binaries of pure and impure, religious and worldly. These are, after all, the same categories that the old man uses throughout the dialogue to evaluate the details of Hoccleve's life and beliefs – from marital relations to Eucharistic doctrine. In the *Regiment*, however, Hoccleve presents a text that *begins* rather than *ends* with a consideration of literature in terms of such binaries. Rather than write a *Canterbury Tales*-like text and then append a text retroactively (and ambiguously) withdrawing anything that might 'sownen into synne', Hoccleve begins with a dialogue that focuses on the moral probity of the text to come, and foregrounds the moral aspirations of the given text. Hoccleve's figure of Chaucer emerges as a remodeled *auctour*, capable of presiding over this new approach to poetry: we witness the appearance of a Chaucer-figure capable of emblematizing literary 'holsumnesse' and 'mateere of sadnesse'.

In his short prologue to the *Regiment* proper, Hoccleve also evokes the end of *Troilus and Criseyde*, and this serves to further position the version of Chaucer that he puts forward in the *Regiment*. Just before using the characteristically Troilean word 'combreworld' to describe Death, Hoccleve renders Chaucer's renown in relation to Virgil, saying, 'The steppes of Virgile in poesie / Thow folwedist eek'

(2089–90).[38] The phrase recalls Chaucer's *envoi* to *Troilus*, wherein the author directs his 'litel bok' to 'kis the steppes where as thow seest pace / Virgile, Ovide, Omer, Lucan, and Stace' (V.1790–92). In removing the other four poets from his rendition of this motif, and having Chaucer follow only the 'steppes [footsteps]' of Virgil, Hoccleve would seem to return the motif to its source in Statius's *Thebaid*, where Statius instructs his poem not to approach Virgil's *Aeneid* but instead to 'follow her footsteps from afar in adoration':

> vive, precor; nec tu divinam Aeneida tempta,
> sed longe sequere et vestigia semper adora.
>
> [live, I pray; and essay not the divine Aeneid,
> but ever follow her footsteps from afar in adoration.]
>
> (*Theb.* 12.816–17)[39]

Notably, in Hoccleve's rendition, the object in question is not a book (as in Statius's and Chaucer's renditions), but the poet himself. Where Statius has one book (the *Thebaid*) follow the footsteps of another book (the *Aeneid*), and where Chaucer has his book (*Troilus*) kiss the footsteps of five literary predecessors, Hoccleve summons to mind Chaucer-the-individual following the footsteps of Virgil-the-individual.

This positioning of Chaucer-the-individual has implications for the broader context of literary fame that we have been tracing thus far. Chaucer adapts his list of authors in *Troilus* V.1792 from the figures that Dante encounters in *Inferno* IV – Dante's *bella scola*.[40] In the *Inferno*, these figures invite Dante to join them, and Dante is thereby implicated into this honorable company of *auctours*.[41] This episode – like much of the *Commedia* – is notable because it imagines writers that Dante would likely only have encountered through their books as individuals – or, rather, as

38 Hoccleve's use of 'combreworld' here, as in the *Male Regle* (l. 225), appears to derive from Chaucer's use of the word at *Troilus*, IV.279. See Charles Blyth's discussion of Hoccleve's usage in *The Regiment of Princes*, TEAMS Middle English Texts (Kalamazoo, MI: Medieval Institute Publications, 1999), 219.

39 Statius, *Thebaid; Achilleid*, ed. D.R. Shackleton Bailey, 2 vols (Cambridge, MA: Harvard University Press, 2003), 2.309; K.P. Clarke, *Chaucer and Italian Textuality* (Oxford: Oxford University Press, 2011), 70.

40 See *Inferno* 4.85–96. Dante's list of venerable authors includes Homer, Horace, Ovid, and Lucan (as well as Virgil). Chaucer adapts this list to exclude Horace and include Statius.

41 See *Inferno* 4.100–2.

the 'shades' that remain after the respective individuals have died. As a result, the given author can often serve as a metonym or symbol for his works, insofar as Dante 'knows' the author from his works. When Dante first meets Virgil, for instance, he immediately aligns the Virgil-figure with the *Aeneid*, and Dante connects his own 'long study' of Virgil's 'volume' with the journey he finds himself on now – his passage through the three places of the afterlife (and, by extension, the writing of the *Commedia*):

> O de li altri poeti onore e lume,
> vagliami 'l lungo studio e 'l grande amore
> che m'ha fatto cercar lo tuo volume.
>
> Tu se' lo mio maestro e 'l mio autore,
> tu se' solo colui da cu' io tolsi
> lo bello stilo che m'ha fatto onore.
>
> [O light and honor of all other poets,
> may my long study and the intense love
> that made me search your volume serve me now.
>
> You are my master and my author, you –
> the only one from whom my writing drew
> the noble style for which I have been honored.]
>
> (*Inferno* I.82–87)

Chaucer's use of Virgil, Ovid, Homer, Lucan, and Statius in the *envoi* to *Troilus* likewise invites the reader to imagine these authors – whom Chaucer himself only encountered through their books – as living individuals who pass by and leave footsteps in their wake. In doing so, Chaucer, like Dante, insinuates himself into the company of these eminent authors. He may order his 'litel book' to be humble or deferential ('subgit be to alle poesye' (V.1790)), but he nevertheless directs his poem in the direction of this august company. Hoccleve's use of the 'footsteps' motif differs insofar as Hoccleve claims to have actually known Chaucer – not only through his books, but as a living, breathing person. The old man points out that he was 'aqweyntid with Chaucer', and Hoccleve later suggests that Chaucer served as his teacher – 'My deere maistir … / And fadir, Chaucer, fayn wolde han me taght, / But I was dul and lerned lyte or naght' (2077–79).[42] Hence,

[42] Linne Mooney has also recently found a document in Hoccleve's hand, written as a Privy Seal clerk, requesting that Chaucer be paid 'ten pounds in arrears for his annuity

the motif of Chaucer following Virgil's footsteps takes on a different significance: where Chaucer sends his book to join the company of his departed literary predecessors, Hoccleve sends his 'maistir' – as an individual – in the direction of literary exemplarity, as emblematized by Virgil. Hoccleve enacts a transition here between Chaucer-the-man (with whom Hoccleve claims to have been acquainted) and Chaucer-the-*auctour* (who will exist hereon as an exemplary literary figure).

Fame, Dante, and the *Speculum Principis*

As we have seen, many of Chaucer's own meditations on fame, literary memorializing, and poetic tradition build on his response to Dante's *Commedia*. We see this most in the *House of Fame*, with its three-book structure and its journey to three distinct places, as well as its specific textual allusions to the *Commedia*, and the instance of Geffrey's flight through the heavens in the grip of an Eagle, which echoes *Purgatorio* 9.19–33. But Chaucer also uses Dantean allusion or translation in *The Parliament of Fowls*, 'The Monk's Tale', and *Troilus and Criseyde*, and the extent to which Chaucer responds to Dante in his works should suggest an enduring, rather than passing, interest in the Italian *auctour*.[43] The *envoi* to *Troilus*, which draws on Dante's *bella scola*, gives way to an account of Troilus's death, which, in turn, gives way to the prayer that eventually ends *Troilus*, based on Dante's Trinitarian prayer from *Paradiso* 14.28–30.[44] This prayer completes a transition in *Troilus*'s Book V from the pagan world of the poem to the contemporary, Christian world of Chaucer, his contemporaries, and his

granted him by Richard II'. This document – dated 9 November 1399 – serves as further evidence that the two were at least 'aqweyntid'. See 'Some New Light', 312, 323.

43 See Schless, *Chaucer and Dante* for an overview of Chaucer's use of Dante throughout his works. Barry Windeatt offers a thorough survey of Dantean allusion in *Troilus and Criseyde* in his *Oxford Guides to Chaucer: Troilus and Criseyde* (Oxford: Clarendon Press, 1992), 125–37. There has been much critical attention paid to Chaucer's use of Dante in *Troilus*: some of the more prominent studies include Winthrop Wetherbee, 'The Descent from Bliss: *Troilus*, III, 1310–1582', in *Chaucer's 'Troilus': Essays in Criticism*, ed. Stephen A. Barney (London: Scolar Press, 1980), 297–317; R. Allen Shoaf, 'Dante's *Commedia* and Chaucer's Theory of Mediation: A Preliminary Sketch', in *New Perspectives in Chaucer Criticism*, ed. Donald M. Rose (Norman, OK: Pilgrims Books, 1981), 83–103; Bonnie Wheeler, 'Dante, Chaucer, and the Ending of *Troilus and Criseyde*', *Philological Quarterly* 61 (1982): 105–23; Taylor, 'A Text and Its Afterlife'; and Winthrop Wetherbee, *Chaucer and the Poets: An Essay on 'Troilus and Criseyde'* (Ithaca, NY: Cornell University Press, 1984).

44 See Windeatt, *Oxford Guide*, 132–33.

readers. It also indicates the ways in which Chaucer navigates Dante's world – he draws on the *Commedia* on one hand when considering the fate of his poem and the nature of poetic tradition, and on the other hand when marking a transition from the pagan past to the Christian present.

Hoccleve's *Regiment* betrays a clear interest in these topics – the role of Christian morality in poetry, and the worldly afterlife of specific poets and poems. And while we cannot claim Dantean influence for Hoccleve based on the parallels examined above, we might profitably raise the question of the degree to which Dante – and the Italian humanist tradition more generally – entered into late medieval notions of fame, literary memorializing, and authorship beyond Chaucer. Lydgate credits Chaucer for writing 'Daunt in Inglissh' in his *Fall of Princes*, a remark that has been taken as a description of Chaucer's *House of Fame*, but which also raises the possibility of Chaucer actually having attempted an English translation of Dante's *Commedia*.[45] A Latin translation of the *Commedia* was commissioned in the decade following the writing of the *Regiment* at the Council of Constance, and one of the commissioners was Hoccleve's one-time colleague in the Privy Seal Office, Nicholas Bubwith (Bubwith served as Keeper of the Privy Seal from March 2, 1405 to October 4, 1406, during which time Hoccleve would have been a senior clerk in the office).[46]

Dante also gains attention from John Gower and Christine de Pizan in the period before the writing of the *Regiment* – and Gower's and Christine's engagement with Dante indicate his role not only as a 'poet of heaven and hell', but also as a political philosopher. Gower uses an anecdote about Dante in his *Confessio amantis* to emphasize the limits of the poet's power, and to expose the effects of false flattery. In Book 7 of his *Confessio*, Gower relates how Dante responds to a flatterer in a foreign court: 'Ther ben many mo / Of thy servantes than of myne. / For the poete of his covyne / Hath non that wol him clothe and fede, / But a flatour may reule and lede / A king

45 Lydgate, *Fall of Princes*, 1.303.

46 The other commissioner was Robert Hallum, bishop of Salisbury. The most extensive discussion to date of this translation of the *Commedia* is Wallace, *Premodern Places*, Chapter 3; for Bubwith's position in the Privy Seal, see *Handbook of British Chronology*, ed. S. Porter and I. Roy, 3rd ed. (London: Offices of the Royal Historical Society, 1986), 95. Jeremy Catto reads Bubwith and Hallum's commissioning of the *Commedia* – considered in tandem with Archbishop Thomas Arundel using his exile of 1397–9 to nurture an intellectual exchange with Coluccio Salutati – as evidence of the 'convergence' of the academic world with the 'court and metropolitan milieu of the Lancastrians'. See 'After Arundel: The Closing or the Opening of the English Mind?' in Gillespie and Ghosh, *After Arundel*, 43–54 (49–50).

with al his lond aboute' (7.2332–37; first recension).[47] Diane Watt reads this episode as a means by which Gower 'uses Dante to reflect on the limitations on his own role as poet and author of a mirror for princes';[48] the anecdote highlights the challenges that the poet faces as a truth-teller in a court where a lying flatterer can exert much more control over the king. Dante comes to stand in for Gower here: as a poet whose attempts to speak the truth put him at risk of alienating himself in the very court that he wishes to improve and guide with counsel. (This use of the poet chimes with the Dante we see in the *Legend of Good Women*, where Chaucer warns, 'Envie ys lavendere of the court alwey, / For she ne parteth, neither nyght ne day, / Out of the hous of Cesar; thus seith Dante' (*LGW* F.358–60).)

The most detailed early fifteenth-century poetic response to Dante outside Italy, however, comes from Christine de Pizan – the poet whose *Epistre au dieu d'amours* Hoccleve translated into English in 1402. Christine's *Chemin de long estude* (c. 1402–03) draws from the *Commedia* on a number of levels: from the title of the work (which is taken from Dante's first words to Virgil in the *Inferno*), to specific references to Dante throughout, to the journey that Christine undertakes in the first section of her poem, in which she undergoes a guided journey through the world (including Earthly Paradise) and then through the heavens.[49] Christine's guide for the journey is the Cumaean Sybil of Virgil's *Aeneid*, rather than the Virgil and Beatrice of Dante's *Commedia*. The work provides a compelling parallel to Hoccleve's *Regiment* in large part because of its experimentation with the genre of *speculum principis*. Like Hoccleve, Christine begins her poem in a state of despondency, a state brought on (as with Hoccleve) by both personal and political circumstances. This format allows Christine to offer specific details about her life – she recounts, for instance, her misfortune at losing her husband at a young age, and her resulting depression – much as Hoccleve offers autobiographical details throughout the first section of the *Regiment*. Christine attempts to console herself by reading Boethius's *Consolation*, and then falls asleep and experiences the vision within which she undertakes her Dantean journey.

---

47 See *Confessio Amantis* in *The English Works of John Gower*, ed. G.C. Macaulay, EETS E.S. 81–2 (London: Oxford University Press for the Early English Text Society, 1957).

48 Diane Watt, 'Literary Genealogy, Virile Rhetoric, and John Gower's *Confessio Amantis*', *Philological Quarterly* 78.4 (1999): 389–415 (404).

49 Christine de Pizan, *Le Livre du Chemin de Long Estude*, ed. Robert Püschel (Paris: H. le Soudier, 1887). All quotations from the *Chemin* in the present study come from this volume. English translations of Christine's text come from: *The Selected Writings of Christine de Pizan: New Translations, Criticism*, trans. Renate Blumenfeld-Kosinski and Kevin Brownlee (London: Norton, 1999).

In both the *Regiment* and the *Chemin*, the journey that constitutes the first part of the poem (a dreamed experience for Christine; a waking walk for Hoccleve) positions the writer in question to write the *speculum principis* portion of the poem. This involves a demonstration of their roles as sophisticated readers, as well as self-positioning with regard to literary genealogy – that is, the positioning of literary father figures. We will expand on these parallels here in order to better situate Hoccleve's poem – and Hoccleve's moral rendition of Chaucer – within a broader international context of poetic identity, political advice-giving, mediation, and literary tradition.

In both the *Regiment* and the *Chemin*, the respective poet's preliminary journey indicates the particular barrier that must be surmounted before the poet can position himself or herself to advise royalty. In Hoccleve's case, as discussed above, this involves verifying the poet's own moral credentials, and crafting Chaucer into an exemplary moral figure who can preside over Hoccleve's own poetic making. For Christine, the barrier would appear to be Christine's own position as a female clerk hoping to contribute to an exclusively male poetic tradition. Christine's writing of the *Chemin* fell within the period that saw her most active contributions to the *Querelle de la Rose*, and Kevin Brownlee has persuasively argued that Christine uses Dante in her *Chemin* as an alternate poetic father figure to the French *auctour* Jean de Meun, and as a means of navigating around what she saw as the misogynistic French literary tradition that Jean de Meun had come to represent.[50] By using Dante's *Commedia* in her *Chemin*, Christine is able to indicate her own authority as a writer with access to both French and Italian poetic traditions. While Brownlee notes the degree to which Christine emphasizes her limits as a woman writer throughout the *Chemin*, Christine's ability to translate portions of the *Commedia*, and to use Dante's poem as a narrative framework, advertises a cultural capital of its own. The title of the poem indicates its focus – the path of long study – and the poem itself becomes a means of demonstrating Christine's unique 'path', and the specific advantages available to her as a clerk who can read Italian as well as French.

---

50 Brownlee suggests that 'Christine counters the negative literary genealogy embodied for her by the *Rose* in the French vernacular with a positive literary genealogy embodied for her by the *Commedia* in the Italian vernacular.' See Kevin Brownlee, 'Literary Genealogy and the Problem of the Father: Christine de Pizan and Dante', *Journal of Medieval and Renaissance Studies* 23.3 (1993): 365–87 (370). See also Earl Jeffrey Richards, 'Christine de Pizan and Dante: A Reexamination', *Archiv für das Studium der neueren Sprachen und Literaturen* 222 (1985): 100–11, where Richards notes that 'Christine's preoccupation with Dante coincides clearly with her participation in the Quarrel over the *Roman de la Rose*' (102).

At the beginning of this chapter, we discussed Hoccleve's attempts to evade his interlocutor's questions and to insinuate himself thereby into an order apart. I suggested that Hoccleve's positioning of Chaucer allowed him to move from the old man's limiting religious discourse to a more fruitful poetic discourse. Christine uses 'the path of long study' to a similar end in the *Chemin*. She describes 'the path' as a space to which she can repair to gather strength, and as a symbol that affords her courage in dangerous situations. Christine specifically links this phrase – and this space – to her reading of Dante, and to Dante's first meeting with Virgil in the *Inferno*:

Mais le nom du plaisant pourpris
Oncques mais ne me fu apris,
Fors en tant que bien me recorde
Que Dant de Flourence el recorde
En son livre qu'il composa
Ou il moult biau stile posa:
Quant en la silve fu entrez
Ou tout de paour yert oultrez
Lors que Virgille s'apparu
a lui dont il fu secouru,
Adont lui dist par grant estude
Ce mot: Vaille moy long estude
Qui m'a fait cerchier tes volumes
Par qui ensemble acointance eusmes.
Or congnois a celle parole
Qui ne fu nice ne frivole
Que le vaillant poete Dant,
Qui a long estude ot la dent,
Estoit en ce chemin entrez,
Quant Virgille y fu encontrez
Qui le mena parmy enfer,
Ou plus durs liens vit que fer.
Si dis que je n'oublieroie
Celle parole, ains la diroie
En lieu d'ewangille ou de crois
Au passer de divers destroys
Ou puis en maint peril me vis;
Si me valu, ce me fu vis.

> [In any case, I had never learned the name of this pleasant route, except in so far as I remember that Dante of Florence records it in the book he composed in such a beautiful style. When he had entered the wild wood, and was completely overcome by fear, at the moment when Virgil appeared to help him, Dante exclaimed with great enthusiasm: 'May the long study that has made me pore over your volumes, through which we first came to know each other, now avail me.' At that point, I knew that with these words, neither silly nor frivolous, the valiant poet Dante, whose taste for learning was fierce, had embarked upon this path when he encountered Virgil, who afterward led him into hell, where he saw chains much stronger than iron. I thereupon declared that I would not forget this phrase, but would use it instead of the Gospel or the sign of the Cross when I encountered various dangers and perils. In my opinion, it served me well in such cases.]
> (1.125–52; pp. 74–75)

The route that Christine follows serves, on one level, as a figure for her read-knowledge – her experience in books.[51] But the phrase itself also has a particular function: Christine uses it to gather courage, she tells us, in much the same way that others use the Gospel or the sign of the Cross. Christine indicates how she uses the phrase soon after this point in the narrative, when being pursued by serpents and other frightening beasts in the territory of the Sultan: 'Si m'eussent moult tost devouree, / Se je fusse entre eulx demouree, / Sanz le conduit qui me menoit; / Mais tout ades me souvenoit / Du bon mot qui vault en tel cas, / Car quant j'estoie en un fort pas / Ou a passer je fusse rude, / Disant: Vaille moy long estude!' (1.385–92).[52] 'Long estude' serves as a charm – instigated by her reading of Dante – that protects Christine in her journey. But 'long estude' simultaneously refers to the 'path' on which the reader travels, with Christine, through the poem; and, furthermore, it refers to the extent of Christine's read-knowledge. It is a means to courage, and a way of foregrounding Christine's credentials as a highly literate clerk. Much as Hoccleve relies on 'Chaucer' to deliver him from his dialogue with the old man, Christine relies on 'long estude' to advance her narrative (and to protect herself, as a character). Both figures

---

51 Cf. Brownlee, 'Literary Genealogy', 379.

52 'They would have very quickly devoured me if I had stayed among them without the guide who was leading me, but right away I remembered the good phrase that is effective in such a case, for when I was in a tight spot which would have been difficult to get out of, I escaped safely and without hindrance by saying "May long study avail me!"' (77–78).

also advertise the poets' personal affiliations – Christine's status as an Italian poet; and Hoccleve's status as an acquaintance of Chaucer.

Both poets also use these respective figures to reach remarkably similar ends in their poems: Hoccleve, bolstered by his acquaintance with Chaucer, advises Prince Henry on the qualities befitting an upstanding, Christian monarch, and he culminates his *speculum* with a treatise on peace, in which he recommends a truce (and a marriage) between England and France. Christine, on the other hand, completes her 'path of long study' with an allegorical debate between Wealth, Nobility, Chivalry, and Wisdom on the qualities needed in a universal ruler who might bring peace to Christendom. Christine performs her role as a good clerk, and writes down the entire debate, and is then sent to convey it 'aux grans princes francois' [to the great French princes] (6.327). In both poems, the 'clerkly' role of the given writer is emphasized: Christine does not participate in the debate – she merely acts as scribe, even going to so far as to show Reason her transcripts, so that Reason might make any necessary corrections ('Mais de son bien lui oy dire / Qu'il n'y avoit riens a redire, / Et moult s'en tint pour bien content' (6.361–63)).[53] Hoccleve's credentials as a scribe are likewise advertised throughout the first section of the *Regiment*, and he makes clear that writing the *Regiment* proper is a matter of drawing exempla from other texts, not writing original advice – he writes, that is, as if compiling documents.[54]

In both poems, too, the ultimate focus on peace between England and France proceeds from the authority of the *speculum principis* portion of the text, while simultaneously gesturing towards concerns that are not only public and political, but also personal. That is, in both poems, the individual subject performs his or her melancholy in the opening lines of the poem with a dual focus on personal misfortune and political strife. The two are thereby linked, indicating that the positive political solutions and the fruits they would bring – peace and stability – would have a personal effect on the given subject, as well as a broader effect on the health of the nation. Hoccleve's melancholy at the beginning of the *Regiment* proceeds in part from the instability resulting from England's 'estate rial' being thrown into 'mescheef':

> Me fil to mynde how that nat longe agoo
> Fortunes strook doun thraste estat rial

[53] 'But I heard her say, because of her beneficence, that there were no corrections to be made, and that she was quite happy with my text' (87).

[54] See especially *RP* ll. 801–05, 988–1029, 1856–68, 2129–35. For further discussion, see Chapter 4 of the present study.

Into mescheef, and I took heede also
Of many anothir lord that hadde a fal.

(22–25)

Hoccleve calls to mind here the actions that renewed tensions between England and France at the dawn of the fifteenth century: Henry IV's deposition of Richard II, and his seizing of the throne. Christine, likewise, opens her poem by meditating in part 'aux ambicions, / Aux guerres, aux afflictions, / Aux traisons, aux agais faulx / Qui y sont et aux grans deffaulx / Que l'en fait' (323–27).[55] She goes on to note the omnipresence of war, and the need for peace, particularly between Christians: 'Mais des crestiens c'est dommages, / Qui pour envie des hommages / Et d'estranges terres conquerre, / S'entreoccient par mortel guerre' (351–54).[56]

The ends of the respective poems offer specific solutions for the problem of warfare between Christian nations, and they portray peace as a Christian virtue of paramount importance. In demonstrating this, Hoccleve turns to address not only Prince Henry, but rather all princes of England and France:

Of France and Engeland, o Cristen Princes,
Syn that your style of worthynesse is ronge
Thurghout the world in al the provinces,
If that of yow mighte be red or songe
That yee were oon in herte, ther nis tonge
That mighte expresse how profitable and good
Unto al peple it were of Cristen blood.

Yee hem ensamplen, yee been hir miroures;
They folwen yow.

(5321–29)

Hoccleve goes on to cite St Bridget of Sweden's prophecy that England and France must achieve peace in order to harbor the true spirit of Christ ('I am pees verray, there I wole abyde' (5386)).[57] Taking steps to ensure peace

55 '... the ambitions, the wars, the afflictions, the betrayals, the deceitful traps that are found everywhere in the world, and the great wrongs that people commit there' (64).

56 'It is, however, sad to state that Christians kill each other in deadly wars, because of greed for power or for newly conquered lands' (65).

57 In Chapter 2, we examined Hoccleve's call for peace within the context of poetic mediation.

between the two Christian nations of England and France, then, will not only present the princes of the two nations as exemplary Christians – it will enable the spirit of Christ to dwell in the nations, rendering them truly Christian. In Christine's poem, the movement towards peace, and towards the potential for a universal ruler who might bring about peace, is effected by virtue of her Dantean 'path of long study'. In Hoccleve's poem, Chaucer comes to serve as guide and go-between – as an authority shaped to suit the necessities of poetic writing circa 1410, and a means through which Hoccleve can achieve the authoritative position he needs to speak with confidence to the rulers of these Christian nations.

'Chaucer' constitutes for Hoccleve, after all, not only a historical figure, but also a figure of learning – a 'mirour of fructuous entendement' as Hoccleve puts it. We have seen how Hoccleve not only names Chaucer in the *Regiment*, but also dwells in Chaucerian poetics and in Chaucerian *poetry*. It is in this sense that the figure of Chaucer most nearly approaches the figure of Philosophy, as used in Boethius's *Consolation*: Philosophy denotes, on one level, a personification of Boethius's read-knowledge, his experience in reading philosophy.[58] Chaucer might be seen to represent, similarly, Hoccleve's composite reading experience – not only, that is, his knowledge of Chaucer's texts, but also his knowledge of Boethius, the Vulgate Bible, a range of biblical commentary and moral philosophy, and the specific texts on which Hoccleve bases the *Regiment* proper.[59] This composite authority allows Hoccleve to move beyond the church-centered authority of the old man, into an authoritative discourse that can speak to matters of importance for the contemporary Christian – such as the need for peace between Christian nations – without presuming to encroach on the ecclesiastical domain. As we have seen, Hoccleve serves as a mediator in bringing this new version of Chaucer to light: this involves reading Chaucer in another way, both in the sense of repurposing Chaucer's language so that it literally contributes to contemporary dialogues on faith, heresy, and personal reform, and in the sense of molding Chaucer-the-individual into a figure of unquestioned moral and literary authority.

[58] See Boethius, *Consolation*, 1.2–3.

[59] On the intermixture of biblical citation and commentary with Hoccleve's three named sources in the *Regiment*, see Perkins, *Hoccleve's Regiment*, 93–99.

Chapter Four

Reforming Thought: The Making of 'Thomas Hoccleve'

The last chapter introduced us to the figure of Chaucer as he appears in the *Regiment*, and offered a comparative, international context for Hoccleve's moral version of Chaucer. In this chapter, we will consider the figure of Hoccleve in greater detail, and will explore other English poetic discourses that contribute to Hoccleve's self-presentation. We will situate Hoccleve with respect to extra-Chaucerian, English literary traditions concerned with Christian allegory and ecclesiastical critique, including *Piers Plowman* and the texts that comprise the *Piers Plowman* tradition. In doing so, we will indicate how the figure of Hoccleve emerges at a crossroads between historical personal identity and communal scribal identity, and how 'Hoccleve' constitutes in itself an intermingling of English poetic voices – an embodied dialogue concerning the possible applications of English poetic discourse. The advertising (and exercise) of the virtue of prudence proves paramount here: we study Hoccleve's use of the virtue throughout his works, and the prudent examples Hoccleve sets for his contemporaries to follow. Hoccleve's prudent examples indicate a means of reforming English literary 'thought' in the early fifteenth century: Hoccleve offers himself as a model for readers, a medium for examining and reflecting on personal and literary reformation in a time of ecclesiastical and political turbulence.

Hoccleve's self-naming in the *Regiment* occurs almost 1,900 lines into the first section of the poem, and it arrives – as we have seen – with the mention of Hoccleve having been 'acquainted' with Chaucer. However, Hoccleve's identity evolves, in its unnamed form, across the span of this first section, in the sequence leading up to the poet's meeting with the old man, and throughout his itinerant dialogue; and this identity emerges at a crossroads between what would appear to be real, biographical details specific to Hoccleve – such as the period in which he has worked for the Privy Seal[1] and the information regarding his marriage[2] – and what might be referred to as his communal identity, his position as a scribe working among scribes and administrators in Westminster.[3] Hoccleve notes having worked at the Privy Seal for almost twenty-four years (ll. 804–05), and his discussion of his financial concerns culminates in what might be called a communal defense – a discussion of the pains and virtues of working as a 'wryter' (ll. 981–1029). Hoccleve begins this discussion by echoing the parable of the unjust steward (Luke 16:1–8):[4]

> With plow can I nat medlen ne with harwe,
> Ne woot nat what lond good is for what corn,
> And for to lade a cart or fille a barwe,
> To which I nevere usid was toforn;
> My bak unbuxum hath swich thyng forsworn,
> At instaunce of wrytynge, his werreyour,
> That stowpynge hath him spilt with his labour.
>
> (981–87)

In the parable of the unjust steward, a master approaches his steward and asks him to make an account of his stewardship; he has heard rumors of the steward's wastefulness, and he tells the steward that he will have to relieve him of his duties if this is true. The steward worries about losing his position and what he might do afterwards, saying, 'To dig I am not able, to beg I am ashamed' (Lk. 16:3).

The way in which Hoccleve expands on this conceit of not being able to conduct agricultural labor – describing the specific ways in which he would make a poor plowman, his inability to tell which crops grow where – has a more specific parallel in Langland's C.5 *apologia* in *Piers Plowman*, where Will, called to account for his lifestyle, approaches his

1 See ll. 799–805, 1023–24.

2 See ll. 1449–56, 1555–61.

3 See ll. 988–1029.

4 Kathryn Kerby-Fulton notes Hoccleve's allusion to the parable of the unjust steward, in the context of Langland's similar use of the allusion, in 'Langland and the Bibliographic Ego', in Justice and Kerby-Fulton, *Written Work*, 67–143 (90–91 and 95). Anne Middleton also discusses Langland's use of the parable in 'Acts of Vagrancy: The C Version "Autobiography" and the Statute of 1388', in Justice and Kerby-Fulton, *Written Work*, 208–317 (249–55, 280; for discussion of medieval commentary on the passage, see p. 307). Hoccleve also alludes to the parable in the *Male Regle*, ll. 367–68.

own self-defense by way of a discussion of his unsuitability to serve as an agricultural laborer:[5]

> Y am to wayke to worche with sykel or with sythe
> And to long, lef me, lowe to stoupe,
> To wurche as a werkemen eny while to duyren.
>
> (*Piers*, C.5.23–5)[6]

In both *Piers* and the *Regiment*, this approach comes in the midst of a discussion in which the subject is under pressure to present the details of his life. As we saw at the beginning of the last chapter, the old man takes an interest in the details of Hoccleve's life, and he questions Hoccleve in a manner redolent of the prologue to the *Legend of Good Women*, but also reminiscent – we note here – of Conscience and Reason's questioning of Will in Passus 5 of the *Piers Plowman* C-text.[7] For Will, this agricultural laborer analogy leads to what would appear to be biographical details about Langland's own life – the nature of his education, his place of residence, and the means by which he earns his living.[8] This section of the poem

5 On the significance of the addition of this passage during Langland's C-text revisions, in the context of labor law and attempts to contain heresy, see Kerby-Fulton, 'Bibliographic Ego', and Middleton, 'Acts of Vagrancy'.

6 All quotations from the C-text of *Piers Plowman* are from *Piers Plowman: A New Annotated Edition of the C-text*, ed. Derek Pearsall, Exeter Medieval Texts and Studies (Exeter: University of Exeter Press, 2008). All quotations from the B-text are from *The Vision of Piers Plowman: A Complete Edition of the B-Text*, ed. A.V.C. Schmidt (London: Everyman's Library, 1987).

7 David Lawton notes this parallel in 'Voice After Arundel', in Gillespie and Ghosh, *After Arundel*, 133–51 (141).

8 See especially C.5.35–52, where Will describes his education, his life in 'London and opelond bothe', and his manner of religious service. Talbot Donaldson and Ralph Hanna both draw upon this section in their discussions of Langland's life: see Ralph Hanna, *William Langland*, Authors of the Middle Ages (Aldershot: Variorum, 1993); and E. Talbot Donaldson, *Piers Plowman: The C-Text and Its Poet* (New Haven, CT: Yale University Press, 1949). George Kane has warned against the dangers of reading as autobiographical the poetry of Chaucer and Langland, concluding with respect to Langland, 'We can … have no biography of Langland, only speculative "lives", without historical necessity' (see *The Autobiographical Fallacy in Chaucer and Langland Studies* (London: H.K. Lewis, 1965), reprinted in *Chaucer and Langland: Historical and Textual Approaches* (Los Angeles: University of California Press, 1989), 14). Even as we approach such passages with caution, and keep in mind conventional contexts, we note – as Pearsall says – that such passages 'are not all necessarily fictitious' (Pearsall, *Piers Plowman*, 21). The continuing critical discourse examining the interplay between

has been read, on one level, as a defense of Will's activities – his manner of religious service and begging.[9] For Hoccleve, the agricultural laborer analogy similarly leads to the poet encoding autobiographical details into his text: it gives way to Hoccleve's discussion of the toils of scribal labor, and Hoccleve makes clear that he speaks from experience: 'What man that three and twenti yeer and more / In wrytynge hath continued, as have I', Hoccleve writes, 'I dar wel seyn, it smertith him ful sore / In every veyne and place of his body' (1023–26).

The entire first section of the *Regiment* proves exceptional for the degree to which it allows Hoccleve to focus on the biographical details of his life, and to offer a self-portrait that surpasses any other such English poetic self-portrait in the period.[10] We can read Hoccleve's concern with evaluating the particulars of his own person not only in this short sequence describing the toils of 'wrytyng', but throughout the entirety of the first section. The portrait of Hoccleve that emerges indicates that the poet shares some vital characteristics with Langland's Will. For instance, Hoccleve says he 'whilom Thoughte / Han been a preest', but after having been denied a benefice for too long, he decided to marry (1447–56). Langland's Will positions himself similarly: in *Piers* C.5, Will discusses having gone to 'scole'

fictional narrative and historical personhood in *Piers Plowman* remains one of the most enduring discussions in Langland scholarship. For other important studies that consider the identity and role of 'Will', see David Lawton, 'The Subject of *Piers Plowman*', *YLS* 1 (1987): 1–30; Anne Middleton, 'William Langland's "Kynde Name": Authorial Signature and Social Identity in Late Fourteenth-Century England', in Patterson, *Literary Practice and Social Change*, 15–82; and J.A. Burrow, *Langland's Fictions* (Oxford: Clarendon Press, 1993).

9 See Middleton, 'Acts of Vagrancy', where Middleton discusses the C.5 *apologia* in the context of the second Statute of Labourers of 1388. Kerby-Fulton, in 'Bibliographic Ego', reads Langland's C.5 *apologia*, in tandem with revisions that appear in Passus 9 of the C-text (ll. 66–281), in terms of Langland's attempt to defend himself, and his *modus vivendi*, against seditious imitators such as John Ball; in response to the conclusions drawn in the Blackfriars' Council of 1382; and as a means of distinguishing his mode of begging against the mode of those 'lollares' who threaten the social structure. See 'Bibliographic Ego', 86–89.

10 With Hoccleve, as with Langland, the line between 'autobiography' and 'poetry' must be treated with caution. Burrow begins his study of the poet's life with the caveat that the 'autobiographical passages' in Hoccleve's poems 'are not above suspicion' (Burrow, *Thomas Hoccleve*, 3). However, as Burrow notes, the substantial amount of extant documentation related to Hoccleve's life and career, compiled from the records of the Chancery and the Exchequer, and – we might add – from Hoccleve's own *Formulary* (London, British Library, MS Additional 24062), give us a firmer historical context with which to approach Hoccleve's poetic self-presentations.

[university] to 'wyste witterly what holy writ menede' (5.37), but says that his education was interrupted owing to loss of patronage. Will also mentions having a 'wyf' (see C.5.2; cf. 'Kytte my wyf' (and 'Calote my doghter') at B.18.426; and 20.193–98).[11] Talbot Donaldson suggests that Langland might have advanced to the level of acolyte, the highest of the minor orders (i.e., the orders before 'the holy orders' of priest, deacon, and subdeacon);[12] and, as Ralph Hanna notes, 'upon his marriage, Will's status would have become anomalous: he could not have advanced beyond minor orders and so become capable of fulfilling a priestly function'.[13] This leaves Will as an unbenificed clerk with a 'wyf', who must learn to use his training and talents to other ends.

Piers Plowman was being copied in the same London environment in which Hoccleve himself lived and worked: Hoccleve worked alongside Scribe D, responsible for the Ilchester manuscript of the *Piers Plowman* C-text (London, University Library, MS SL V.88), on the Cambridge, Trinity College, MS R.3.2 copy of Gower's *Confessio amantis*.[14] Anne Middleton points out that *Piers Plowman*'s 'survival to the present century in over fifty manuscripts, none clearly a direct copy of any of the others, implies that copies of the poem must have numbered in the hundreds by 1400'; and she notes that 'the poem was immediately and widely imitated'.[15] It becomes possible to talk about a *Piers Plowman* 'tradition' as early as

---

11 Ralph Hanna notes that Will's 'fall' may have been into either concubinage or matrimony: 'it is difficult to say which, as "wyf" might then mean either "woman" or "wife"' (Hanna, *William Langland*, 22).

12 Donaldson, *C-Text and Its Poet*, 202–06.

13 Hanna, *William Langland*, 22.

14 A.I. Doyle and M.B. Parkes, 'The Production of Copies of the *Canterbury Tales* and the *Confessio Amantis* in the Early Fifteenth Century', in M.B. Parkes, *Scribes, Scripts, and Readers: Studies in the Communication, Presentation and Dissemination of Medieval Texts* (London: Hambledon Press, 1991), 201–48. Linne Mooney and Estelle Stubbs put forward the theory that Scribe D is John Marchaunt, who was common clerk of the City of London from c.1399–1417, in *Scribes and the City: London Guildhall Clerks and the Dissemination of Middle English Literature, 1375–1425* (Woodbridge: York Medieval Press; Boydell Press, 2013), Chapter 3. They argue, furthermore, that 'many of the earliest and most authoritative manuscripts of works by Geoffrey Chaucer and his contemporaries John Gower, John Trevisa, and William Langland were copied by clerks employed at the London Guildhall' (7); and they position Scribe B ('Adam Pinkhurst') among these clerks. We will return to Scribe B later in this chapter. Mooney and Stubbs briefly discuss Hoccleve in the context of the Guildhall scribes, suggesting that Hoccleve may have served as a distributor of quires during the copying of MS R.3.2: see pp. 123–31 (125).

15 Middleton, 'Kynde Name', 15–16.

the first decade of the fifteenth century: the poems *Pierce the Ploughman's Crede*, *Richard the Redeless*, *Mum and the Sothsegger*, and the *Crowned King* use alliterative verse and Langlandian characters and themes as means to political and ecclesiastical commentary.[16] The author of *Richard* and *Mum*, and the author of the *Crowned King*, have both been situated within the Westminster environs in which Hoccleve himself worked. The author of *Richard* and *Mum* is thought to be a member of Sir Thomas Berkeley's household. The poet's knowledge of the events of Richard's deposition and Henry IV's accession to the throne would then come from Berkeley's own active role in these proceedings, and from his presence at Henry IV's councils.[17] The author of *The Crowned King* has been put forth as a 'Chancery clerk or comparable member of the Westminster bureaucracy'.[18] Kathryn Kerby-Fulton and Steven Justice have suggested, furthermore, that the immediate audience of *Richard the Redeless* would have been 'Westminster and its satellites – the writing offices, the inns where their clerks lived, and the scriveners and lawyers who came into contact with them'.[19]

The likelihood of a Westminster readership for these *Piers Plowman* tradition poems, and the popularity of *Piers Plowman* itself during the period in which – and in the place where – Hoccleve came of age,[20] raise the question of the extent to which Hoccleve might be responding to Langland in the *Regiment*, and also the extent to which at least some of his readers

16 The '*Piers Plowman* tradition' poems are collected in *The Piers Plowman Tradition: A Critical Edition of Pierce the Ploughman's Crede, Richard the Redeless, Mum and the Sothsegger, and The Crowned King*, ed. Helen Barr (London: Everyman's Library, 1993).

17 Barr, *Socioliterary Practice*, 161–64.

18 Nuttall, *Lancastrian Kingship*, 120; Derek Pearsall, '*Crowned King*: War and Peace in 1415', in *The Lancastrian Court: Proceedings of the 2001 Harlaxton Symposium*, ed. Jenny Stratford, Harlaxton Medieval Studies, 13 (Donington: Tyas, 2003), 163–72 (171).

19 'If the poem was released within a reading community constituted less by a few named individuals than by a professional group, geographically defined but too large for face-to-face intimacy, then one can understand how the author might expect his poem to "hap into the hands" of those to whom he had not given it and still remain, potentially and for a time, secret. Westminster and its satellites – the writing offices, the inns where their clerks lived, and the scriveners and lawyers who came into contact with them – would have provided this Langlandian poem with a civil service audience of just this description.' See Kathryn Kerby-Fulton and Steven Justice, 'Langlandian Reading Circles and the Civil Service in London and Dublin, 1380–1427', *NML* 1 (1997): 59–83 (78).

20 Ralph Hanna, Kathryn Kerby-Fulton, and Steven Justice suggest an initial audience for *Piers Plowman* itself in London and Westminster. See Hanna, *William Langland* 23–24; Kerby-Fulton and Justice, 'Langlandian Reading Circles'.

would register Langlandian parallels in the poem.[21] Hoccleve foregrounds that element of his persona that most clearly recalls Langland – his status as a married clerk who never advanced beyond minor orders. Langland set a precedent for Hoccleve not only in this regard, but also in his decision to mine the details of his historical person for the content of a vernacular poem, for his interest in using poetry to comment on contemporary ecclesiastical and political events, and for his use of authorial signature. As we saw in the last chapter, Hoccleve's instance of self-naming at the end of the first section of the *Regiment* interacts with an international tradition that considered matters of fame, literary memorializing, and interpersonal apotheosis. But Hoccleve's self-naming also bespeaks something more recognizably Langlandian, in that it marks the progression of an authorial identity, and it indicates the way in which this identity evolves progressively and dialogically over the course of the poem. For Middleton, Langland's complicated authorial signatures denote a gradual revelation of identity that parallels the given reader's ability to follow Langland's sustained narration, and to 'apprehend the applied ethical and subjective importance of the difficult and abstract questions broached by the poem's discursive wanderings'.[22] Hoccleve's identity in the *Regiment* likewise evolves incrementally, and his self-naming as 'Hoccleve' forms a boundary, a point at which the narratorial 'I' meets its formal signifier. Leading to this point, we gather

---

[21] Critics have highlighted a series of thematic and stylistic similarities between the poetry of Langland and Hoccleve: A.C. Spearing suggests that Hoccleve's 'persistent use of small-scale personification … may conceivably indicate the influence of *Piers Plowman*' (*Medieval to Renaissance*, 119); Sarah Tolmie places Hoccleve into the 'proximity' of Langland by noting the authors' shared interest 'in satire, metaphysics, and language', and in 'veer[ing] between the material and immaterial, concrete and abstract, personal and public, resisting any final resolution' ('*Prive Scilence*', 285); Lee Patterson likens the narrator of the *Male Regle* to Langland's Haukyn in Passus 13 of the *Piers* B-text ('What Is Me', 469); Ethan Knapp suggests Langlandian affinity in Hoccleve's adoption of 'the tones of *clergie*' (*Bureaucratic Muse*, 71), and compares the poets' portrayals of scribal labor, in the context of agricultural and monastic labor ('Poetic Work and Scribal Labor in Hoccleve and Langland', in *The Middle Ages at Work: Practicing Labor in Late Medieval England*, ed. Kellie Robertson and Michael Uebel (New York: Palgrave, 2004), 209–28; John Bowers notes that the *Regiment*'s 'uneasy hybrid of authorial autobiography and Mirror of Princes … resembles poetry of the Langlandian tradition', and also likens the *Regiment* to the *Piers Plowman* tradition poem, the *Crowned King* (*Chaucer and Langland*, 198–200); and David Lawton notes the Langlandian 'thread' woven through the first section of the *Regiment*, emphasizing especially the similarity between the old man's role and the role of Conscience and Reason in Passus 5 of the *Piers* C-text ('Voice After Arundel', 141).

[22] Middleton, 'Kynde Name', 42.

hints at Hoccleve's professional identity, his personal habits and affiliations, and his geographical setting, but only at the end of the poem's first section do the fragments of this 'I' concretize around the name 'Hoccleve'. Hoccleve's authorial signature, unlike Langland's, is clear and direct.[23] But the passage to this moment of self-naming indicates a *process* of inscribing the self, progressively and dialogically – a process that characterizes the poetry of Langland more readily than that of Chaucer. To illustrate this, and to indicate the way in which we move from a 'communal' narrator to an individual Hoccleve, we will turn to examine Hoccleve's use of an agential 'Thought' figure in the first section of the *Regiment*. We will engage in a comparative reading of Hoccleve's and Langland's respective iterations of an agential 'Thought' in order to illustrate the journey that Hoccleve's narrator takes towards his designation as 'Hoccleve'. Then, we will explore how this aspect of Hoccleve's self-presentation interacts with his use of Chaucer to demonstrate a more prudent poetics and an approach to writing centered on 'endytyng'.

Thought

In *Piers Plowman*, the character Thought plays a pivotal role: he is the first in a series of personified faculties that Will interrogates in the interest of learning how to live a virtuous life. Thought introduces Will to the triad Dowel–Dobet–Dobest and, while his definition of these three does not entirely satisfy Will, he nonetheless forms the first link in the chain along which Will travels in his understanding of 'Dowel'. Without Thought, Will might not meet Wit, and so might not move on to Study and Clergy, and so on. Most importantly, Thought appears to Will just after Will's first interaction with Piers. In arriving at that moment in the poem, Thought enables Will to begin working through the problems presented in the 'Pardon from Truth' episode (B.7/C.9). The pardon received from Truth – which directs Will to 'dowel' – does not hearten Will, so much as it further confuses him. He grapples with the notion of doing well, and more specifically, the notion of how *any* human work – any *doing* – might be seen as valuable before God.[24] Thought's appearance to Will initiates his

[23] The most extensive discussion of Langlandian authorial signature is Middleton, 'Kynde Name'. Middleton records each instance of authorial signature in the appendix to her study, pp. 79–82.

[24] For an overview of Langland's Thought, see James Simpson, *Piers Plowman: An Introduction*, 2nd rev. ed., Exeter Medieval Texts and Studies (Exeter: University of Exeter Press, 2007), 90–91; see also 98–99.

(and the reader's) meditation on the status of one's work, and the ability to make one's work accord with God's will.

In the first stanzas of the *Regiment*, by contrast, we encounter a personified Thought who serves as a destructive and obstructive force. Rather than leading the narrator forward along a chain of interpretation, and thereby maintaining the sequential integrity of the dream narrative, Thought actively keeps the narrator from falling asleep and thereby even beginning such a sequence.[25] Where Will drifts to sleep, and in sleep encounters the series of interlocutors that enable him to test ideas of 'Dowel', Hoccleve opens his poem stranded in a state of wakefulness, Thought – his 'cruel fo' – having chased away 'Reste' and 'Sleep' (71–77). Where Langland's Thought spurs the narrator to contemplate the status of good works before God, Hoccleve's Thought spurs his narrator to contemplate only his own despair. Far from preparing the narrator to conceive good works, this Thought sows its 'wastyng seed' (201) and produces the 'fruyt of bittirnesse' (3).

Hoccleve's first exchange with the old man arrives in the wake of this destructive iteration of Thought. The old man approaches our narrator with the same greeting that Holy Church uses to confront Will in Passus I: 'Sleepstow?'[26] And Hoccleve's response is emphatically negative: 'Voide fro me, me list no compaignie.' He shoos the man away, accusing him of trying to 'encresse' his 'greef' (141–42). As the two characters begin to talk, the old man recognizes the presence of this latter-day Thought in Hoccleve, and refers to it as if an established concept: without Hoccleve's prompting, the old man knows to refer to it as 'Thought', and he begins listing Thought's destructive tendencies. He warns Hoccleve about Thought's 'wastyng seed', calls Thought 'perillous', and directs Hoccleve to 'voide [Thought's] poisoun' (201, 267, 203). The old man's duty is to 'twynne' the poet–narrator from this suspicious and ruinous iteration of 'Thought' (276).

'Thought' is represented in Hoccleve's passage as a provocateur, serving not as a way forward for Hoccleve (as it is for Will), but rather as an

---

25 The poem begins with an illustration of Thought's disruptive nature: in the opening stanza of the poem, it is Thought, rather than the 'I' narrator, who has agency. As the narrator lies 'in [his] bed upon a nyght' (l. 6), Thought muses 'upon the restlees bysynesse / Which that this troubly world hath ay on honde' (ll. 1–2), and thereby robs the narrator of rest: 'Thoght me byrefte of sleep the force and might' (l. 7).

26 Cf. *Piers* B.1.5: 'Sone, slepestow?' Notably, Langland's Holy Church appears as the antithesis to Hoccleve's old man: she is a 'lovely lady of leere in lynnen yclothed' (B.1.3); whereas Hoccleve's interlocutor is a 'poore old hoor man' (122).

impasse. Later in the narrative, Hoccleve indicates the extent to which Thought overcame his senses, rendering him unable to discern what he thought or said:

> Thogh I nat slepte, yit my spirit mette
> Ful angry dremes; Thoght ful bysyly
> Vexid my goost so that nothyng wiste I
> What that I to yow spak or what I thoghte,
> But heer and there I myselven soghte.
>
> (759–63)

The final line in this stanza – 'heer and there I myselven soghte' – seems to echo the frame of Will's journey, albeit with a bleak distinction. As Will 'meets' with his separate faculties (such as Thought and Wit) in the interest of seeking answers on how to 'Dowel', Hoccleve's poet–narrator 'meets' with 'ful angry dremes', not hoping to understand Dowel, but only searching for some evidence of who he is, and scrambling for solace.

Importantly, the old man's concern with ridding Hoccleve of what appears as 'Thought' is rooted in the way Thought makes the poet seem like a heretic. When the old man asks Hoccleve if he 'wrappid been in this dampnacioun' (373) – that is, if he is associated with John Badby – he aligns Hoccleve explicitly, if momentarily, with a man recently executed for heresy.[27] Hoccleve's Thought becomes the author's means of delineating this suspicious aspect. He foregrounds his own potential to be misread and dedicates the first 2,000 lines of his poem to dramatizing his own reformation and, more importantly, the reformation of his Thought: from a faculty that produces bitter fruit to a faculty that produces good fruit.[28]

---

27 Perkins notes the connection between 'bisy thoght' and the 'dangers of heresy' in the early moments of the old man's dialogue with Hoccleve in 'Haunted Hoccleve', 113–14, 117.

28 In this respect, Hoccleve's self-presentation might be seen to parallel that of Langland in his C-text revisions. If, as Kerby-Fulton suggests, Langland uses his C-text revisions – and his C.5 *apologia* in particular – as a means of self-defense and self-differentiation after the Peasants Revolt of 1381 ('Bibliographic Ego', 86–88), then Hoccleve can be seen, in a similar light, highlighting his ability to be misread and offering a poetic self-defense in the first section of his poem. We should remember, too, that John Ball was by no means the last person to use Langland's poem to his own political ends. *Pierce the Plowman's Crede*, for instance, culminates in the creation of a pro-Wycliffite version of Piers Plowman, who publishes his politically freighted 'Crede' at the end of the poem (c. 1393–1400). *Richard the Redeless* puts *Piers*-ian tropes to the service of criticizing the newly deposed Richard II (c. 1400). And *Mum and the Sothsegger*

As Hoccleve's stanzas describing scribal labor in the first section of the *Regiment* constitute in many ways a communal autobiography for Hoccleve and his fellow 'wryters', the first section of the poem as a whole can be read, on one level, as a communal defense.[29] By refusing to settle his identity as 'Hoccleve' until the end of this section, the poet offers his reader the opportunity to inhabit his 'I' narrator and thereby partake in a sympathetic act of reformation. Hoccleve dramatizes the process of 'unlocking' his 'conceit' at the end of this first section:

> With herte as tremblyng as the leef of asp,
> Fadir, syn yee me rede to do so,
> Of my symple conceit wole I the clasp
> Undo and lat it at his large go.
>
> (1954–57)

This passage serves to bookend the old man's early demand that Hoccleve 'voide [Thought] and lat him twynne, / And walke at large out of thy prisoun' (276–77). As 'Thought' is reborn here as 'Conceit', Hoccleve, through the old man, authorizes his release from 'prisoun' and into the world at large. This stanza marks Hoccleve's successful shedding of one skin (Thought) in the interest of inhabiting another skin – renewed and revitalized Thought, in the person of Conceit. In restoring Thought as 'Conceit', Hoccleve activates medieval meanings more specific to that word

---

employs a Langlandian mode of inquiry to question the efficacy of Henry IV's rule and to criticize friars (c. 1408–1410). On the relationship between Lollardy and *Mum* and *Crede* specifically, see D.A. Lawton, 'Lollardy and the "Piers Plowman" Tradition', *The Modern Language Review* 76.4 (1981): 780–93. Lawton notes that the 'case for [*Mum*'s] Lollard sympathies … is far from conclusive', but suggests a 'serious possibility that *Mum* may belong to the same Lollard subculture as *Piers the Ploughman's Creed*' (791). If Hoccleve did encounter poems such as *Mum and the Sothsegger* in his position as a clerk in Westminster and London, he would have encountered, at any rate, an approach to political and ecclesiastical critique that contrasts strongly with the approach taken in the *Regiment*. I consider the implications of these contrasting approaches in greater detail below.

29 Knapp considers Hoccleve's 'communal' identity as a Privy Seal clerk in detail in his *Bureaucratic Muse*. Whereas Knapp focuses on the interplay between 'reticence' and 'assertion' in Hoccleve's self-presentation (34), I focus on how this self-presentation serves as a self-defensive strategy. In my view, the most salient feature of Hoccleve's self-presentation is not only the interplay between namelessness and namedness, or anonymity and identity, but rather the more specific ends to which these dynamics are being used and, moreover, the literary contexts with which they affiliate.

– the mind in a more holistic sense, the 'complex of mental faculties', and also mental powers.[30]

But this process also proves very personal. Hoccleve's choice to delay giving his own name until the end of this process, and to proffer his name along with Chaucer's, is emblematic of the nature of his own self-defense. In the stanzas describing the labor of writing, the narrator speaks as a 'we' – and this plural first person defines itself by silence and stillness: 'we laboure in travaillous stilnesse; / We stowpe and stare upon the sheepes skyn, / And keepe moot our song and wordes yn' (1013–15). After 1,860 lines of conversation and Thought-reformation, the old man finally asks Hoccleve to name himself:

'What shal I calle thee, what is thy name?'
'Hoccleve, fadir myn, men clepen me.'
'Hoccleve, sone?' 'Ywis, fadir, that same.'
'Sone, I have herd or this men speke of thee;
Thow were aqweyntid with Chaucer, pardee –
God have his soule, best of any wight!'

(1863–68)[31]

As Thought becomes Conceit, one scribe among many becomes 'Hoccleve', and Chaucer emerges – quite suddenly, in fact – as the presiding figure who authorizes Hoccleve's identity. The book imagery that Hoccleve employs in the stanza confirming Thought's reformation – the trembling 'leef', the image of Hoccleve 'undoing' the 'clasp' of Conceit – emphasizes the process of bookmaking here. It foreshadows Chaucer's 'bookes of ornat endytyng' (1973) – those books that survive Chaucer on earth, and that carry on his legacy. It reflects back, simultaneously, on the book that Hoccleve is making – the book, indeed, that we are reading. Hoccleve teases the line between 'speech' and 'text' here: the dialogue that we have been 'listening' to exists as text, and it is manifested as text even as we experience it simultaneously as speech.[32]

30 *Middle English Dictionary Online*, s.v. 'Conceit (n.)', http://ets.umdl.umich.edu/m/med/.

31 We examined this stanza in Chapter 3, in the context of fame and literary affiliation. Here, our focus is instead on how the naming of Chaucer aligns with the transformation of Hoccleve's 'Thought'.

32 For a consideration of medieval orality and textuality, see David Lawton, 'English Literary Voices, 1350–1500', in *The Cambridge Companion to Medieval England*, ed. Andrew Galloway (Cambridge: Cambridge University Press, 2011), 237–58. Lawton

The transition that Hoccleve undergoes at the end of this first section is also enacted through a transition between 'wrytyng' as scribal activity and 'endytyng' as poetic composition. Early in the dialogue, Hoccleve describes the Privy Seal as the place where 'I wone [dwell] / And wryte' (803). When describing the toils of scribal labor, similarly, Hoccleve uses 'wryte' and 'wrytyng' to describe the work undertaken, and 'wryter' to describe the person performing the task (see 'wrytynge, his werreyour' (986); 'Many men, fadir, weenen that wrytynge / No travaille is' (988–89); 'A wryter moot thre thynges to him knytte' (995); 'Whoso shal wryte …' (1002); 'Wrytyng also dooth grete annoyes thre …' (1016); etc.). 'Enditing', on the other hand, denotes composition rather than the act of writing or copying; and the introduction of 'endite' into the *Regiment* coincides with the first mention of Chaucer, and with Hoccleve's self-naming. The old man's first suggestion that Hoccleve 'Endite in Frenssh or Latyn thy greef cleer' gives way to his asking for Hoccleve's name (1854). After establishing that he is talking to the same Hoccleve who was acquainted with Chaucer, the old man suggests Hoccleve 'endyte' a piece 'In Englissh tonge' (1871–72). Hoccleve then uses the word 'endytyng' to align his writing with Chaucer's, describing Chaucer's 'bookes of … ornat endytyng' (1973); he then employs a modesty topos to draw attention to his own 'endytyng' twice more (see ll. 2056, 5458). The word cooperates not only with a sense of composing, rather than copying, but also with a specifically Chaucerian approach to poetic composition, insofar as Chaucer is presented in the poem as the only other individual capable of 'endytyng' – and, indeed, as the highest standard of the form.[33]

---

draws attention to the fact that 'in medieval usage, voice, *vox*, has twin, somewhat paradoxical, meanings: as quotation, the trace of an authority cited if not always endorsed; and, notwithstanding, as independent human utterance. The usage binds together senses modern theory has wanted to draw apart – textuality and orality, presence and absence' (239).

[33] Cf. Anne Middleton's discussion of the importance of the word 'enditing' to Chaucer's poetics: 'For Chaucer, the idea of "enditing" was one that reconciled two contrasted aspects of literature and the writer's role he had considered repeatedly in his earlier work: on the one hand, the mode of existence of the "maker" as participant-entertainer and celebrant of the cult values of love, and on the other, that of the "poete," who was absent in his own person from the world of the living, but endured as it were in petrified form, through books … . In reconciling "making" and "poetry," "enditing" offered a middle way through which vernacular writing could attain both high style and broad public rather than coterie standing.' See Anne Middleton, 'Chaucer's "New Men" and the Good of Literature in the *Canterbury Tales*', in *Chaucer, Langland, and Fourteenth-Century Literary History*, ed. Steven Justice (Farnham: Ashgate Variorum, 2013), 27–60 (38–39).

Immediately after Hoccleve has 'undone' the clasp of Conceit, he delivers a paean to Chaucer infused, as we noted in the last chapter, with the language of Chaucer's *Book of the Duchess*: Hoccleve's 'What eiled deeth? Allas, why wolde he sle the?' (1967) recalls the Black Knight's 'Allas, deth, what ayleth the, / That thou noldest have taken me ...' (*BD* 481–82).[34] Upon beginning the *Regiment* proper, Hoccleve underscores his ability to 'endite' by doing exactly what the Black Knight does in the *Book of the Duchess*: expressing himself through chess-related metaphors. Hoccleve seizes upon the name of one of his sources for the *Regiment* – Jacob de Cessolis's 'Ches Moralysed'[35] – to demonstrate his mastery of chess puns: where the Black Knight describes the process by which his 'fere' (his queen) was taken by a pawn, Hoccleve says his time in the Privy Seal has enabled him to learn the 'kynges draght' (the king's move (i.e., in chess)), and so has equipped him to counsel Prince Henry on how to act as a king. Hoccleve then goes on to show his skill in navigating the metaphorical possibilities of a single word: his use of 'draght' in lines 2120–21 could mean 'move', 'draft (i.e., a draft of a letter)', and also 'trick'; his use in line 2128 intimates a king's 'training' or 'education'; and in line 2144 the word means at once 'inclination' and 'body of water'. Hoccleve also puns on 'th'eschequeer': a word that refers at once to a chessboard, and to The King's Exchequer.[36] Hoccleve says he has 'aventured many a yeer / My wit therin' and positions 'th'eschequeer' as a place where 'a man may lerne to be wys and waar' (2116–19). Within this matrix of chess metaphors, then, Hoccleve's workplace undergoes its own transformation: it becomes a site in which Hoccleve is not anonymous and overworked, but rather knowledgeable ('wys') and also crafty and prudent ('waar'). Hoccleve's focus on the *king's* 'move' in the following stanzas diverts attention from the move that Hoccleve has already achieved for himself in this first section of his poem: he has moved from a position of relative anonymity into a position in which he can be appreciated as a named and capable writer. Hoccleve progresses from a position amid many other 'wryters' to

34 We noted this allusion at the beginning of Chapter 3, in the context of the old man's dissonant dialogue with Hoccleve. Here, we explore the relevance of the given allusion to chess, writing, and Chaucer's own wordplay.

35 On the importance of Jacob de Cessolis's *De ludo saccorum* to the *Regiment*, see Perkins, *Hoccleve's Regiment*, 94–114, 122–25. Perkins notes, 'If the only criterion for influence on the *Regiment* were the volume of borrowings from each source, any argument could quickly be settled in favour of *De ludo saccorum*' (94). See also Jenny Adams, *Power Play: The Literature and Politics of Chess in the Late Middle Ages* (Philadelphia: University of Pennsylvania Press, 2006), Chapter 4.

36 Blyth draws our attention to some of these chess puns: *Regiment*, 219–20.

a position of singularity; and, in the course of this move, he transforms into a more authoritative version of himself.

But Hoccleve's self-presentation as 'waar' here proves equally as important as his self-presentation as 'wys'. Indeed, writing for Prince Henry in 1410, some three years before the prince would ascend the throne, with the recent deposition of Richard II in mind, and even more recent rumors of quarrels between Prince Henry and his father in the air, to be wise was to be wary, attentive, and prudent.[37] And it is exactly this quality – prudence – with which Hoccleve endows Chaucer: 'Allas that thow thyn excellent prudence / In thy bed mortel mightest nat byqwethe!' (1965–66). 'Prudence' carries the meaning of 'intelligence' here, but also 'discretion' and 'good judgment'. Hoccleve indicates that Chaucer was associated with this virtue as early as 1410. We must remember here that Chaucer-the-pilgrim's own contribution to the *Canterbury Tales* features the central character of Prudence, and is referred to in its *explicit* in the Ellesmere manuscript as 'Chaucers tale of Melibee and of Dame Prudence'.[38] Paul Strohm has also noted Chaucer's ability to navigate factional politics in the 1380s, particularly as they contrast with the less tactful approaches of Thomas Usk: 'No single step saved Chaucer from indictment, but rather a whole series of prudent adjustments of his relations with the court party.'[39] For Strohm, this prudent approach dovetails with Chaucer's approach to poetry and, specifically, with his ability to 'suppress the particular coordinates of his own worldly situation' in favor of a poetics that situates itself in the trans-historical tradition of *poesie*.[40]

In moving from the interior setting of Chester's Inn in the opening stanzas of the *Regiment* into the streets of London, and in moving from his own internal meditations to open dialogue with a stranger, Hoccleve exhibits the momentum of his own speech (simultaneously his own text) from private to public spheres. The *Regiment* announces itself as a poem that operates outside, among individuals who pronounce their religious orthodoxy openly and who willingly engage in processes of self-reform and

37 As Perkins notes, 'The Prince wrested control of the Council from his father in 1409–10, and the position of Henry IV himself came under scrutiny before the King regained his hold over the Council in late 1411.' See Perkins, *Hoccleve's Regiment*, 69.

38 *The Ellesmere Manuscript of Chaucer's Canterbury Tales: A Working Facsimile*, Introduction by Ralph Hanna III (Woodbridge: D.S. Brewer, 1989).

39 Strohm, 'Politics and Poetics', 96.

40 'Chaucer shows a marked tendency to suppress the particular coordinates of his own worldly situation, and to connect his work with a tradition of 'poesye' (*Troilus* 5.1790) that existed before him and will survive him.' Strohm, 'Politics and Poetics', 109.

self-emendation. Indeed, Hoccleve's opening section progresses towards an illustration of prudence – both in the example of Chaucer's prudence, and in Hoccleve's own self-presentation as 'wys' and 'waar'. In approaching the *Regiment* proper, in which Hoccleve takes on the task of writing his *speculum principis*, the poet proves similarly prudent: he is careful to emphasize both the moral credentials and the authority of the texts on which he will be drawing. He will translate Aristotle's letters to Alexander (the *Secreta Secretorum*), whose 'sentence' he describes as 'holsum' and 'growndid on treewe entente', echoing the old man's instructions that Hoccleve write a 'tretice / Growndid on his estates [the Prince's] holsumnesse' (2040–41; 1949–50). He mentions also wanting to 'translate' Giles of Rome's 'Regiment / Of Princes' and Jacob de Cessolis's 'Ches Moralysed' – the latter author, Hoccleve says, is 'a worthy man', 'Of the ordre of prechours maad' (2110–11). Hoccleve distances himself from the content of these texts by saying he will merely 'compyle' stories that these other 'clerkes' wrote (2132, 2151) – stories that the prince has likely already read:

> I am seur that tho bookes alle three
> Red hath and seen your innat sapience;
> And as I hope, hir vertu folwen yee.
> But unto yow compyle I this sentence
> That, at the good lust of your excellence,
> In short yee mowen beholde heer and rede
> That in hem thre is scatered fer in brede.
>
> (2129–35)

This approach would appear to follow a Chaucerian poetics, wherein the 'already-written' and 'already-read' status of these old texts underscores the degree to which Hoccleve distances himself from any hazardous, contemporary political disputes. As we shall see in the following section, however, far from suppressing 'the particular coordinates of his own worldly situation', Hoccleve uses the *Regiment* proper to move towards increasingly timely political concerns. His figure of Chaucer adapts to suit this poetic approach, which in substance recalls less the poetry of Chaucer and more the approach of the *Crowned King* and portions of *Piers Plowman*, in which a given clerk speaks on behalf of the people in the interest of curbing instances of political willfulness or misconduct.

A Poetics of Prudence

In order to illustrate how Hoccleve portrays Chaucerian authority in the final pages of the *Regiment*, we will turn now to read the poem in the formatting of its two earliest extant manuscripts. These manuscripts – London, British Library, MSS Harley 4866 and Arundel 38, both of which have been dated by John Burrow to 1411–12 (i.e., immediately after the poem's composition) – follow exactly the same page layout, in terms of which stanzas are included on which pages.[41] As Charles Blyth notes, these manuscripts 'have the closest imaginable relationship apart from the fact that they were written by two distinct scribes'.[42] They have 'page for page, an identical textual format: when one manuscript departs from the norm of four complete stanzas to the page, so does the other one'.[43] There is, for example, the memorable instance in both manuscripts of a man lassoing a stanza (the same stanza in each manuscript), and attempting to pull it into the body of the page, where, one might assume, the common exemplar gave instruction for the scribe to do so.[44] This intimation of an imposed order is further underscored by what Blyth calls 'the strong probability that they were executed with some degree of supervision by Hoccleve himself'.[45] As we shall see, this uniform *mise-en-page* allows for a particular dynamic between text and image in the *Regiment*, and it also allows for a unique interplay between political advice-giving and exemplary prudence.

In the penultimate section of the *Regiment*, which concerns 'counsel', Hoccleve entertains the question of who might serve best as a counselor for the king. Towards the end of folio 87r in MS Harley 4866, Hoccleve

41 Burrow, *Thomas Hoccleve*, 50; Blyth, *Regiment*, 14–17.

42 Blyth, *Regiment*, 15.

43 Ibid.

44 This occurs on f. 65r of MS Arundel 38, and f. 62r of MS Harley 4866.

45 Blyth, *Regiment*, 16. The copy of the *Regiment* preserved in San Marino, Huntington Library, MS HM 135 indicates a similar scribal concern with following a precise 'imposed order'. The scribe miscopies a sequence of lines on f. 51r of the manuscript; upon realizing his error, he draws a box around each miscopied stanza, and marks each with a small cross and the word 'n*u*l'. That the scribe wanted to follow the exact presentation of his exemplar is suggested by the fact that he copies the two stanzas that should have been there directly next to the canceled stanzas, then continues copying underneath. When he runs out of room on the given page, he then fits more text in the margin, to enable him to fit four (new) stanzas on the page. If he had not wanted to follow the exact format of his exemplar, he would have kept copying the text directly below the canceled stanzas. I thank Daniel Wakelin for bringing my attention to this instance.

discusses which factors make for a good counselor.[46] He warns the prince against Favel, or false flattery, then moves on to discuss the element of experience. This leads to Hoccleve's suggestion that the prince take counsel from old and experienced men, rather than young men:

> He that is fressh and lusty now this day
> By lengthe of yeeres shal nothyng be so;
> Fresshnesse and lust may nat endure alway;
> Whan age is comen, he commandith ho.
> But let see, who considerith this, who?
>
> (4957–61)

The page ends. With this question lingering in mind – who considerith this, who? – we turn the page to read on. Upon turning the page, however, we are less inclined to finish the present stanza, and more inclined to take in the sudden appearance of Chaucer on the facing page, reaching beyond the frame and into the very poem we are reading:

Figure 1. Chaucer figure in London, British Library, MS Harley 4866, f. 88r.

46 Blyth uses the two manuscripts in question – MSS Harley 4866 and Arundel 38 – as the copy texts for his edition of the *Regiment*. I use his edition in quoting the text from the relevant portion of the *Regiment*. As noted above, the two manuscripts share the same page layout and format; I refer here to folio numbers from MS Harley 4866, as that manuscript keeps all relevant pages intact.

We read on. Coming to the end of the next page, Hoccleve's 'mateere' shifts: he seizes the occasion to offer the prince a piece of advice: specifically, that he should avoid holding his councils on holy days. 'Thynkith wel this', Hoccleve says, 'yee wel apaid be nolde / If your soget nat by youre heestes tolde. / Right so our lord God, kyng and commaundour / Of kynges alle, is wrooth with that errour' (4967–70). Hoccleve continues:

> To God your herte bowe
> If yee desyre men hir hertes bende
> To yow. What kyng nat dredith God offende
> Ne nat rekkith do him disobeissance,
> He shal be disobeied eek, par chance.
>
> (4973–77)

The poet seizes the occasion to further submit the future king to the 'kyng and commaundour / Of kynges alle' – God – and to remind him that if he does not respect his king, he risks being disobeyed by his own subjects.

The connection between the king's respect for God and a respect for his own people links this passage to several other passages in the *Regiment.* For example, earlier in the *Regiment* proper Hoccleve advises Prince Henry:

> my good Lord, wynneth your peples vois,
> For peples vois is Goddes vois, men seyn.
> And He that for us starf upon the Crois
> Shal qwyte it yow, I doute it nat certeyn.
>
> (2885–88)

This notion – that the voice of the people is God's voice – derives from 'Vox populi vox dei', a favorite maxim of John Gower.[47] The marginal gloss 'Vox populi vox dei' beside this stanza, along with the phrase 'men seyn', would suggest Hoccleve is merely restating a convention here. But the emphasis on speaking on behalf of the people, in the interest of reminding the prince of his duty to the people, also places the *Regiment* in the context of contemporary political poems such as the *Crowned King.* In the *Crowned King,* Prince Henry – now Henry V – is beseeched to bow his head to that

47 See especially Russell A. Peck, *Kingship and Common Profit in Gower's Confessio Amantis* (Carbondale: Southern Illinois University Press, 1978). On the role of 'vox populi, vox dei' in late medieval English literature and culture, see Matthew Giancarlo, *Parliament and Literature in Late Medieval England* (Cambridge, Cambridge University Press, 2007), especially Chapter 3.

other 'crowned Kyng' – 'Crist … that on Cros didest' (l. 1). A clerk kneels before the king on behalf of the population and asks him to reconsider the heavy taxes he has laden upon his people in the name of warfare. 'The condicion of a kyng shuld comfort his peple', the clerk says, ' … euere in your mynde haue hym that you made [he that made you], / And taketh a siker ensample that Crist hym-self sheweth' (133; 136–37). This kneeling clerk, in turn, recalls the 'lunatik' who kneels 'to the Kyng clergially' in the Prologue to *Piers Plowman* (B.123–24), and says, 'Crist kepe thee, sire Kyng, and thi kyngryche, / And lene thee lede thi lond so Leaute thee lovye, / And for thi rightful rulynge be rewarded in hevene!' (125–27). In each case, the resident clerk emerges to remind the king of his duty to the people, and to link this duty to a sense of reverence for – and answerability to – his own king, God. In the *Regiment*, as in the *Crowned King*, this reminder comes hand in hand with a specific request made to the king on behalf of the people – a request, that is, to keep holy days sacred and not let the business of royal meetings impinge on sacred time.[48]

The lines that immediately follow Hoccleve's request have caused some confusion for critics. After delivering this pointed and timely suggestion to the prince on behalf of the people, Hoccleve's *mateere* shifts again:

> The first fyndere of our fair langage
> Hath seid, in cas semblable, and othir mo,
> So hyly wel that it is my dotage
> For to expresse or touche any of tho.
> Allas, my fadir fro the world is go,
> My worthy maistir Chaucer – him I meene
>
> (4978–83)

Charles Blyth notes that Hoccleve's reference, in line 4979, is unclear: if the line refers to Chaucer, then where is the Chaucerian precedent for what Hoccleve has written regarding councils and holy days? Jeanne

48 Hoccleve's reminder that 'peples vois is Goddes vois' has an analogue, too, in the Digby Poems – the sequence of lyrics collected in Oxford, Bodleian Library, MS Digby 102, with an incomplete copy of the *Piers Plowman* C text, Richard of Maidstone's *Seven Penitential Psalms*, and *The Debate between the Body and Soul.* (Helen Barr, ed., *The Digby Poems: A New Edition of the Lyrics*, Exeter Medieval Texts and Studies (Exeter: University of Exeter Press, 2009)). Poem 13, 'Dede Is Worchyng', appears to have been written in response to the same occasion as *Crowned King* – the November 1414 parliament. The poet warns the prince, 'þe puple is Goddis and noȝt ȝoures: / þey paye ȝoure rente to gouerne lawe' (51–52). The poet uses the same sentiment in other poems: see Poem 1, line 19; and Poem 3, line 131.

Krochalis suggests Chaucer's 'Lak of Stedfastnesse' as a possibility,[49] but the narrator's encouragement there to 'Dred God, do law, love trouthe and worthinesse' (l. 27) does not necessarily equate to the specific advice Hoccleve has just issued. Nor does it suggest 'othir mo' situations in which Chaucer has written with a timely and direct suggestion on behalf of the people. Instead, I wish to suggest, this stanza posits Chaucer as an authority at a conspicuously un-Chaucerian moment – un-Chaucerian insofar as Chaucer's poetry eschews direct reference to current political events, thereby maintaining a prudent distance from politically sensitive material. Rather than a historical Chaucer, Hoccleve indicates here the version of Chaucer that he has put forth within the text of his poem – the Chaucer who serves both as an authority figure, and as an enabling mechanism for the type of poetry that Hoccleve writes.

Hoccleve emphasizes the artifice in applying Chaucerian authority here by delaying the delivery of Chaucer's name. The poet is referred to first, obliquely, as 'The first fyndere of our fair langage' (4978), and then as 'my fadir'. The final line – 'My worthy maistir Chaucer – him I meene' – resolves the ambiguity, albeit in a particularly Chaucerian way. Consider, for instance, the scene in which Pandarus falls to his knees to pray in *Troilus* Book 3:

> Fil Pandarus on knees, and up his eyen
> To heven threw, and held his hondes highe:
> 'Immortal god,' quod he, 'that mayst nought deyen,
> *Cupide I mene*, of this mayst glorifie;
> And Venus, thow mayst maken melodie!'
>
> (III.183–87; italics mine)

Line 185 presents an ambiguity as to whether Pandarus refers here to the monotheistic Christian God or to a pagan god. The following line resolves this ambiguity with 'Cupide I mene', but the addition of 'I mene' denotes playfulness – a need for clarification after the fact. The following line then adds Venus to Pandarus's address, indicating an even wider gap between the initial, singular subject ('Immortal god'), and the plural gods that Pandarus assigns to clarify his initial subject. The sequence points up a distance between the pagan world that Pandarus inhabits, and the contemporary, Christian world that Chaucer's readers inhabit. Hoccleve's 'Chaucer – him I meene' has a similar effect. It resolves the initial ambiguity, while giving

[49] Jeanne Krochalis, 'Hoccleve's Chaucer Portrait', *Chaucer Review* 21 (1986): 234–45 (240); for 'Lak of Stedfastnesse', see Benson, *Riverside Chaucer*, 654.

the impression of a signifier being added on after the fact. It also admits a distance between this signifier and the claim being made for it: Chaucer has not spoken of the matter of councils and holy days 'in cas semblable, and othir mo', but he is nevertheless offered as the presiding authority. The world of Chaucer and the world of Hoccleve's Chaucer overlap here, much as the pagan past and the Christian present overlap in the *Troilus* passage. Hoccleve's unwillingness to name a specific work of Chaucer's – a practice that he follows throughout the *Regiment* – indicates that Hoccleve's Chaucer proceeds less from Chaucer's self-portrayals in his own works, and more from Hoccleve's own needs in the present poem. The Chaucer figure serves in this instance to divert Hoccleve from a potentially sensitive moment: 'Chaucer' changes the subject, much as – in the first section of the *Regiment* – the appearance of Chaucer enables Hoccleve to advance from the dialogue with the old man to the writing of the *Regiment* proper. Chaucer serves as an authority figure, but also as a 'mene' – as an intermediary through which Hoccleve ventures from one textual place to another.

Hoccleve indicates that he refers here to his morally recast version of Chaucer by immediately linking Chaucer to the Virgin Mary. Much as Hoccleve affirmed Chaucer's good standing in the eyes of the devout old man in the first section, here Hoccleve asks for the Virgin's intercession and approval:

> My worthy maistir Chaucer – him I meene;
> Be thow advocat for him, hevenes queene.
>
> As thow wel knowist, o blessid Virgyne,
> With lovyng herte and hy devocioun,
> In thyn honour he wroot ful many a lyne.
> O now thyn help and thy promocioun!
> To God thy sone make a mocioun,
> How he thy servant was, mayden Marie,
> And lat his love floure and fructifie.
>
> (4983–91)

The line in which Hoccleve names Chaucer forms the first half of a couplet, in which Chaucerian authority gives way to Marian authority. 'Him I meene' finds its rhyme in 'hevenes queene' – Hoccleve's literary 'mene' preceding Christ's 'mene', the official 'advocat' (or mediator) between Christ and man. Hoccleve reminds Mary here of Chaucer's service to her. Then, with the line 'To God thy sone make a mocioun', the page ends in the Harley manuscript, and our eyes move to the top of the facing page, where we read the stanzas accompanying the vivid illumination of Chaucer. The final lines of the stanza present their own ambiguity: 'To God thy sone make a mocioun, / How he thy servant was, mayden Marie, / And lat his love floure and fructifie.' The 'his' in the final line can refer either to Chaucer or to Christ, and this intermixture of Christian identity with Chaucerian identity deepens the sense of devotion that Hoccleve brings to the fore.

The fruitful language – 'lat his love floure and fructifie' – also recalls the status of that particularly unfruitful Thought, as we experienced him in the first section of the *Regiment*: the iteration of Thought that Hoccleve presents sowing his 'wastyng seed' (201) and bringing forth the 'fruyt of bittirnesse' (3).[50] After having presented his 'peynture' of Chaucer, Hoccleve seizes the opportunity to discuss the proper function of images in terms of 'thoght':

> The ymages that in the chirches been
> Maken folk thynke on God and on his seintes
> Whan the ymages they beholde and seen,
> Where ofte unsighte of hem causith restreyntes
> Of thoghtes goode. Whan a thyng depeynt is
> Or entaillid, if men take of it heede,
> Thoght of the liknesse it wole in hem breede.
>
> (4999–5005)

The beginning of this stanza discusses the process by which 'unsighte' of religious images restrains 'thoghtes goode'.[51] The last three lines refer to images more generally ('whan a thyng depeynt is / Or entaillid'), indicating the way in which Hoccleve's own image might 'breede' not only thoughts of the likeness of Chaucer in the viewer, but also 'thoghtes goode' – the likes of which can serve to counteract that negative iteration of Thought that we experienced earlier in the poem: the Thought that not only unsettled

[50] Perkins also remarks on this interplay between destructive and fruitful thought, albeit in a different context, in 'Haunted Hoccleve', 117.

[51] The Chaucer image and the accompanying presentation stanzas have attracted much attention from scholars. See, for instance, James H. McGregor, 'The Iconography of Chaucer in Hoccleve's *De Regimine Principum* and in the *Troilus* Frontispiece', *Chaucer Review* 11.4 (1977): 338–50; David R. Carlson, 'Thomas Hoccleve and the Chaucer Portrait', *Huntington Library Quarterly* 54 (1991): 283–300; Krochalis, 'Hoccleve's Chaucer Portrait'; Knapp, *Bureaucratic Muse*, 120–24; Perkins, *Hoccleve's Regiment*, 114–21, 155–59; James Simpson, 'Chaucer's Presence and Absence 1400–1550', in *A Chaucer Companion*, ed. Jill Mann and Piero Boitani, 2nd ed. (Cambridge: Cambridge University Press, 2003), 251–69; R.F. Yeager, 'Death Is a Lady: *The Regiment of Princes* as Gendered Political Commentary', *SAC* 26 (2004): 147–93; and Gayk, *Image, Text, and Religious Reform*, 48–54.

Hoccleve, but also made him appear suspicious to the old man. This image of Chaucer, after all, is a representation of the specific figure of Chaucer that Hoccleve has used throughout the *Regiment*. Taking 'heed' of this figure denotes, on one level, taking heed of Hoccleve's poetic example. Doing so enables the reader to convert hazardous or limiting thought into productive and useful thought. Hoccleve packages his poetic approach in the form of an image here – an image that can represent not only a historical Chaucer, but also an emblem of the ends to which Hoccleve uses Chaucer in the *Regiment*: as a moral authority, as an enabling mechanism, and as a means of distancing himself from politically sensitive situations.

It is instructive that Hoccleve completes his presentation of the Chaucer image by signaling back to that first section of the *Regiment*, where he portrayed himself as one of many scribes who spend each day in silence and stillness: 'al my lust is qweynt with hevynesse, / And hevy spirit commandith stilnesse', Hoccleve writes. 'And have I spoke of pees' – that is, after he has written the next and final section of the poem – 'I shal be stille' (5016–18). This comment directs the reader back to Hoccleve's description of himself among fellow 'wryters' who 'laboure in travaillous stilnesse' and 'keep moot [their] song and wordes yn' (1013–15). The juxtaposition points up the distance Hoccleve has traveled over the course of the poem – from his status as a nameless 'wryter' to a named Hoccleve who advances English *poesie* with this more authoritative version of Chaucer, and who advises the prince on matters of contemporary ecclesiastical and political importance.

'Fructuous Intelligence': London Readers and Prudence

Hoccleve's movement from one among a group of unnamed scribes to a named and authoritative 'Hoccleve' mirrors Chaucer's own movement within the *Regiment* towards a position of singularity and moral authority. Whereas we can track Hoccleve's movement through his trajectory from anonymity to namedness, and from his identity as a scribe to his actions as an individual capable of 'endytyng', Chaucer's new position manifests first in Hoccleve's paeans for his master (at the end of the first section of the poem), and then in Hoccleve's presentation of Chaucer as an image (towards the end of the *Regiment* proper). The movement between the Chaucer that predates Hoccleve's *Regiment* and the Chaucer who emerges in the *Regiment* can also be traced visually through the images preserved in the Ellesmere manuscript of the *Canterbury Tales* (San Marino, Huntington Library, MS EL 26 C 9), and the British Library, MS Harley 4866 copy of the *Regiment* (Figures 2 and 3). We will turn to examine these images briefly as a means of considering in greater detail Hoccleve's 'prudent' positioning of his master.

The Ellesmere manuscript dates to the earliest years of the fifteenth century, and would have been complete by 1405.[52] MS Harley 4866, by contrast, has been dated to 1411–12.[53] The similarities between these two images have been noted.[54] For our purposes, we might focus specifically on the way in which Hoccleve's Chaucer appears here in a more conspicuously devout form. In both images, Chaucer wears a black cloak and points towards the text of the poem in question. In Hoccleve's image, however, Chaucer's horse reins have given way to a rosary. This rosary stands out in the foreground and chimes with the text of the poem itself, which – as we have seen – introduces the image of Chaucer by way of an invocation to the Virgin. The frame around Chaucer adds to the sense of *gravitas* that the image conveys – particularly when we compare it with the Ellesmere image. In Ellesmere, Chaucer's disproportionately short legs offer a comic effect. And here, too, the corresponding text enhances our reading of the image: Chaucer points to the 'Tale of Melibee', but in arriving at the beginning of this tale he arrives at the juncture between the tale that has just ended abruptly – the 'Tale of Sir Thopas', Chaucer's first attempt at a contribution – and the 'Tale of Melibee'. The mixture of comedy and seriousness – of 'game' and 'ernest' – effected by the juxtaposition of these tales finds its counterpart in the image – in the mixture of Chaucer's sober black robe and his plump body and foreshortened legs. In MS Harley 4866, the sober Chaucer has been singled out by the frame and made more conspicuously Christian by the prominently displayed rosary.

Looking at these images in isolation also obscures one of the more significant ways in which Harley's presentation differs from Ellesmere's: whereas the Ellesmere image of Chaucer appears in a series of images, in which Chaucer is but one of many pilgrims illustrated, the Harley image appears as one of very few images in the manuscript. (Harley is missing a leaf where, we assume, the manuscript once had a presentation portrait similar to the one found in the copy of the *Regiment* in MS Arundel 38. The only other image in the manuscript is the comical image of a man lassoing a stray stanza into the body of the poem.) This aspect of Harley's presentation

---

52 On the dating of Hengwrt and Ellesmere, see Scott, 'Hours and Psalter', 106.

53 Burrow, *Thomas Hoccleve*, 50.

54 For recent appraisals of the relationship see, in particular, Kathleen Scott, *Later Gothic Manuscripts, 1390–1490*, 2 vols (London: H. Miller, 1996), II: 160–61; and Derek Pearsall, *The Life of Geoffrey Chaucer: A Critical Biography* (Oxford: Blackwell, 1992), 285–89.

Figure 2. Chaucer figure in San Marino, Huntington Library EL 26 C 9 ('Ellesmere'), f. 153v.

Figure 3. Chaucer figure in London, British Library, MS Harley 4866, f. 88r.

also reflects the textual aims of Harley: rather than depict Chaucer as one among many – an individual who passes so unknown among his fellow travelers as to provoke the host's 'What man artow?'[55] – in the *Regiment* Chaucer has transformed into a figure of singular authority. In Ellesmere, the pilgrim portraits contribute to what Kathleen Scott calls an 'a-hierarchical design' – a design reflected both in the scribes' refusal to distinguish decoratively between prologues and tales, and the reluctance to 'indicate through illustration any relative importance among the narrators'.[56] Each decorative element in Ellesmere is made equal – each 'washed down to a standard (if handsome) size, shape, and position'.[57] Such a presentation suggests an equal standing among Chaucer's narrators. In Harley, Chaucer's singularity is evoked by his ability to stand alone. His appearance in the text is exceptional and unexpected: whereas in Ellesmere we encounter the Chaucer pilgrim much as we have encountered the other pilgrims – as an illustrative companion to the coinciding tale – in Harley Chaucer is set apart, and this placement reinforces the version of Chaucer put forth within the poem itself.

In the *Regiment*, Hoccleve presents his image of Chaucer as an image that he causes to be made ('I have heere his liknesse / Do make …' (4995–96)). We cannot know for certain whether Hoccleve encountered this image of Chaucer originally in Ellesmere, or whether he worked from an exemplar from which the Ellesmere and Harley versions derived, but in considering Hoccleve's relationship to books such as Ellesmere, it is important to note Hoccleve's position as a scribe who worked in the London circles within which Chaucer's works were being actively copied. Hoccleve's contribution to the Cambridge, Trinity College, MS R.3.2 copy of Gower's *Confessio amantis* would have put him in the company of Scribe D, who copied two manuscripts of the *Canterbury Tales* in addition to the Ilchester manuscript of the *Piers Plowman* C-text;[58] and also of Doyle and Parkes's Scribe B ('Adam Pinkhurst'), the main scribe for the Ellesmere and Hengwrt copies of the *Canterbury Tales* (San Marino, Huntington Library, MS EL 26 C; and Aberyswyth, National Library of Wales, MS Peniarth 392D, respectively).[59] The copying of MS R.3.2 would have been undertaken

55 The question occurs at VII.695 in the *Canterbury Tales.*

56 Scott, 'Hours and Psalter', 89–90.

57 Ibid., 90.

58 The manuscripts of the *Canterbury Tales* written by Scribe D – London, British Library, MS Harley 7334; and Oxford, Corpus Christi College, MS 198 – were identified by Doyle and Parkes in 'Production of Copies', 202, 212–20.

59 Doyle and Parkes, 'Production of Copies'. The identity of Scribe B as Adam

just prior to the writing of the *Regiment* – c. 1408. Doyle and Parkes suggest, furthermore, that Hoccleve served as one of the supplementary scribes on Hengwrt, and Derek Pearsall has suggested that Hoccleve would have been well positioned to serve as an editor for both Hengwrt and Ellesmere.[60] The Harley manuscript of the *Regiment* also has textual ties to Ellesmere: it is very similar in format not only to the British Library, MS Arundel 38 copy of the *Regiment*, but also, indeed, to Ellesmere itself.[61] This suggests affiliation with that early illuminated manuscript of the *Canterbury Tales* on both a professional level and a textual level.

It is important to remember that Hoccleve's position in Westminster administrative circles would have put him in the proximity not only of Langland's first readers, after all, but also of Chaucer's first readers. Richard Sotheworth, a Chancery clerk, owned a copy of the *Canterbury Tales*, which he bequeathed to his fellow clerk, John Stopyndon, in 1419.[62] The Privy Seal clerk Thomas Kent, who would rise to the position of Secondary of the Privy Seal in 1444, also owned a copy of the *Canterbury Tales*.[63] Henry Somer, who is the dedicatee of two of Hoccleve's poems, rose to the position

Pinkhurst was advanced by Linne R. Mooney in 'Chaucer's Scribe', *Speculum* 81 (2006): 97–138 and is discussed in Mooney and Stubbs, *Scribes and the City*, Chapter 4. Jane Roberts offers a dissenting view in 'On giving Scribe B a name and a clutch of London manuscripts from *c.*1400', *MÆ* 80 (2011): 247–70. Roberts notes that the 'Adam Pynkhurst canon has elaborated quickly and perhaps ill-advisedly', and concludes that, 'Convincing evidence that Adam Pynkhurst was scribe B remains uncertain' (263). I refer to 'Scribe B' and 'Scribe D' throughout to indicate that the process of identification is still evolving and has not reached a point of scholarly consensus.

60 A.I. Doyle and M.B. Parkes, 'Paleographical Introduction', in *The Canterbury Tales: A Facsimile and Transcription of the Hengwrt Manuscript, with Variants from the Ellesmere Manuscript*, ed. Paul Ruggiers (Norman, OK: University of Oklahoma Press, 1979), xlvi; see also Simon Horobin, 'Adam Pinkhurst and the Copying of British Library, MS Additional 35287 of the B Version of *Piers Plowman*', *YLS* 23 (2009): 61–83 (82–83). Mooney and Stubbs also discuss this possibility in *Scribes and the City*, 125–26. On Hoccleve as a possible editor of Ellesmere and Hengwrt, see Pearsall, *Life of Geoffrey Chaucer*, 338 n. 9. Simon Horobin offers new evidence for the suggestion that Hoccleve served as the editor of Hengwrt and Ellesmere in a recent article. See Simon Horobin, 'Thomas Hoccleve: Chaucer's First Editor?' *The Chaucer Review* 50.3–4 (2015): 228–50.

61 Burrow, *Thomas Hoccleve*, 18.

62 Malcolm Richardson, 'The Earliest Known Owners of *Canterbury Tales* MSS and Chaucer's Secondary Audience', *Chaucer Review* 25 (1990): 17–32.

63 Perkins, *Hoccleve's Regiment*, 160–61. See also John M. Manly and Edith Rickert, *The Text of the 'Canterbury Tales'*, 8 vols (Chicago, IL: University of Chicago Press, 1940), I, 166–69.

of Chancellor of the Exchequer, and was himself acquainted with both Geoffrey Chaucer and his son Thomas.[64] Hoccleve's peers in the Privy Seal also had wider interests in, and connections to, late medieval vernacular poetry: one individual who worked with Hoccleve in the Privy Seal from c. 1388 to 1400 appears to be the William Denne who served as executor of John Gower's will;[65] and Guy de Rouclif, under whom Hoccleve trained in the Privy Seal, knew John Gower and later bequeathed Hoccleve 'uno libro vocato Bello Troie' [a book called the War of Troy].[66] As mentioned in the last chapter, Nicholas Bubwith, who served as Keeper of the Privy Seal from 1405–6, was later responsible for commissioning a Latin translation of Dante's *Commedia* at the Council of Constance, during his tenure as the bishop of Bath and Wells.[67] Such facts help to position Hoccleve within a professional context comprised in part of highly literate clerks with interests in contemporary vernacular poetry, and with personal connections to the authors who created such poetry. Such individuals indicate the type of reader who would have appreciated Hoccleve's positioning of Chaucer in the *Regiment*.[68]

The poems collected in San Marino, Huntington Library MSS HM 111 and 744, Hoccleve's autograph verse manuscripts, give us a broader view of both Hoccleve's audience among the nobility, and his affiliation with individuals who worked in an administrative capacity under the nobility and the crown.[69] Some pieces shed light on the more prudent poetics that Hoccleve associates with Chaucer in the *Regiment*, while also indicating a stratified approach to reading – with the nobility receiving the poem officially, and other administrators reading the poem more closely and

64 Nuttall, *Lancastrian Kingship*, 123.

65 Perkins, *Hoccleve's Regiment*, 160. See also Malcolm Parkes, 'Patterns of Scribal Activity and Revisions of the Text in Early Copies of Works by John Gower', in *New Science Out of Old Books: Studies in Manuscripts and Early Printed Books in Honour of A.I. Doyle*, ed. Richard Beadle and A.J. Piper (Aldershot: Scolar Press, 1995), 81–121 (97); John H. Fisher, *John Gower: Moral Philosopher and Friend of Chaucer* (London: Methuen, 1965), 67; and Watt, *Making*, 52.

66 Burrow, *Thomas Hoccleve*, 9; Nuttall, *Lancastrian Kingship*, 121.

67 Watt also notes Hoccleve's proximity to Denne, Rouclif, and Bubwith in *Making*, 52.

68 For a recent discussion of Hoccleve's peers and readers, see Watt, *Making*, Chapter 1. See also Nuttall, *Lancastrian Kingship*, 120–23 for a discussion of textual transmission and readership among administrative circles in early fifteenth-century London and Westminster.

69 The autograph verse manuscripts are printed in facsimile edition in Burrow and Doyle, *Facsimile*. John Bowers examines the manuscripts in detail in 'Hoccleve's Huntington Holographs'.

prudently. One such piece is a dedicatory verse in which Hoccleve presents his *Regiment of Princes* to John, duke of Bedford (HM 111, fol. 37v).[70] The poem begins by addressing Bedford directly, but with the second stanza Hoccleve's attention shifts to another subject – a figure called 'Massy', who Hoccleve anticipates will read the poem. Turville-Petre and Wilson have identified this individual as William Massy, who served as Receiver-General and General Attorney to Bedford.[71] David Watt notes that, as part of this position, Massy 'almost certainly had business with at least one of the courts in Westminster Hall', and that he would have 'lodged at the Inns of Court when in London during the law term'.[72] Such an arrangement would indicate one means through which Hoccleve knew Massy: Hoccleve depicts himself at the beginning of the *Regiment* in Chester's Inn, one of the inns in which Westminster lawyers, clerks, and scribes lived and worked.[73]

The verses in which Hoccleve refers to Massy prove significant for our purposes, however, for the way in which they invite Massy's help in improving the manuscript, and for the way in which Massy is praised in language that echoes Hoccleve's praise for Chaucer in the *Regiment*:

> I dreede lest þat my maistir Massy
> þ*a*t is of fructuous intelligence,
> Whan he beholdith how vnconnyngly
> My book is metrid / how raw my sentence
> How feeble eek been my colours; his prudence
> Shal sore encombrid been of my folie;
> But yit truste I / þat his beneuolence
> Compleyne wole myn insipience
> Secreetly / and what is mis / rectifie
>
> (ll. 10–18)

---

70 This poem is collected in *Hoccleve's Works*, pp. 56–57. I quote from that edition here.

71 Thorlac Turville-Petre and Edward Wilson, 'Hoccleve, "Maistir Massy" and the Pearl Poet: Two Notes', *RES* 26 (1975): 129–43 (130). Massy was previously thought to be the Pearl-poet: see Ormerod Greenwood, *Sir Gawain and the Green Knight* (London: Lion and Unicorn Press, 1956), 6–12; Barbara Nolan and David Farley-Hills, 'The Authorship of *Pearl*: Two Notes', *RES* 22 (1971): 295–302. David Watt reviews the evidence for Massy's identity in *Making*, 46–48. For further discussion, see Malcolm Andrew and Ronald Waldron, eds., *The Poems of the Pearl Manuscript: Pearl, Cleanness, Patience, Sir Gawain and the Green Knight*, Exeter Medieval Texts and Studies (Exeter: University of Exeter Press, 2011), 5–12 (especially 8–9).

72 Watt, *Making*, 47.

73 See *Regiment* line 5; Blyth, *Regiment*, 201.

The phrase 'fructuous intelligence' echoes the phrase that Hoccleve uses to present Chaucer in the *Regiment*: in his first paean to Chaucer, Hoccleve calls Chaucer 'Mirour of fructuous entendement' (l. 1963). By replacing the word 'entendement' with 'intelligence', Hoccleve retains the same syllable count while shifting praise from his 'maistir' Chaucer to 'maistir Massy'. (The word 'fructuous' is used on only one other occasion in the *Regiment*: in the stanzas leading up to the presentation of the Chaucer portrait, in which the advice of older men is described as 'fructuous' (4946).) Chaucer is referred to as 'my maistir' repeatedly throughout the *Regiment* – indeed, the word refers to him far more than it refers to any other subject in the poem – and he is linked, as with Massy, explicitly to the virtue of prudence. Hoccleve will go on to connect prudence to 'entendement' in the *Regiment* proper, in the section 'De Regis Prudentia' – where Hoccleve notes, 'Prudence is vertu of entendement' (4761) – much as Massy's own prudence pairs with his 'intelligence' in this short poem.

Massy's prudence is manifested not only in his ability to serve as a close reader of Hoccleve's text, but also in his ability to practice discretion in addressing Hoccleve's faults. Hoccleve requests that Massy 'compleyne' his 'insipience / Secreetly', and he invites him to 'rectifie' 'what is mis'. The focus on secrecy in the process of textual correction stands out here, particularly given the politically freighted subject matter of the *Regiment*. It has a parallel in the language of the anonymous *Richard the Redeless*, which presents itself as a 'secrette' poem and invites its readers, similarly, to correct it: the narrator discusses his intentions in writing a 'tretis to teche men … / To be war of wylffulnesse' and invites the given reader – should this book 'happe to youre honde' – to engage in emendation:

And if ye fynde fables or foly ther amonge,
Or ony fantasie yffeyned that no frute is in,
Lete youre conceill corette it and clerkis to-gedyr,
And amende that ys amysse and make it more better:
For yit it is secrette and so it shall lenger,
Tyll wyser wittis han waytid it ouere,
That it be lore laweffull and lusty to here.

(ll. 57–63)[74]

As with Hoccleve's narrator, this narrator admits the possibility of his own misgivings and looks to other, wiser readers for assistance. In both poems,

74 I use Helen Barr's edition of this poem in *Piers Plowman Tradition*, 101–33.

the process of emendation is posited as secret – in Massy's case, as a task to be undertaken 'secreetly'.

Of course, Hoccleve's request that Massy correct him 'secreetly' occurs in a poem addressed directly to Bedford. It does not imagine circulation among an anonymous group, but rather expects to be delivered into the hands of Bedford and then possibly into the hands of Massy. This raises the question of what would be involved in Massy 'rectifying' 'what is mis': would this involve Massy literally correcting the manuscript that Hoccleve delivers to Bedford, and thereby serving as a custodian for the manuscript while it is in Bedford's keeping? Or is it, rather, a case of maintaining Hoccleve's own reputation in the household? In the final stanza of the poem, Hoccleve turns to address his poem directly and, in doing so, he personifies the poem, much as he does in his *envoi* for Prince Henry: 'Thow book … / I charge thee, go shewe thow thy face / Before my seid maistre' (ll. 19, 21–22). As Hoccleve refers to Massy as 'my maistir Massy', the 'seid maistre' that Hoccleve posits here would appear to be Massy himself. Hoccleve tells his poem, 'to him [my seid maistre] preye / On my behalue / þ*a*t he peise and weye / What myn entente is…' (ll. 22–24). The book acts on Hoccleve's behalf here – it shows its face on his behalf – and Massy is left to 'peise and weye' Hoccleve's 'entente'. Here, as in *Richard the Redeless*, the narrator recognizes the potential for the poem to speak 'amiss', and he invites the reader to take an active role in correcting – or 'rectifying' – the poem. For Hoccleve, however, this involves specifying both a recipient – Bedford – and a separate reader who will 'peise and weye' the text, and will 'rectifie' it when it goes amiss. It suggests one reader who will receive the poem officially, and another reader who will take an active interest in its contents.

This dynamic surfaces in another poem found in HM 111, a dedication to a book given to Prince Edward, duke of York (MS HM 111, fol. 32v).[75] Here, too, Hoccleve posits both an official recipient – Prince Edward – and a reader who will serve to 'amende' Hoccleve's text. This reader, Picard, is thought to have been a clerk of the chapel 'who had [been given] power of attorney from the Duke of York in 1394'.[76] In Hoccleve's poem, the poet highlights his own potential to 'speke vnfittyngly' and invites Picard 'to amende and to correcte' his text – particularly those aspects which 'nat to the ordre of endytyng obeye' (ll. 48, 53, 50). The phrase 'ordre of endytyng' brings to mind Hoccleve's discussion of the 'orders' of wedlock and

75 This poem is included in *Hoccleve's Works*, pp. 49–51. I quote from that edition here.

76 Clifford Peterson and Edward Wilson, 'Hoccleve, the Old Hall Manuscript, Cotton Nero A.x., and the Pearl-poet', *RES* 28 (1977): 49–56 (52). See also Watt, *Making*, 50–51; Knapp, *Bureaucratic Muse*, 154.

priesthood in the first section of the *Regiment*, and, indeed, the mythical 'order of love' that Chaucer presents in *Troilus*, which we discussed at the beginning of the last chapter. Hoccleve's suggestion that his poems should 'obeye' the 'ordre of endytyng' offers a playful religious context for the practice of reading and writing poetry: it posits a community wherein clerks work to 'reform' each other's texts – or, as in Massy's case, to 'rectifie' them – and where the community follows a certain rule, in the monastic sense, to which each member must adhere.

Such language also indicates, however, how Hoccleve's approach to political advice-giving and 'endytyng' departs from the approach of the author of *Richard the Redeless*: Hoccleve employs the language of 'secret' or prudent correction, but he does so in the context of poetry that imagines its circulation not among a closed network of readers, but rather among a wider public. In the *Regiment*, similarly, he learns to present himself not as an anonymous commentator, but as a named 'Hoccleve' who clarifies where he works, what he believes in, with whom he is associated, and where he can be found. Rather than circulate poems 'secreetly', among a closed group of readers, he learns to create poetry that intends to be disseminated widely, but that also acknowledges that it can experienced differently by different types of reader. As these presentation poems imply, the 'prudence' of Hoccleve's poetics rests in the reader as much as in the poet: 'endytyng' emerges as a communal and reciprocal activity, whereby the 'fructuous intelligence' of a given reader is defined, in part, by that reader's ability to practice prudence and good judgment when responding to the poem.

'Go My Will': Hoccleve's Seal

We might conclude by considering one more Hocclevian image. The image in question is Hoccleve's personal seal, recently unearthed by Linne Mooney in the National Archives. The seal was found attached to a Privy Seal document dated November 27, 1402, about eight years prior to the *Regiment*, and it is 'written, signed, and sealed by Hoccleve' himself.[77] In the seal, a scribal hand points to a cross, and this hand is circumscribed by what we assume to be Hoccleve's motto: 'VA MA VOLUNTEE'.[78] Ethan Knapp and Richard Firth Green, who translate the motto as 'Go, my will [to God or heaven]', note Hoccleve's 'emphasis [in his poetry] on the need

[77] Mooney, 'Some New Light', 315–16.

[78] Mooney transcribes the motto as 'va illa voluntee' in 'Some New Light', 317. R.F. Green and Ethan Knapp offer the 'va ma voluntee' reading as a correction in 'Thomas Hoccleve's Seal', *MÆ* 77 (2008): 319–21 (319).

Figure 4. Thomas Hoccleve's Seal, attached to Kew, National Archives E 43/554.

to properly orient will ("voluntee") towards some permanent virtue beyond the fickle snares of the world'.[79] This is certainly an emphasis that we can track throughout Hoccleve's poetry. There is an extent, too, to which this motto could serve as a defensive mechanism in itself – a means by which the morally driven poet might claim to focus his efforts on according with God's will, rather than any particular human or political will. The narrator's initial anxiety in the *Regiment* derives in part from the political instability brought on by the 'estat rial' being thrown into 'mescheef' (23–24), and from the fact that 'many another lord … hadde a fal' as a result (25). Directing one's will towards God suggests one means of navigating the mutability of political life in the early fifteenth century.

The image of Chaucer that Hoccleve presents in the Harley manuscript provides an intriguing counterpoint to the image on Hoccleve's seal. Both images feature a maniculum: in the case of the seal, the maniculum gestures towards the cross; in the Chaucer image, the maniculum is, of course, connected to the body of Chaucer, and it gestures towards the text of the poem. The cross (the symbol of the church) gives Hoccleve's seal a devotional emphasis and, in the Harley manuscript, Chaucer's stance gives the impression of the poet presiding over the text. But the Chaucer image is also authorized by the text of the poem: Chaucer may preside over an

[79] Green and Knapp, 'Thomas Hoccleve's Seal', 320.

'ordre of endytyng' (to use Hoccleve's phrase), but it is the presence and nature of the 'endytyng' here that brings the image into being and, indeed, that positions Chaucer as a figure capable of presiding over the making of a 'holsum' vernacular work of poetry.

Hoccleve's seal also reminds us of the more conspicuously religious aspects of Hoccleve's own self-presentation in the *Regiment*, and throughout his works. In the *Regiment*, Hoccleve's discussion of the process by which he decided not to pursue the priesthood comes across as relatively lighthearted: 'I gazid longe first and waytid faste / Aftir sum benefice, and whan noon cam, / By procees I me weddid atte laste' (1451–53). The language reflects back on those unworthy priests that the old man has just described – 'Ful many men knowe I that gane and gape / Aftir sum fat and ryche benefice' (1408–09). These priests crave the benefice rather than the duty of priesthood, going so far as to secure a plurality of benefices and then ignoring their respective flocks (1415–28). In presenting himself as 'gazing' 'Aftir sum benefice', Hoccleve seems to align himself – if only in jest – with that group of priests who want the financial benefits more than the actual role of spiritual mediator. Hoccleve's decision to marry, similarly, arrives as if in afterthought – a consolation for never having received the benefice after which he had 'gazid longe ... and waytid faste' – rather than as a gift from God, as the old man later suggests ('God woot and knowith every hid entente; / He for thy beste a wyf unto thee sente' (1469–70)). That Hoccleve's self-presentation proves more playful than sincere is suggested by the poet's role as a devout intermediary elsewhere in the poem: for instance, when Hoccleve speaks out to protect the sanctity of holy days (4964–77), when he refers to the prophesies of St Bridget of Sweden to remind England and France of the Christian obligation to strive for peace (5384–5439), and when he meditates on the life and sacrifice of Christ (e.g., 5160–80).

A focus on enabling devotional experience for others also recurs throughout Hoccleve's poetry. In the *Series*, Hoccleve's inspiration for translating a chapter from Henry Suso's *Horologium sapientiae* comes not from Chaucer, but from an unnamed 'devout man'.[80] As we move from the public, outdoor space of the *Regiment* to the more interior, private space of the *Series*, the Thomas narrator announces an interest in publishing both his 'Complaint' and his Suso treatise as spurs to penance and contemplation.[81]

---

80 See 2.232–36: 'Not hath me stirid my deuocioun / To do this labour, ȝe shullen vnderstonde, / But at the excitinge and mocioun / Of a deuoute man, take I here on honde / This labour ...'.

81 See 2.57–98, 2.211–31.

Hoccleve's 'collected poems' in Huntington Library, MSS HM 111 and 744 contain numerous poems of Marian devotion, prayers to God, Christ, and the Holy Spirit, and a second copy of Hoccleve's Suso translation.[82] In the *Regiment*, as in the *Series*, Hoccleve also betrays an interest in bringing the specific details of his own life into dialogue with ecclesiastical doctrine. The conversation between Hoccleve and the old man in the *Regiment* has a parallel not only in the exchange between Will and Holy Church in Passus I of *Piers*, but also in the dialogue between 'Haukyn the actif man' and Patience in Passus 14 of the *Piers* B-text.[83] There, Haukyn presents the details of his life – from his soiled cloak to his 'houswif' and children – and grapples with the advice of his interlocutor on matters of penitence, contrition, and virtuous poverty. At one point, Patience offers Haukyn 'liflode' in the form of 'a pece of the *Paternoster – Fiat voluntas tua*' (B.14.49), and invites him to sate his hunger with this. Hoccleve's old man proves less uncompromising than Patience, yet nevertheless intent on encouraging Hoccleve to appreciate a life of virtuous poverty; and, in response, Hoccleve complains that he is 'nat so parfyt / To take it so' (1219–20). As with Haukyn, Hoccleve's dialogue becomes, on one level, a meditation on whether the active life can nevertheless bear spiritual fruit. In both cases, the protagonist's status as a married man bespeaks the active role that he plays in the world.[84]

---

[82] The contents of the autograph verse manuscripts are listed in Burrow and Doyle, *Facsimile*, xii–xx: see specifically MS HM 111 items 1, 7, 10, 19; and MS HM 744 items 1–6(b), 11.

[83] Cf. Patterson, 'What Is Me', 469: Patterson likens Hoccleve's narrator from *Male Regle* to Haukyn. Patterson's comparison there focuses not on the active life in a religious context, however, but rather what Patterson sees as the Hoccleve narrator's defining stance – 'a man filled with self-doubt and a sense of isolation who compensated by a brittle tavern gaiety'.

[84] Hoccleve also highlights his role as a married man in the *Series*: see 2.739–42. Walter Hilton's prose devotional treatise, *The Mixed Life* (c.1384–96) provides an intriguing point of comparison to Hoccleve and Haukyn's respective situations. Hilton advises his reader not to leave behind one's active life, but rather to 'meedele' active and contemplative lives by attending to each in turn: 'Thou schalt not uttirli folwen thi desire for to leuen occupacioun and bisynesse of the world, whiche aren nedefull to usen in rulynge of thi silf and of alle othere that aren undir thi kepynge, and ȝeue thee hooli to goostli occupaciouns of praiers and meditaciouns, as it were a frere or monk or an othir man that were not bounden to the world bi children and seruauntes as thou art, for it falleth not to thee, and ȝif thou do soo, thou kepest not the ordre of charite' (ll. 89–96). See Walter Hilton, *The Mixed Life*, ed. S.J. Ogilvie-Thomson (Salzburg: Institut für Anglistik und Amerikanstik, Universität Salzburg, 1986). Haukyn's interlocutor proves far more uncompromising in *Piers*; and Hoccleve's proves decidedly less helpful. Yet,

In some respects, Hoccleve's old man manifests the more devotional side of Hoccleve's self-presentation, which appears in more conspicuous forms in the *Series* and in the religious verse in the collected poems manuscripts. Whereas Will converses with different faculties such as Wit and Thought, and different abstract concepts such as Patience and Conscience, Hoccleve converses with the old man, who serves at once as a person with discernable physical features and as a vehicle for Christian doctrine and occasional ecclesiastical critique. It is through the old man that we hear the same critique of inattentive priests that Clergy offers in Passus 10 of the *Piers* B-text: where Clergy refers to 'religiouse that han no routhe though it reyne on hir auters' (B.10.312; cf. C.5.164), the old man opines on priests for whom, 'Thogh that his chauncel roof be al totorn / And on the hy auter it reyne or sneewe, / He rekkith nat' (1422–24).[85] Hoccleve-the-character proves reticent when pronouncing his own opinions on ecclesiastical issues – he indicates a preference for being seen as neither inclined to, nor capable of, meditating on '[God's] hy knowleche and His mighty werkis' (see ll. 375–79); and he issues but one statement of faith: that he believes 'in the sacrament / Of the auter' and 'alle othir articles of the feith … / as fer as that Holy Writ seith' (380–85). Where the old man lectures, Hoccleve practices prudent self-deprecation and silence. The irony in this approach is apparent: Hoccleve shapes the old man's discourse as well as his own, and, in doing so, he presents himself as simultaneously learned and simple; he indicates the performance of prudent piety as well as the motivations for appearing prudent; he foregrounds the role of heresy in engendering his self-presentation, and he pronounces a willingness to appear childish, and to reform and rectify his own faults; he reveals how close he came to becoming a priest, while also claiming ignorance and distancing himself from a priest-like self-presentation.

When considering Hoccleve's discussion of having wanted to become a priest, and when exploring the devotional use of Hoccleve's poetry, we must also remember the nature of Hoccleve's peer group, and specifically the movement between positions in the Privy Seal and ecclesiastical office. As we have seen, Nicholas Bubwith advanced from Keeper of the Privy Seal to bishop of Bath and Wells. Thomas Langley, who had served as Keeper of the Privy Seal prior to Bubwith, went on to serve as bishop of Durham.[86]

---

nevertheless, the *Regiment* and *Piers* indicate the way in which Hoccleve and Haukyn both follow mixed lives of their own sorts.

85 Kerby-Fulton, 'Bibliographic Ego', 83–84.

86 Burrow and Doyle, *Facsimile*, xiv. Burrow and Doyle note that item 12 in MS HM 111 (fol. 38r–v) is 'probably addressed to Thomas Langley, Chancellor and Bishop of

Furthermore, the 'Prentys and Arondel' that Hoccleve refers to in the context of drinking and socializing in 'La Male Regle' served as clerks of the King's Chapel, with Prentys later becoming dean of St Stephen's, Westminster, in 1418, and Arundel advancing to dean of St George's, Windsor, in 1419.[87] Hoccleve's immediate social and professional context, then, included not only anonymous 'devout men', but also specifiable peers who followed careers as professional religious – in some cases after having worked alongside Hoccleve in the Office of the Privy Seal. The bifurcation between 'Hoccleve' and the 'old man' in the *Regiment* becomes in some ways a meditation on Hoccleve's own limits as someone who falls short of the 'order of priesthood' and who exists, rather, in the active life – in the 'order of wedlock'. The devout version of Chaucer that Hoccleve introduces in the *Regiment* suggests a solution of sorts – an indication of what Hoccleve can achieve outside the 'order of priesthood' and in the 'ordre of endytyng'. If such an approach admits to limitations in Hoccleve's self-presentation, it also suggests the formal strategies that Hoccleve can use, nevertheless, to comment on matters of ecclesiastical importance. It offers new manifestations of Hoccleve's wit, as well as new applications of his will.

Durham, 1406–7'; see also Burrow, *Thomas Hoccleve*, 15. Hoccleve refers to Langley in the poem in question as 'fadir in God', and puts himself forward as 'your clerc' (ll. 1, 18).

87 A.B. Wathey, 'Music in the Royal and Noble Households in Late Medieval England: Studies of Sources and Patronage' (Ph.D. diss., University of Oxford, 1987), 152, 166–67. See also Nuttall, *Lancastrian Kingship*, 68–69; Watt, *Making*, 28–29.

Chapter Five

Hoccleve's Eucharist

In this chapter, we will deepen our focus on the role that ecclesiastical discourse plays in Hoccleve's poetry, by focusing specifically on the role of the Eucharist in Hoccleve's works. In doing so, we will approach a clearer definition of how the old man and the Friend operate in Hoccleve's poetry, and will expand on Hoccleve's status as a religious poet – that is, as a vernacular writer with evident interests in the role and function of priesthood, the spiritual health of the institutional church, the treatment of laypeople within the church, and the ability of poetry to act as a conduit for prayer, penance, and devotional reflection. We will also further explore the communal role that the figure of Chaucer plays in Hoccleve's *Regiment*, and its implications for Hoccleve's own role as a spiritual and literary intermediary.

In the last chapter, I suggested a parallel between the old man's role in the *Regiment* and the role of Holy Church in Passus I of *Piers Plowman*. Hoccleve's old man proves unhelpful, however, not just because he expounds on lofty theological concepts of which the narrator has no natural understanding (or 'kynde knowyng' (C.I.137)), as in Will's case, but rather because he approaches the layperson as suspicious and potentially dangerous. Will's Holy Church expresses theological truths that, while lofty, are nonetheless potentially helpful; Hoccleve's old man does not even arrive at this point. He refers to Hoccleve as 'my chyld' (e.g., 441), and warns him that not following his advice would be an indication of Hoccleve's 'childissh misreuled conceit' (195). Such language – as well as the father/son terminology that Hoccleve and the old man use for each other throughout the first section – might seem to align the *Regiment* with prose spiritual guides such as *Book to a Mother*, where, in learning the 'text' of Christ, the reader becomes like a child learning the ABC, with a view to becoming literate through spiritual ascent.[1] Other late fourteenth-century

[1] Cf. *'Book to a Mother': An Edition with Commentary*, ed. Adrian James McCarthy (Salzburg: Institut fur Anglistik und Amerikanistik, 1981), 23.15–24.3.

spiritual guides, such as *Life of Soul* and Walter Hilton's *Mixed Life*, use similar language to emphasize collaborative engagement: they focus on a 'shared search for knowledge' that can potentially 'realize shared forms of intellectual authority'.[2] Hoccleve's old man, however, seems less interested in positioning Hoccleve as a fellow traveler, and more interested in verifying his orthodox credentials and reinforcing the hierarchy of the church.

The old man's identity in the *Regiment* is constituted in large part by this approach, and by his identification with the church. Rather than answering Hoccleve's initial question – 'who is there?' (134) – by offering his name or his specific office, the old man presents himself in the *Regiment* by way of a discussion of the dangers of heresy, John Badby's rejection of the Eucharist, Badby's subsequent execution, and the 'souffissant' and hierarchical nature of the institutional Church.[3] This opening salvo serves to position the old man clearly as an opponent of heresy and as a proponent of orthodox Christianity:

Presumpcion, a benedicitee!
Why vexest thow folk with thy franesie,
Thogh nothyng elles were, I seye for me?
But see how that the worthy prelacie,
And undir hem the souffissant clergie,
Endowid of profounde intelligence,
Of al this land werreyen thy sentence.

That selve same to me were a brydil
By which wolde I governed been and gyed,
And elles al my labour were in ydil.
By Holy Chirche I wole be justified;
To that al hoolly is myn herte applied,
And evere shal.

(358–70)

2 Nicole R. Rice, *Lay Piety and Religious Discipline in Middle English Literature*, Cambridge Studies in Medieval Literature 73 (Cambridge: Cambridge University Press, 2008), 53. Rice presents a good overview of these texts. See Hilton, *Mixed Life*; and *Þe Life of Soule: An Edition with Commentary*, ed. Helen M. Moon (Salzburg: Institut für Englische Sprache und Literatur, Universität Salzburg, 1978).

3 For an overview of the context and significance of Badby's execution, see especially Peter McNiven, *Heresy and Politics in the Reign of Henry IV: The Burning of John Badby* (Woodbridge: Boydell Press, 1987). Studies that explore Hoccleve's discussion of the execution include Pearsall, 'Hoccleve's *Regement*', 403–05; Perkins, *Hoccleve's Regiment*, 135–36; Cole, *Literature and Heresy*, Chapter 5; Antony Hasler, 'Hoccleve's Unregimented Body', *Paragraph* 13 (1990): 164–83.

The old man emphasizes the hierarchical nature of the Church, stressing the position of the 'prelacie' (or episcopal authority) above the 'clergie', and indicating his adherence to this understanding of the Church.[4] In this opening sequence, the old man indicates both the Church's power and its willingness to use this power against those who question ecclesiastical authority. He does this by specifically referring to Badby and the Eucharist, and to the central position that the Eucharist plays in the struggle between the Church and its opponents.

By opening his poem thus, Hoccleve locates it in the contentious space occupied by the Eucharist in early fifteenth-century England.[5] The Church's focus on the importance of the Eucharist during this period emphasized the integral role of priests and the hierarchy of the clergy ordained by the Church: the Eucharist was the only sacramental object at the time 'which doctrinally endorses clerical power, and centralizes it, rather than diffusing it to popular or other control'.[6] Hoccleve's old man grounds his discussion of the Eucharist in precisely this context: he stresses the power of the 'prelacie' (or episcopal authority) as well as the role of 'the souffissant clergie' (the locally approved clergy). The emphasis on the Eucharist, and the concomitant focus on the hierarchy of the Church, proved to be of utmost importance because the Church faced the challenge of positioning its definition of the Eucharist not only against that of the Lollards, but also against 'the competing claims of other images, relics and icons' used within the Church.[7] The Church was

---

4 Here, we continue our analysis of the old man, having looked first at the role he plays in the emergence of Hoccleve's Chaucer (in Chapter 3) and then at the role he plays in the making of Hoccleve himself (in Chapter 4). In this chapter we focus more deeply on the old man's ability to reflect the English Church and its response to heresy.

5 See Margaret Aston, 'Lollardy and Sedition, 1381–1431', *Past and Present* 17 (1960): 1–44; Mervyn James, 'Ritual, Drama, and Social Body in the Late Medieval English Town', *Past and Present* 98 (1983): 3–29; Hudson, *Premature Reformation*, Chapter 6; Robert N. Swanson, *Church and Society in Late Medieval England* (Oxford: Blackwell, 1989); Miri Rubin, *Corpus Christi: the Eucharist in Late Medieval Culture* (Cambridge: Cambridge University Press, 1991); Miri Rubin, 'The Eucharist and the Construction of Medieval Identities', in Aers, *Culture and History*, 43–63; Sarah Beckwith, *Christ's Body: Identity, Culture and Society in Late Medieval Writings* (London: Routledge, 1993); Sarah Beckwith, *Signifying God: Social Relation and Symbolic Act in the York Corpus Christi Plays* (Chicago, IL: University of Chicago Press, 2001).

6 Sarah Beckwith, 'Ritual, Church and Theatre: Medieval Dramas of the Sacramental Body', in Aers, *Culture and History*, 65–89 (67).

7 Ibid.

anxious, in other words, to centralize the Eucharist as *the* sacramental object of importance.[8] In emphasizing clerical power in his discussion of Badby, the old man indicates that this struggle over the meaning of the Eucharist – and its implications for the Church as a whole – is taking place in the very streets of London. Hoccleve uses the old man's 'street sermon' – and the specific example of John Badby – to reflect on the role that the Eucharist plays in contemporary ecclesiastical disputes.

It makes sense, for instance, that the old man frames John Badby's rejection of transubstantiation as working hand in hand with a rejection of clerical power:

> The precious body of our Lord Jhesu
> In forme of brede he leeved nat at al;
> He was in nothyng abassht ne eschu
> To seye it was but brede material.
> *He seide a preestes power was as smal*
> *As a rakers or swich anothir wight,*
> *And to make it hadde no gretter might.*
>
> (288–94; italics mine)

Badby's heresies are presented as twofold: he refuses to accept the real presence of the 'body of our Lord Jhesu' in the Eucharistic bread, and he downplays the special authority of 'preestes'.[9] The power of the priest is reduced here to that of a 'raker' – a street-cleaner or refuse collector – who deals daily not with the body of Christ, but rather with refuse, mud, and 'donge'.[10]

The old man's description of Badby's execution also highlights the central role that Prince Henry plays in attempting to convince Badby to

---

8 The Feast of Corpus Christi, reaffirmed by Pope Clement V in 1311, was instated to centralize the position of the Eucharist in the church. On the significance of the feast, and the function and manifestation of the Corpus Christi plays, see especially V.A. Kolve, *The Play Called Corpus Christi* (Stanford: Stanford University Press, 1966); James, 'Ritual, Drama, and Social Body'; Rubin, *Corpus Christi*; Beckwith, *Signifying Signs*. For early fifteenth-century poetic treatments of the Corpus Christi, see Lydgate, 'A Procession of Corpus Christi', in MacCracken, *Minor Poems of John Lydgate*, 35–43; and 'Poem 23: Of the Sacrament of the Altere', in Barr, *Digby Poems*, 296–303.

9 See also Thomas Walsingham's account of Badby's interrogation and execution in *The Chronica Maiora of Thomas Walsingham, 1376–1422*, trans. David Preest (Woodbridge: Boydell Press, 2005), 375–76.

10 See *Middle English Dictionary Online*, s.v. 'raker(e)', http://ets.umdl.umich.edu/m/med/.

recant his heresies. He depicts the sacrament being conveyed to Badby at Prince Henry's request:

> Also this noble prynce and worthy knyght –
> God qwyte him his charitable labour –
> Or any stikke kyndlid were or light,
> The sacrament, our blessid Sauveour,
> With reverence greet and hy honour,
> He fecche leet, this wrecche to converte,
> And make our feith to synken in his herte.
>
> (309–15)

The sacrament is equated with 'our blessid Sauveour' and we are told that, in causing the Eucharist to be brought to Badby, Henry uses 'reverence greet and hy honour'. This line proves integral to an orthodox presentation of the Eucharist because, as we have seen, the Church was working to centralize the host in Christian ritual, and treating the host with the 'reverence greet and hy honour' that the old man describes proved crucial to affording the host a central position. In the setting of a church the priest demonstrated this 'hy honour' of the Eucharist by elevating it for all to see and by marking its elevation with incense and the ringing of bells.[11] In Hoccleve's poem the presentation of the Eucharist is overseen not by a priest, but by the prince, who serves here as a 'mene' – or intermediary – for his father, Henry IV.[12] As Archbishop Arundel has presided over Badby's deposition, Prince Henry – 'worthy knyght' and future military hero of Agincourt – presides over the execution.[13] The old man recounts that Prince Henry promised Badby his 'lyf' (306), and 'souffissant lyflode' (307) should he recant his error and 'come unto our good byleeve ageyn'. 'Lyf' and 'lyflode' – life and the sustenance needed to sustain it – exist here, for Badby, only within the terms established by the church. They are presided over in these stanzas, however, not by the church, but rather by the prince.

[11] Rubin, 'The Eucharist', 50; cf. Rubin, *Corpus Christi*, 49–62, 155–63. See also: Eamon Duffy, *The Stripping of the Altars: Traditional Religion in England c.1400–c.1580* (New Haven, CT: Yale University Press, 1992), 95–102. The laity's view of the altar was often obscured by veil or screen, a marked boundary between 'the people's part of the church and the holy of holies'. As Duffy shows, the veil 'heightened the value of the spectacle it temporarily concealed'. *Stripping of the Altars*, 111.

[12] See ll. 302–03: 'This good lord highte him to be swich a mene / To his fadir, our lige lord sovereyn …'.

[13] See McNiven, *Heresy and Politics*, Chapter 10; Walsingham, *Chronica Maiora*, 375–76.

When the old man asks Hoccleve if he 'wrappid been in this dampnacioun' (373), Hoccleve responds by offering, in as succinct a manner as possible, that he believes 'in the sacrament / Of the auter', and that he believes 'in alle othir articles of the feith' according to the standards of 'Holy Writ':

Of our feith wole I nat despute at al,
But at o word, I in the sacrament
Of the auter fully byleeve and shal,
With Goddes help, whil lyf is to me lent,
And in despit of the feendes talent,
In alle othir articles of the feith
Byleeve as fer as that Holy Writ seith.

(379–85)

Hoccleve insists that his 'wit' is too 'derk' to consider theological material; he will not 'despute at all' any element of 'our feith'. Hoccleve promises to continue believing what he believes 'whil lyf is to me lent' (382). And, in the wake of Badby's execution, this phrase takes on an especially ominous cast: while the more traditional meaning of the phrase would be that life is 'lent' to Hoccleve by God, the narrative context highlights instead the role that powerful secular figures such as Prince Henry play in giving or taking an individual's life.

Hoccleve's account of Badby shows the English Church to be in a decidedly conflicted state: at the center of this conflict is not the greediness of friars, as in the final pages of *Piers Plowman*,[14] but rather the way in which competing definitions of the Eucharist threaten to tear the Church apart.[15] This representation of the Eucharist – and by extension, the Church – evolves through what Hoccleve chooses to include in his narrative, as much as what he chooses to exclude. *Piers Plowman* provides a good point of comparison here. As David Aers notes, Langland's presentation of the Eucharist in *Piers* proves exceptional for the way in which it avoids 'current devotional, ritual, and theological norms': *Piers* offers no 'processions in

[14] I refer here to the *Piers Plowman* B-text, Passus 20; and the C-text, Passus 22.

[15] On the ability of the Eucharist to signify, as Christ's body, the unity of the church – and, by the same token, discord within the church – see Beckwith, *Christ's Body*, Chapter 2. Beckwith describes 'the signification of Christ's body' as a 'contested social arena in late medieval English society'; 'Ostensibly an image of the unity of Christian society, the strain in the model, and the questioning to which it is put, the different, conflicting uses which agents use it for, are easily apparent' (25).

which the consecrated host [is] carried by clerics', wherein the hierarchy of the Church is reinforced.[16] Furthermore, Conscience's call to partake in the sacrament of the altar, late in the poem, is irregular in its suggestion that Christians take the sacrament as often as they need to – even in excess of once a month:

> Here is bred yblessed and godes body therunder.
> Grace thorw godes word gaf Peres the plouhman power,
> Myhte to make hit and men for to eten hit aftur
> In helpe of here hele ones in a monthe
> Or as ofte as they hadden nede, tho that hadden payed
> To Peres pardon the plouhman *Redde quod debes.*
> (C.21.385–90)

As Aers points out, 'this calls people to communion far in excess of even the practices of the especially devout laity'.[17] Langland's representation of the sacrament, then, invites a particular and peculiar vision of the Church – one in which hierarchy and ritual are downplayed in favor of communality.[18]

Hoccleve's presentation of the Eucharist in the *Regiment*, on the other hand, focuses on those aspects of the sacrament that Langland's presentation elides. By opening the poem with the old man's discussion of Badby, Hoccleve depicts the Eucharist in terms that centralize the position of the clergy and affirm the hierarchy of the Church. We do not see the Eucharist serving to nourish Christians, or to bind them together. The Badby episode is marked not by Badby accepting the host, but rather by his refusal to accept it and by his subsequent execution: the Eucharist emerges as the site of conflict, as an emblem of a divided church. Insofar as Hoccleve stands in for a devout layperson in this first section, he models the appropriate response to the Eucharist: he uses minimal words to signal his agreement with the church and to declare his belief in the sacrament of the altar.

This presentation of the Eucharist is by no means specific to the *Regiment.* Elsewhere in Hoccleve's works the sacrament is mentioned either in terms

16 David Aers, 'The Sacrament of the Altar in *Piers Plowman* and the Late Medieval Church in England', in *Images, Idolatry, and Iconoclasm in Late Medieval England: Textuality and the Visual Image*, ed. Jeremy Dimmick, James Simpson, and Nicolette Zeeman (Oxford: Oxford University Press, 2002), 63–80 (76–77).

17 Ibid., 79.

18 The obligation 'Peres pardon the plouhman *Redde quod debes*' is by no means an easy task. Nevertheless, the invitation to partake in the sacrament – and to do so often – is extended here openly.

of conflict and division or in terms of absence and withholding. We will turn now to consider the way in which the Eucharist manifests throughout Hoccleve's poetry, in order to illustrate both Hoccleve's emphasis on the Eucharist's role in contemporary ecclesiastical disputes, and his concomitant focus on instances wherein the Eucharist is withheld or otherwise made inaccessible to the given layperson.

Hoccleve refers to the Eucharist explicitly in 'To Sir John Oldcastle', and it is represented there in much the same terms as in the *Regiment* – in response to the heterodox challenge to priestly power:

> Yee seyn, 'a preest in deedly synne falle,
> If he so go to messe / he may nat make
> Crystes body' / falsly yee erren all*e*,
> þat holden so / to deepe yee ransake!
>
> (325–28)

Hoccleve refers to the sacrament only briefly in this poem, and he uses it only to elucidate Oldcastle's error in attempting to limit the power of priests.[19] In framing the Eucharist within this polemical context, Hoccleve's presentation recalls Nicholas Love's *Mirror of the Blessed Life of Jesus Christ*, in which Love centralizes the role of the Eucharist and explicitly links the orthodox definition of the Eucharist to the struggle against heresy. Love introduces his discussion of the Last Supper by advising his reader to take special note: 'For in þis processe is þe most strengþe & gostly fruyte of alle þe meditaciones þat bene of þe blessed lif of oure lord Jesu...' (145.11–13).[20] The section describes Christ's actions at the Last Supper, and then ends with a word of reproach for those who misunderstand the sacrament of the Eucharist (151.19–30) – aptly glossed 'Contra lollardos' – which he follows with a formal statement of orthodox doctrine on the Eucharist (151.31–152.1). The central role that the Eucharist plays in Love's *Mirror* – and the degree to which it is used 'contra lollardos' – is emphasized even more in those manuscripts of the *Mirror* that contain both a memorandum from Archbishop Arundel authorizing the work to be used against heretics, and a separate treatise devoted to 'þat excellent & most worþi sacrament of Cristies blessede bodye'.[21]

19 For the broader context of Oldcastle's rebellion, see K.B. McFarlane, *John Wycliffe and the Beginnings of English Noncomformity* (London: English Universities Press, 1952), Chapter 6; and Strohm, *England's Empty Throne*, Chapters 3 and 5.

20 Sargent, *Mirror*.

21 Sargent, *Mirror*, 36–37.

In Hoccleve's *Series*, on the other hand, the Eucharist is defined by its absence. It appears in the final text of the *Series* – the moralization to the 'Tale of Jonathas'. There, the second water that Jonathas encounters in his journey is described as 'holy communion aftir penance' (5.721). The role of the water within the tale proves significant, however, not for the way it is used, but rather for the way in which it is withheld: after finding the second water and proving its efficacy for the reader, Jonathas purposely withholds it from Fellicula after she delivers her confession. Instead of offering Fellicula the water that symbolizes Holy Communion and the fruit that symbolizes restoration and healing (see ll. 5.724–26), Jonathas applies instead 'the fruyt of sharpnesse' and 'the watir of penance', and as a result Fellicula dies in a particularly gruesome manner:

> And as blyue in hir wombe gan they frete
> And gnawe so þat change gan hir herte.
> Now herkneth how it hir made smerte.
> Hir wombe opned and out fil eche entraille
> That in hir was.
>
> (5.661–65)

The poem – and the *Series* as a whole – ends with this image: Fellicula's entrails pouring from her stomach as a result of her being denied the water of 'holy communion aftir penance'.[22] The moralization expands on the idea of the water serving as communion by equating it explicitly with Christ: it is 'holy communion aftir penance, wherof spak our sauueour, "I am the welle. Whoso drynkith of þat watir, he shal nat thriste ageyn"' (5.722–23). Given this description, Fellicula's death results from being denied both the sacrament of Holy Communion and the opportunity to commune with Christ.

The earliest and most authoritative scribal copy of the *Series* – Oxford, Bodleian Library, MS Selden supra 53 – presents the *Series* in full directly following the *Regiment*. The *Series* begins on the same page on which the *Regiment* ends, with only a small 'explicit' and a stanza's space to separate the two texts (see f. 76r). The two poems in Selden would therefore offer

22 In the context of the moralization, Fellicula is situated as Jonathas's 'wrecchid flessh' (5.701), so the scene can be read, alternatively, as Jonathas shedding his 'wrecchid flessh' through the actions described in the poem. But the vivid image of Fellicula's death – and the sense of vengeance on Jonathas's part – counters this interpretation. Hoccleve's decision to end the poem – and the *Series* – with this image of disembowelment invites the viewer to question the multiplicity of meanings at play here.

a symmetry in their presentations of the Eucharist: whereas the *Regiment* begins with Badby's Eucharistic heresy and his subsequent execution, the *Series* ends with Fellicula being denied the water of 'holy communion' and dying as a result. The substance of both poems extends between these two moments. Whereas Badby refuses to accept the host that the prince offers him – and therefore refuses the orthodox definition of the sacrament of the altar – Fellicula confesses openly but is denied Holy Communion, and so is denied communion with Christ and the restoration and healing that it brings.[23]

Hoccleve refers to the Eucharist once more in the *Series*, in the opening stanzas to his translation of the *Ars moriendi* chapter from Henry Suso's *Horologium sapientiae.* Thomas has already made clear in the 'Dialogue' that he intends only to translate the 'Lerne for to Die' portion of the *Horologium* (2.205–17), but when actually translating the text he includes Suso's prefatory material for the chapter, in which he also describes the contents of the three chapters following this one. This gives the impression that Thomas actually intends to translate these chapters as well, which, in turn, heightens the drama when Thomas stops translating after the *Ars moriendi* chapter. Including the prefatory material also allows Hoccleve to indicate the substance of the chapters that he has chosen not to translate:

> First, how lerne dye telle wole Y;
> The iide, how þat a man lyue shal;
> The iiide, how a man sacramentally
> Receyue me shal wel and worthyly;
> The iiiie, how with an herte cleene and pure
> That man loue me shal and honure.
>
> (4.24–28)

The 'Lerne for to Die' chapter serves as the first in a sequence, in which the reader, having first learned to die, then learns to live, then learns to receive the Eucharist, and then learns how to love and honor divine wisdom 'with an herte cleene and pure'. The synopsis depicts a trajectory through

23 In three scribal copies of the *Series*, the *Regiment* follows the *Series* and Lydgate's *Dance Macabre*. This places the two references to the Eucharist in closer proximity, and inserts between them Lydgate's own meditation on mortality: the mention of Holy Communion at the end of the *Series* immediately precedes the *Dance Macabre*, which then gives way to the opening of the *Regiment*, and Badby's execution. The manuscripts in question are Oxford, Bodleian Library, MS Bodley 221; Oxford, Bodleian Library, MS Laud misc. 735; and New Haven, Yale University, Beinecke Library, MS 493.

these four lessons towards a state of purity and love for divine wisdom. Importantly, the Eucharist stands at the center of this textual progression.

When Thomas stops translating after the *Ars moriendi* chapter he refers back to his description of the other three sections of the book, even as he declares his inability to translate any of these sections:

> The othir iii partes which in this book
> Of the tretice of deeth expressid be,
> Touch Y nat dar. þat labour Y forsook,
> For so greet thyng to swich a fool as me
> Ouer chargeable is, by my leautee,
> To medle with.
>
> (4.918–23)

The *Series* uses the recurring trope of announcing a given text's unavailability. The most obvious example of this is the Friend conspicuously appending a moralization to Hoccleve's 'Tale of Jereslaus's Wife' – the moralization that Hoccleve says his source text lacked. The trope also occurs in the 'Complaint', where Hoccleve borrows a text from a friend – Isidore of Seville's *Synonyma* – only to have the friend recall it unexpectedly.[24] In the case of the *Horologium sapientiae*, however, the problem is not textual availability, but rather suitability. Hoccleve has access to the full book, and he highlights his deliberate choice not to translate these three chapters – including, that is, the chapter concerning the Eucharist. He connects the decision to 'forsake' this 'labour' to his professed foolishness, and in doing so he recalls his response to the old man in the *Regiment*, when asked whether he 'wrappid been in this dampnacioun'[25] – whether he is involved in the debate over the meaning of the Eucharist: 'I thanke it God', Hoccleve says there, 'noon inclinacioun / Have I to laboure in probacioun / Of His hy knowleche and His mighty werkis, / For swich mateere unto my wit to derk is' (375–8).[26] In both instances, Hoccleve rejects the dangerous 'laboure' at hand and cites his own foolishness, his own dim wits.

[24] A.G. Rigg identifies this text as the *Synonyma* in 'Hoccleve's Complaint and Isidore of Seville', *Speculum* 45 (1970): 564–74. John Burrow responds to this argument, suggesting that Hoccleve might have used an epitome of the *Synonyma* instead, in 'Hoccleve's Complaint and Isidore of Seville Again', *Speculum* 73 (1998): 424–28.

[25] We also explored this question of the old man's in Chapter 4, where we noted its role in defining Hoccleve's Thought.

[26] Here, Hoccleve's humility topos aligns with what David Lawton calls 'the ultimate – one might say transcendent – dullness': 'dullness before the name of God' ('Dullness

In both instances, Hoccleve depicts himself quite clearly navigating the perimeter of this sensitive subject – not dwelling long in his discussion of the Eucharist, but moving swiftly along, keeping his distance, and admitting ignorance. Hoccleve's decision not to translate the 'othir iii partes' would have been positioned in MS Selden supra 53 (as we have seen) between two fatal encounters in which the Eucharist plays a central role – Badby's execution at the beginning of the *Regiment*, and Fellicula's death at the end of the *Series*. In both cases, importantly, the conveyer (or withholder) of the Eucharist is not a member of the clergy, but a secular man. Jonathas is presented as a 'Cristen man which is sliden or fallen into synne' (5.700–01) in the tale's moralization. When he hears Fellicula's confession and withholds the water of 'holy communion', he does so only as a 'Cristen man', not as a professional religious.

The prince, by contrast, acts as a 'mene' for his father, the king. He assumes a para-ecclesiastical role in Badby's execution by conveying the sacrament to Badby, and he does so by claiming the role outright. In positioning himself thus, Prince Henry may well have been presenting a challenge to Archbishop Arundel, as Peter McNiven has suggested, and he may have hoped to succeed where the church had failed; but in doing so, he also blurs the line between secular and religious authority.[27] He encroaches on the domain of the church, and positions himself as an intermediary not only between Badby and the king, but also between the church and the crown. This action lends credence to Jeremy Catto's evaluation of the first decades of the fifteenth century as being defined by an increasing intermixture of secular and religious power. Catto sets 1400 as the date before which 'religion was outside the competence of the secular power' and notes that, by the end of Henry V's reign, 'more than a century before the title could be used, Henry V had begun to act as the supreme governor of the Church of England'.[28] Hoccleve indicates such an intermixture of secular and religious responsibilities in his presentation of the Badby execution. In doing so, he also indicates the dangerous potential of such a mixture: Prince Henry's actions, while presented by the old man as 'charitable labour' (310), are unsuccessful insofar as they ultimately lead to

---

and the Fifteenth Century', *ELH* 54.5 (1987): 761–99 (769)). Cf. Hoccleve's use of poetic deference before Christ, in an explicitly devotional context, in 'Inuocacio ad Patrem': 'Alle his tormentes may nat be reherced / By noon enditour ne by translatour, / Ne no wight elles, for so many a stour, / And so greuous, souffrid he for our synne, / þat to telle al, mannes wit is to thynne' (*Hoccleve's Works*, 278, ll. 115–19).

27 McNiven, *Heresy and Politics*, 209–19.

28 Jeremy Catto, 'Religious Change Under Henry V', in *Henry V: The Practice of Kingship*, ed. G.L. Harriss (Stroud: Alan Sutton Publishing, 1993), 97–115 (97, 115).

the death of a layperson. The secular performance of ecclesiastical duties can be seen, through the lens of this presentation, to be noticeably problematic.[29]

This presentation of Prince Henry, arriving as it does in the opening stanzas of a poem that evolves into a *speculum principis* for the prince himself, compels us to reconsider the advice that Hoccleve offers within the *Regiment* proper. As we saw in the last chapter, Hoccleve seizes one opportunity in the *Regiment* to upbraid Henry for holding councils on holy days, and to request that the prince not use sacred time for secular matters. This aligns not only with reminders to respect the people's voice – 'for peples vois is Goddes vois' – but also with reminders that Henry himself is not God, but rather a man, and a leader. In one exemplum, Hoccleve reports how a knight reprimanded Alexander for his cupidity, suggesting that if the gods had made his body large enough to reflect the size of his own greed he would be too big to fit in this world. The knight encourages Alexander to consider whether he is 'a man, or god, or noght' (4059). If he is God, he must follow God's actions and be merciful to his people ('If thow be god, thow folwe muste his trace / And nat men of hir good robbe or byreve, / But hem releeve and do hem ese and grace' (4061–63)). If he is a man, on the other hand, he must consider his own mortality. As Hoccleve had positioned Henry as the 'Alexander' to his 'Aristotle' in the prologue to the *Regiment* proper (2038–53), the character of Alexander in this exemplum can be read, by extension, as a model for Henry, through whom Henry can consider his own mortality and the way in which he might practice mercy as a ruler.

One of the main 'mirrors' that Hoccleve uses for Henry throughout the *Regiment* proper, however, is Christ, in his incarnate form. Whereas Hoccleve avoids discussing the nature of the Eucharist at length, he proves unafraid of using the body of Christ to instruct the prince. More specifically – and more relevant to Hoccleve's initial presentation of the prince in the *Regiment* – Hoccleve positions Christ's body throughout the *Regiment* proper as a means of contemplating the virtues of mercy and humility.[30]

---

29 In this respect, Hoccleve's presentation might be seen to align with contemporary Benedictine anxieties regarding an increasingly secular church. See, for instance, Natalie Calder's argument that the Digby poems, apparently written by a Benedictine monk, evince an anxiety over Henry V's consolidation of ecclesiastical and regal power ('"The puple is godes, and not ȝoures": Lancastrian Orthodoxy in the Digby Lyrics', *RES* (2013): 1–18). See also Catherine Sanok's argument that Lydgate responds in his work to an increasingly powerful secular church, in 'Saints' Lives and the Literary After Arundel', in Gillespie and Ghosh, *After Arundel*, 469–86.

30 Cf. Cole, *Literature and Heresy*, 124–30: Cole emphasizes the integral role of the virtues of pity and mercy in the *Regiment*, albeit without the focus on the manifestation (and legibility) of Christ's body that I concentrate on here.

In the section 'De misericordia', for instance, Hoccleve invites the prince to consider the mercy that Christ showed when he became incarnate and gave his life for all mankind:

> Mercy Cryst causid to been incarnat,
> And humbled Him to take our brethirhede.
> God inmortel, reewynge our seek estat,
> Mortel becam to pourge our synful dede.
> Him lothid nat His precious body sprede
> Upon the Crois, this lord benigne and good;
> He wroot our chartre of mercy with His blood.
>
> Of Him, His handwerk and His creature,
> For to be merciable, aright may lerne.
> This lyf present shul but a whyle dure,
> And, lastyng it, your mercy nat ne werne,
> O worthy Prince, for to God eterne
> It ful plesant is.
>
> (3333–45)

Hoccleve positions Christ's body – and the 'chartre of mercy' that he writes with his own blood – as a model for Henry.[31] By contemplating 'Him, His handwerk and His creature', Henry is invited to grasp the necessity of being a merciful ruler.[32] Hoccleve literally places the body of Christ before Henry here, and asks him to study this 'precious body' in order to consider the virtue of mercy. This leads, in turn, to Hoccleve's suggestion that Henry take the example of 'the ledere / Of bees' who is 'prikkelees': he should avoid stinging people, leading him thereby 'for Goddes sake / to weyve crueltee and tirannye' (3384–85).

---

31 On the 'Charter of Christ' tradition, see *The Middle English Charters of Christ*, ed. Mary Caroline Spalding (Bryn Mawr: Bryn Mawr College, 1914); Rubin, *Corpus Christi*, 306–08; Emily Steiner, *Documentary Culture and the Making of Medieval English Literature*, Cambridge Studies in Medieval Literature 50 (Cambridge: Cambridge University Press, 2003), 50–53, 159–61.

32 Hoccleve uses the word 'handwerk' on only one other occasion in the *Regiment*: in the final stanzas of the poem, urging the princes of France and England towards peace, Hoccleve notes the necessity to show 'love and awe / Of Him that is the kyng of kynges alle', and reminds the princes that in killing Christian men they are killing 'His handwerk soothly' – his own creations, his own images and likenesses (see *Regiment* ll. 5412–25).

In the section on 'De paciencia', similarly, Hoccleve argues that Christ exhibited his humility by taking on 'mortel rynde', and he presents the incarnate Christ as a 'mirour': 'God took upon Him humble buxumnesse / Whan He Him wrappid in our mortel rynde: / That oghte a mirour be to al mankynde' (3575–77). The stanza following these lines goes on to explain that 'verray God and man / Conceyved was thurgh the humilitee' of Mary (3579–80).[33] Later in the same section Christ's body reappears – this time as a spur to considering patience and honorable meekness:

Take heede how, whan that Cryst our Sauveour
Was bobbid and His visage al byspet,
And greet despyt doon Him and deshonour,
Bownden and scourgid and grevously bet,
Crowned with thorn, nayled to the gibet;
Yit for al this torment, no word He speek,
So was He pacient, benigne, and meek.

(3613–19)

Hoccleve focuses the reader's attention on the pains that Christ suffered during his Passion, calling to mind the crown of thorns on Christ's head and the nails in his hands and feet. He then directs this vivid image towards the reader as a model of patience. Only by acting in a charitable manner, Hoccleve tells his reader, can we prove that we are 'disciples' of God: 'Oonly keepyng of charitee us preeveth / That we disciples been of God almighty' (3606–07). This reminder comes hand in hand with a textual representation of Christ's body, beaten and bloody, and an indication of how this body might lead the reader to be more patient and more charitable.

Depictions of Christ's body in the *Regiment* proper, then, contrast with the initial representation of the 'blessid Sauveour', as he appears in the form of the Eucharist. Whereas the Eucharist becomes attached to the death of a layperson, and whereas this presentation of the Eucharist reinforces Prince Henry's own approach to power, Hoccleve reintroduces Christ within the *Regiment* proper not as the sacrament but rather as a human body which renders legible and tactile the values of mercy, humility, patience, and charity. In the final section of the poem, 'De Pace', Hoccleve then explicitly links this body with the institutional church and with the sacraments of the church:

33 The physicality of this process of 'verray God and man' manifesting himself is heightened in MSS Arundel 38 and Harley 4866 by a lasso drawn around this stanza: whether by design or chance, the words are encircled by the rope, and the words thereby become tactile substance, much as Christ (as Word) became flesh.

Makynge of Eeve tokned the makynge
Of Holy Chirche and sacramentz of it;
As of the syde of Adam, him slepynge,
Eeve was maad, so our lord Cryst dyynge
Upon the Crois, Holy Chirche of His syde
And the sacramentz maad were in that tyde.

(5161–66)

This stanza underscores the connection between the sacrament of the altar and the physical body of Christ; it positions 'the sacramentz' in terms of Christ's sacrifice, and in terms of the greater historical significance of this sacrifice: in dying, Christ redeemed the sins of mankind, but he also instigated the foundation of 'Holy Chirche' and the creation of its 'sacramentz'. Hoccleve reminds his reader that the 'sacramentz' reflect this ultimate sacrifice: in handling the sacrament of the altar, one handles Christ's body; in communing with Christ, one reflects on his sacrifice, and contemplates the virtues that he embodies.

Hoccleve's presentation of Christ's body in the *Regiment* has an analogue in the poet's handling of the Corpus Christi in 'Inuocacio ad patrem'. This short poem opens Hoccleve's autograph 'collected poems' manuscript, San Marino, Huntington Library, MS HM 744, and it serves as the first in a series of invocations to God, Christ, the Holy Spirit, and the Virgin.[34] There, Hoccleve uses very similar language to evoke Christ's crucifixion and the wounds that he suffered. Hoccleve addresses God, inviting him to

Beholde [Christ's] sydes / and see how they bleede
His giltlees handes / how they stremen / see
With blody stremes …
His feet and handes w*ith* nayles been perced …
With sharpe thornes / fadir wel thow woost,
Coroned was thy sone / and sore pyned,
And wowndid to the herte …

(ll. 105–07, 113, 120–23)

Hoccleve ends this poem with a request that God consider Christ's wounded body and think thereby of man's own 'substance'. Christ's body indicates the 'substance' of the individual Christian: 'Beholde his toren membres, fadir free / And lat our substance in thyn herte impresse' (129–30). In the

34 This poem is printed in *Hoccleve's Works*, pp. 275–79. I cite from this edition here.

Regiment, Hoccleve uses images of a wounded Christ not to ask that God have mercy on mankind, but rather to encourage the prince to have mercy on his subjects: to practice mercy, humility, and patience, and to consider the source and meaning of the sacraments.

As with the knight who encourages Alexander to consider whether he is 'man, or god, or nought', Hoccleve positions the prince to consider his own mortality (and fragility), and his own answerability to God. Hoccleve's treatment of the body of Christ within the *Regiment* proper suggests a need to reorient the prince towards a respect for the body of Christ, and a consideration of what Christ's body betokens. As we have seen, this comes hand in hand with a reminder that a good leader should respect the bodies of his people: he should be wary of overexerting his powers, and be mindful of his capacity for cupidity.

*

This understanding of Hoccleve's relationship with Prince Henry in the *Regiment* enables us to revisit the question of how Hoccleve himself operates in the poem. In the following section we will explore the way in which Hoccleve positions himself, as a writer, in relation to sacramental discourses on communion and confession. This will lead, in turn, to our consideration of how Hoccleve's positioning of Chaucer interacts with the sacramental discourses we have been considering thus far. One of Hoccleve's accomplishments in the *Regiment* is his repositioning of the body of Christ: from a symbol of internal conflict, to a symbol of peace and humility. Hoccleve enacts a trajectory from an execution rooted in competing definitions of the Eucharist, to a definition of Christ as a living human body, and as peace incarnate – 'I am pees verray; there I wole abyde' (5386).[35] In both instances, Hoccleve foregrounds the question of where Christ 'abides': Badby dies because of his unwillingness to admit that Christ abides in the Eucharistic bread; and, by the end of the poem, Christ 'abides' in manifestations of peace.[36] As we have seen, Hoccleve punctuates

[35] We explored Hoccleve's use of this phrase also at the end of Chapter 3, where it contributed to our discussion of Christine, Hoccleve, and the writers' respective attempts at political peacemaking. Here, we explore how the phrase reflects the nature of Christ's presence throughout the *Regiment*.

[36] This might compel us to consider the nature of the 'meritorie werreyyng' that Hoccleve does promote in the final lines of the *Regiment* (see ll. 5426–39). John Bowers has read this as 'a call for the persecution of heretics' ('Politics of Tradition', 354); David Lawton, on the other hand, reads it as referring to crusade against non-Christians, and

his first meditation on the body of Christ with a description of Christ writing a 'chartre of mercy with His blood'. This image is conventional, but it nevertheless recalls Hoccleve's own descriptions of writing and pain earlier in the poem: writing 'smertith him ful sore / In every veyne and place of his body' (1025–26).[37] Hoccleve's final words before beginning the *Regiment* proper call this self-presentation to mind: 'But sore in me ther qwappith every veyne, ... / The Crois of Cryst my werk speede and avance' (2154, 2156). Here, the pains he embodies – the aching veins – coincide with the 'Crois of Cryst'. Christ's cross often marked the beginning of a piece of writing, and this would have been the most immediate reference here; but the phrase also refers, of course, to Christ's actual cross and the instance of his sacrifice.[38] The phrase enables Hoccleve to link his own bodily sacrifice as a writer ('sore in me ther qwappith every veyne') with Christ's sacrifice. The mention of Christ writing a charter with his own blood, coming as it does in the wake of Hoccleve's meditation on the pains of writing, serves to further link Hoccleve's own treatise – the *Regiment* – with Christ's sacrifice, and his 'chartre' of blood.[39]

---

therefore as following in the footsteps of Gower's 'In Praise of Peace', which positions crusade as among the only acceptable forms of warfare ('Dullness and the Fifteenth Century', 781–82; see 'In Praise of Peace', ll. 246–52). In the context of the present reading of the *Regiment*, I am strongly inclined towards the second reading. The structure of Hoccleve's final address in support of peace also echoes Gower's presentation in 'In Praise of Peace': Hoccleve first addresses Prince Henry (whereas Gower addresses Henry IV), and then his address shifts to the Christian princes of England and France (whereas Gower addresses 'these othre princes Cristene alle' (380)). Both poets also position peace as a patently Christian pursuit – and as Christ-*like* (see 'In Praise of Peace', ll. 155–96). On Gower and Chaucer's relationships with the virtue of peace, see R.F. Yeager, '*Pax Poetica*: On the Pacifism of Chaucer and Gower', *SAC* 9 (1987): 97–121.

37 Cf. Perkins, *Hoccleve's Regiment*, 148.

38 Barr, in *Piers Plowman Tradition*, notes that the cruciform mark was often placed at the beginning of a piece of writing, such as at the start of *Sir Launfal* in BL Cotton Caligula A ii. fol. 35 (213). The opening line of 'Pierce the Ploughman's Crede' plays with this convention: 'Cros, and Curteis Crist this begynnynge spede ...'.

39 The Charter of Christ tradition read the body of Christ in documentary terms. The metaphor of Christ's crucified body as a document extended to all aspects of documentary culture: 'The parchment is made of his skin, which has been stretched on the cross; his blood is the ink (or the sealing wax); the scourges of his enemies are the pens; his wounds, letters; his heart or his pierced flank, the seal.' See Brigitte Miriam Bedos-Rezak, 'In Search of a Semiotic Paradigm: The Matter of Sealing in Medieval Thought and Praxis (1050–1400)', in Adams et al., *Good Impressions*, 1–7 (5). The tradition also included Christ leaving a 'copy of the charter (the Eucharist) with

The stanza in which Hoccleve describes Christ's conception in Mary takes on a parallel significance in MSS Arundel 38 and Harley 4866 – the two earliest extant copies of the *Regiment*. In both manuscripts the stanza detailing Christ's conception is positioned in the margin and is depicted as being lassoed into the body of the poem (see Figures 5 and 6). Not only does the image render the text as a physical object that can be moved (even as the text describes Christ being conceived, and therefore advancing into material form); it also emphasizes the labor involved in positioning such text. These men are depicted much as Hoccleve depicts his fellow scribes in the first section of the *Regiment* – as men whose work constitutes physical labor, not unlike the physical labor of those 'artificiers' who toil outside.[40] This presentation, whether by design or coincidence, highlights the labor involved in the making of this poem at the very point in which Hoccleve presents Christ's 'mortal rynde' as a physical mirror for all mankind.

As we saw in the last chapter, Hoccleve presents his account of scribal labor by alluding to the biblical tale of the unjust steward – the steward who worries about his future employment and announces, 'To dig I am not able, to beg I am ashamed' (Lk 16:3). Hoccleve alludes to the parable once again, later in his dialogue with the old man, as he continues to worry about his 'lyflode': 'To begge, shame is myn impediment; / I woot wel rather sholde I dye and sterve' (1807–08). The parable in question, which Hoccleve also uses in *La Male Regle*, serves in Luke as a vehicle for contemplating the difference between material wealth and spiritual wealth. It culminates in Jesus's memorable moral: 'No servant can serve two masters: for either he will hate the one, and love the other; or he will hold to the one, and despise the other. You cannot serve God and mammon [wealth]' (Lk. 16:13). Hoccleve's choice to evoke this parable twice in the first section of his poem is intriguing. The poem opens, after all, with Prince Henry taking the initiative to mix secular and religious power in his own person. The prince's offerings during the execution similarly reflect his hybrid power: he offers Badby not only the sacrament, but also money – if Badby recants his beliefs, we are told, he can live, and receive sufficient income for the rest of his life ('souffissant lyflode eek sholde he have / Unto the day he clad were in his grave' (307–08)). If we read the prince's actions in part as an attempt to succeed where the church has failed, and as a challenge to the authority of the archbishop, then the proffering of 'souffissant lyflode' in tandem with the sacrament constitutes a conspicuous mixing of the

---

the priest so that future generations would remember and benefit from his sacrifice'. See Steiner, *Documentary Culture*, 50.

40 See ll. 1009–15.

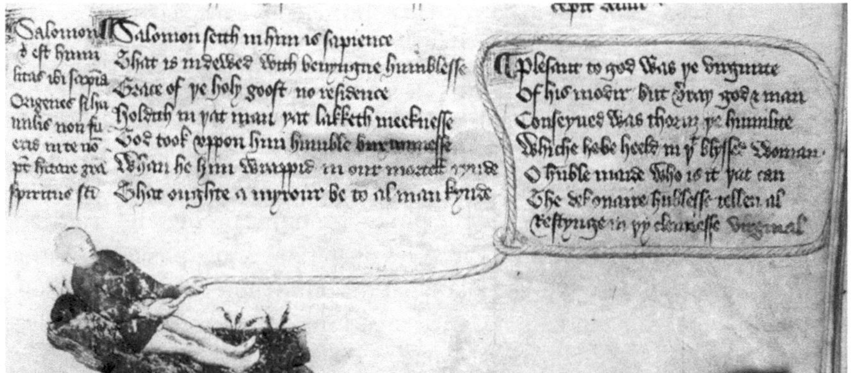

Figures 5 and 6. London, British Library, MSS Arundel 38, f. 65r, and Harley 4866, f. 62r.

defining symbols of the church and the world, of religious and secular power, God and mammon.

The inability of the individual to serve both the world and God becomes a recurring concern in the *Series*. The moralization of the 'Tale of Jereslaus's Wife' builds to the simple and straightforward declaration, 'It is impossible to plese the world and God' (3.1061). In addition, the ninth lesson read on All Saints' Day, which Hoccleve translates after completing his translation of 'Lerne for to Die', ends by employing an economic metaphor to encourage the reader to devote himself or herself to spiritual works: 'And sikirly, syn God of his hy grace and benigne courtesie hath yeuen vs libertee and freedam for *to purchace by our wirkes in this present lyfe* þat oon or þat othir [heaven or hell], al standith in our choys and eleccioun.

To grete fooles been we but if we cheese the bettre part' (4.1007–11; italics mine). The lesson highlights the individual's free will – his or her ability to 'purchase' salvation through the demonstration of good works on earth. Choosing the 'bettre part' is presented through means of this economic metaphor, but it paradoxically points up the need to renounce earthly goods and focus one's energies on the production of spiritual wealth.[41] If the *Series* betrays Hoccleve's fear that the militant hunt for heretics might encroach on the sphere of poetry,[42] the *Regiment* witnesses this concern taking shape: an early stage occurs in Prince Henry's mixing of secular and religious authority – wielding his secular power as both a knight and a prince against heresy and, in doing so, entering into the domain of the institutional church.

This reading might also compel us to reconsider the role of the old man in the *Regiment*. The old man presents himself as conspicuously devout throughout the first section of the *Regiment*, but his specific position remains undefined. As we have seen, the old man refers to 'Holy Chirche' as a 'brydil', and he defines his 'labour' by way of the church – his heart is applied, he tells Hoccleve, 'to that al hoolly is' (see ll. 365–71). Later, the old man imagines what Hoccleve thinks of him, saying he likely believes him to be a 'noble prechour at devys'. The phrase is not meant literally – indeed, its echo of the Pardoner calling the Wife of Bath 'a noble prechour in this cas' (*CT* III.165) underscores its colloquial meaning; but, given the religious context in which the old man has presented himself, the term is suggestive. The old man also uses religious language to refer to his youthful exploits – such as taking a 'pilgrimage to taverne' (615) and offering his 'tythe' there (617). When he refers to his speech as a 'long sermoun', similarly, the phrase activates multiple meanings – at once a speech or long discourse (*MED* senses 1(a) and (b)) and a public religious discourse (*MED* sense 2(a)).[43] The old man ends the dialogue by informing Hoccleve that he can be found daily at the 'Carmes messe' 'aboute the hour of sevene' (2007–08). Derek Pearsall has used this to suggest a possible alignment between the old man

41 The reference to choosing the 'better part' also recalls the story of Martha and Mary (Lk. 10:38–42), in which Jesus commends Mary for 'choosing the better part' by sitting and listening to him speak (rather than attending to worldly matters, as Martha does). This contrasts with the Friend's earlier admonition to 'cheese the bettre part' (2.680), a phrase he uses not to spiritual ends, but rather to convince Hoccleve that he should admit his offense to 'wommen' and pursue the secular penance of writing to please them.

42 See Chapter 1.

43 *Middle English Dictionary Online*, s.v. 'sermoun (n.)', http://ets.umdl.umich.edu/m/med/.

and the Carmelites;[44] but, of course, a Carmelite identity for the old man is never made explicit within the narrative. Indeed, the old man's identity is never settled, beyond the fact that he aligns himself strongly with the orthodox church and its hierarchical organization, and that he undertakes his 'labour' in association with the church. On one level, the old man operates as a 'mene' for the English church as it presents itself in London circa 1410; insofar as he presents Hoccleve with the details of Badby's execution and the prince's role in the execution, as well as the church's need to underscore its own hierarchy and power, he indicates the 'state of affairs' as it stands.

If the old man does not hold a religious office or act in some capacity as a friar or confessor, then he can also be seen to exercise – as with Jonathas and Prince Henry – a quasi-religious role without religious credentials. His efforts to counsel Hoccleve are, after all, similarly unsuccessful: much as Prince Henry's attempt to convert Badby ends in death, and Jonathas's overseeing of Fellicula's confession ends in disaster, the old man's pious dialogue with Hoccleve ends with neither real-world solution nor spiritual absolution and comfort. The dialogue merely transitions to another text and, with it, another discourse. But the dialogue is also referred to in terms of confession – the sacramental counterpart to communion. Before his first extended block of speech in the dialogue, Hoccleve offers to 'confesse' his problems to the old man, and the old man responds, 'Yis, telle on in the name of Cryst' (792; 798). Hoccleve then bookends their dialogue by referring to having been almost entirely 'shriven':

> I am unto so streit a poynt ydryve,
> Of thre conclusions moot I cheese oon:
> Or begge, or stele, or sterve; *I am yshryve*
> *So ny* that othir way ne see I noon
>
> (1800–03; italics mine)

This reference serves doubly to underscore the extent to which the dialogue has not resolved Hoccleve's problems, nor has it offered him solace. He has exhausted his options in the course of being 'shriven' and remains unsettled. The fact that their conversation takes place in the days preceding Easter (see l. 805) adds further meaning: Canon 21 of the Fourth Lateran Council (1215)

---

44 Pearsall, 'Hoccleve's *Regement*', 407. Pearsall suggests, furthermore, that the image of a 'man in white garment with a hood and skull cap' at the beginning of the copy of the *Regiment* in Coventry, City Record Office, MS Accession 325/1 might be intended to 'portray the Old Man of the poem as a Carmelite friar'.

required that each adult confess his sins once a year and receive Eucharist at least at Easter.[45] The days leading to Easter therefore present the last time in which an individual might become shriven and present himself – with pure heart – to receive the body of Christ.[46] Hoccleve's surprise at having the man depart 'sodeynly' after their conversation, rather than 'dyne' with him, suggests a reading more appropriate to the Easter season: Hoccleve has undergone a confession of sorts, but, after doing so, he has not properly communed – he has not received the body of Christ.

The subject of confession recurs throughout the *Series*, and serves as another feature that brings the *Regiment* and the *Series* into conversation with one another. The moralization to the 'Tale of Jereslaus's Wife' identifies the 'earl' as a 'prechour or discreet confessour' who leads the soul 'vnto the hows of holy chirche for to teche and norisshe [her]' (3.1018–20). The description points up the shortcomings of the old man: insofar as he oversees a confession in the *Regiment*, he fails to 'teche' his subject adequately; and his conversation hardly serves to 'norisshe' Hoccleve. The word 'norisshe' carries metaphorical as well as literal connotations of feeding and sustaining.[47] Hoccleve underscores his lack of nourishment at the end of the dialogue by indicating that he still faces starvation (1802); and also in the old man's declining to 'dyne' with him. In the *Series*, Thomas presents his 'Complaint' by way of confession: he says he will make 'an open shrifte' by publishing his poem (2.83). His having been healed by God constitutes a gift, Thomas tells the Friend – 'It to confesse and þanke hym, am I holde' (2.94). The Friend downplays the need for such confession in the *Series*, and instead convinces Thomas to accept a sin he does not believe he has committed (offending 'wommen' in his *Epistle*), and to 'pourge' his 'gilt' through translating a work he had not originally intended to translate (ll. 2.825–26). Thomas's ability to actually purge his guilt is undermined by the fact that the guilt seems to have been invented by the Friend. In the *Regiment*, on the other hand, the old man presides over a confessional dialogue that has little efficacy – Hoccleve completes the dialogue neither 'taught' nor 'nourished'.

45 See H.J. Schroeder, *Disciplinary Decrees of the General Councils: Text, Translation and Commentary* (St. Louis: B. Herder, 1937), 259–63.

46 For Hoccleve, they also indicated the way in which spiritual and material 'lyflode' overlap: Easter was one of two times in the year when Hoccleve received payment of a portion of his annuity (the other time being at Michaelmas). See Burrow, *Thomas Hoccleve*, 11. In traveling 'towards' Easter in the first section of the *Regiment*, then, he might be seen as traveling towards both spiritual and financial fulfilment.

47 *Middle English Dictionary Online*, s.v. 'norishen (v.)', http://ets.umdl.umich.edu/m/med/. See especially senses 1–3.

Confession serves not only as a way into translation in the *Series*, but also as a means of discussing personal identity. By referring to the 'confessour' as 'discreet' in the moralization to the 'Tale of Jereslaus's Wife', Hoccleve echoes the language used to direct the actions of an official confessor in Canon 21 of the Fourth Lateran Council: 'Sacerdos autem sit *discretus et cautus*, ut more periti medici superinfundat vinum et oleum vulneribus sauciati' [Let the priest be *discreet and cautious* that he may pour wine and oil into the wounds of the one injured after the manner of a skilful physician].[48] In the 'Complaint', when discussing the division between appearance and identity, Hoccleve likewise foregrounds the virtues of discretion and prudence:[49]

> And som man lokeþ in foltisshe manere
> As to þe outwarde doom and iugement,
> That, at þe prefe, *discreet is and prudent.*
>
> But algatis, howe so be my countinaunce,
> Debaat is nowe noon bitwixe me and my wit,
> A[l] þouȝ þat ther were a disseueraunce,
> As for a time, bitwixe me and it.
> The gretter harme is myn, þat neuere ȝit
> Was I wel lettrid, *prudent and discreet.*
>
> (1.243–51; italics mine)

If one of the 'voices' at work within the 'Complaint' is the voice of the recovering church,[50] then these stanzas can be read as a reflection of the church's struggle to present itself as upstanding and capable of administering to its laypeople, despite appearances. The repetition of the words 'prudent' and 'discreet' in this passage not only links it to the discussion of discreet confession in the moralization to the 'Tale of Jereslaus's Wife',

48 The Latin text is from *Decrees of the Ecumenical Councils*, ed. Norman P. Tanner, 2 vols (Washington, D.C.: Georgetown University Press, 1990), 1: 245; the English translation is from Schroeder, *Disciplinary Decrees of the General Councils*, 260. These directions to priests and confessors were echoed throughout late medieval devotional guides. See, for instance, the *Speculum Christiani: A Middle English Religious Treatise of the 14th Century*, ed. Gustaf Holmstedt, EETS, O.S. 182 (London: Oxford University Press for the Early English Text Society, 1933), 230–31.

49 We discussed Hoccleve's use of the word (and virtue) prudence in the *Regiment* in Chapter 4. In our present discussion, the virtue is explored in an ecclesiastical – rather than mostly literary – context.

50 See Chapter 1.

but also recalls the proper actions of a confessor or priest, as designated at the Fourth Lateran Council. In doing so, it summons to mind the means by which the given priest effects spiritual healing – using the process of confession to 'pour wine and oil into the wounds of the one injured'. It positions Thomas's own self-examination within the terms used by the institutional church to discuss the process of healing.

This aspect of Thomas's approach, however, intersects with a confession of ignorance in the second stanza: Thomas counters the suggestion that he might appear 'prudent and discreet' – that he might have been spiritually healed – with the assertion that he cannot appear thus, because he never was 'wel lettrid, prudent and discreet'. Thomas uses the same approach that we see the Hoccleve narrator use when asked whether he dabbles in theological debate in the *Regiment*: he insists on his ignorance, his dim wits. Here, however, this assertion paradoxically integrates the language used by the church to describe the process of spiritual healing. The passage links also with Thomas's earlier assertion in the 'Complaint' that, in determining the strength of one's wits, 'commvnynge is the beste assay [test]' (1.217). Thomas immediately follows this line with a clarification: 'I mene, to commvne of thingis mene, / For I am but riȝt lewide, douteles, / And ignoraunt. My kunnynge is ful lene' (1.218–20). These lines – and the declaration of ignorance that they carry – betray a desire to clarify that he refers not to spiritual 'commvnynge' here, or confession; neither does he mean to refer to the 'holy *communion*' that the moralization to the 'Tale of Jonathas' discusses. As with the 'prudent and discreet' stanzas, these lines suggest the language of confession, and then they retreat; they indicate an interest in engaging with the process of confession, but also a concomitant need to be seen as too 'lewide' and 'ignoraunt' to do so. This self-presentation stems at least in part from a need not to be seen as 'wel lettrid'. In the *Regiment*, Hoccleve's admission to being 'lettred' [or educated] 'sumdeel' led to the old man's intensive questioning about Hoccleve's relationship to heresy, and to his fears that Hoccleve 'Nat haddest standen in [his] feith aright' (391). In the *Series*, Thomas presents himself as hesitant to claim even partial status as a 'lettrid' man.

Reading Isidore's *Synonyma* does away with this hesitation, however: Thomas learns to frame his sickness and recovery as an instance of 'Goddis visitacion' (1.382), to position his recovery as 'the benefice of God'. As we have seen, Canon 21 of the Fourth Lateran Council discusses spiritual healing in terms of a 'skilful physician' who pours wine and oil into the patient's wounds. In doing so, it refers to the parable of the Good Samaritan (Lk. 10:25–37), wherein the Samaritan treats a 'semivivo' [half-alive] stranger's wounds with oil and wine (Lk. 10:30; 10:34). Hoccleve refers to this in 'Item de b*eat*a Virgi*ne*', another of the religious poems collected in MS HM 744 (fol. 33r): 'The oyle of thy mercy flowith eu*er*emore … / That licour, our wowndes greuous and sore / Serchith, and is our ful curacion, / That is the way of our sauuacion' (ll. 15, 17–19).[51] In the *Series*, Hoccleve summons to mind the process of divine healing by describing God as a 'leeche', or doctor, whose expertise in curing his wounds deserves to be recognized. The instance of being cured by this divine 'leeche' is, Thomas argues, 'a spectacle' that might magnify for others 'howe greet a lord is he' (2.96–98).

Langland uses the episode of the Good Samaritan in *Piers Plowman* to depict Christ, disguised as the Good Samaritan, encountering the 'semyuief': 'With wyn and with oyle his wounds he can lithe [soothe] / Enbaumed hym and boend his heued and on bayard hym sette / And ladde hym forth to *lavacrum-lex-dei* [the bath of the law of God]' (C.19.71–73). This gives way to a discussion of the necessity of receiving the sacraments of baptism and the Eucharist. Only with these can the half-alive man recover fully:

> Withoute the bloed of a barn he beth nat ysaued,
> The whiche barn mote nedes be born of a mayde
> And with the bloed of that barn enbaumed and ybaptised.
> And thouh he stand and steppe, riht stronge worth he neuere
> Til he haue eten al that barn and his bloed drunken
> (C.19.86–90)

This serves as an orthodox exegesis on the parable of the Good Samaritan: the wine and oil represent the communal wine (or blood) and baptismal oil respectively, and Langland presents the act of nourishing the 'semyuief' back to health in sacramental terms. Eating 'that barn' and drinking his 'bloed' proves of utmost importance: only by eating and drinking Christ can the half-alive man fully regain his strength. What proves so compelling about the conversational passages in the *Series* is that Hoccleve uses the language of confession and spiritual healing without ever approaching (or alluding to) the Eucharist. So, too, in the *Regiment*: the confessional dialogue gives way to a conspicuous display of *not* dining, *not* eating. In both poems, the Hoccleve character takes on the role of 'semyuief' – wounded either by the 'smert of thoght' (*RP* 106) or 'greuous [mental] venim' (*Series* 1.234). In depicting his return to health, Hoccleve suggests the process of confession, but the sacrament of the Eucharist remains ever absent, ever out of reach.

Nevertheless, the process of translation offers a means of cleansing comparable to that of confession and penance. In describing his motivations

[51] This poem is printed in *Hoccleve's Works*, pp. 285–89. I quote from this edition here.

for translating the 'Lerne for to Die' portion of Suso's *Horologium sapientiae*, Hoccleve imagines that the process of translation will purify him:

> And that haue I purposid to translate,
> If God his grace list therto me lene,
> Siþen he of helþe hath opened me þe ȝate,
> For where my soule is of vertu al lene,
> And þoruȝ my bodies gilte foule and vnclene,
> To clense it sumwhat by translacioun
> Of it shal be myn occupacioun.
>
> (2.211–17)

Hoccleve positions this translation as an extension and reflection of the instance of having been healed by God. It offers him the opportunity to cleanse his soul, which has become 'foule and vnclene' through his 'bodies gilte'. In other words, Hoccleve suggests that the act of translation will bring him as close as he comes within the *Series* to the 'second watir' that features in the moralization to the 'Tale of Jonathas' – the water that is otherwise withheld, the water 'wherof spak our sauueour, "I am the welle. Whoso drynkith of þat watir, he shal not thriste ageyn"' (5.721–23).

Much of what renders the act of translation virtuous, after all, is the capacity it has to help others. Hoccleve depicts his translation of 'Lerne for to Die' in these terms: 'For I not oonly but, as that I hope, / Many another wiȝt eek therby shal / His conscience tendirly groope, / And wiþ himsilfe acounte and reckon of al / That he hath in this liif wrouȝt … / While he tyme hath, and freish witt and vigour' (2.218–23). In the *Regiment*, similarly, Hoccleve underscores the mutual benefit that translation facilitates – it not only presents virtuous stories for others to use, but awakens the spirit and allows the writer to avoid sloth: 'The thewes vertuous that to it [the *Regiment*] longe / Wacchen my goost and letten him to [prevent him from] sleepe' (2145–46). Hoccleve indicates the sustenance that he derives from the act of translation at the end of the first section of the *Regiment*. After the old man declines Hoccleve's invitation to 'dine', Hoccleve goes 'hoom to mete' – home to eat dinner. Sated and nourished, he sleeps and then awakes the next morning to write: 'And penne and ynke and parchemeyn I hente, / … / I took corage, and whyles it was hoot, / Unto my lord the Prince thus I wroot:' (2013, 2015–16). Hoccleve's 'mete' gives way in this stanza to the 'hoot' writing at hand – the treatise that he will write for the prince. Eating and writing are aligned, and in this sense the *Regiment* offers its own form of sustenance, its own path to strength.

*

As we have seen in the past two chapters, the figure of Chaucer plays a key role in licensing the production of the *Regiment*. We will conclude our discussion by focusing more on the language that Hoccleve uses to present his version of Chaucer, and by exploring the way his presentation of Chaucer participates in the sacramental discourses we have been considering thus far.

Hoccleve demonstrates the effect that reading has on him in both the *Regiment* and the *Series* – the 'thewes vertuous' that Hoccleve encounters throughout the *Regiment* awaken his 'goost'; and, in the *Series*, reading Isidore's *Synonyma* enables Hoccleve to appreciate his suffering as a gift and to cast off his sorrow. In his first paean to Chaucer in the *Regiment*, Hoccleve describes his dead master in similarly energizing terms:

> O deeth, thow didest nat harm singuler
> In slaghtre of him, but al this land it smertith.
> But nathelees yit hastow no power
> His name slee; his hy vertu astertith
> Unslayn fro thee, which ay us lyfly hertith
> With bookes of his ornat endytyng
> That is to al this land enlumynyng.
>
> (1968–74)

In this passage, Chaucer's 'vertu' survives in the form of 'bookes of his ornat endytyng', which, in turn, vivify ('lyfly hertith') his readers. Hoccleve's use of 'vertu' here brings together a number of different meanings: it means at once 'strength' or 'force' (MED, sense 1); a 'talent' or 'skill' (sense 2); a 'life-sustaining force', as one might find in a plant (sense 3b); and a 'talismanic power' (sense 7a).[52] Hoccleve has already demonstrated the process of being vivified by a book, and here he aligns Chaucerian 'vertu' with this 'lyfly' property.[53]

Thomas Usk's use of the word 'lyfleich' provides a useful analogue here. Usk uses the word to bookend his *Testament of Love*: it is synonymous there with 'spiritual', and is used as a means of bridging philosophy and divine truth. In his prologue to the *Testament*, Usk writes: 'Utterly, these thynges be no dremes ne japes to throwe to hogges. It is lyfelyche meate

52 See *Middle English Dictionary Online*, s.v. 'vertu (n.)', http://ets.umdl.umich.edu/m/med/.

53 Cf. Deschamps's poetic elegy for Machaut, in which Deschamps writes, 'Vo noms sera precieuse relique' (no.124 in Deschamps's *Œuvres complètes*; line 6).

for chyldren of trouthe …' (Prol. 86–87).[54] The phrase recalls Boethius's *Consolation of Philosophy* I, pr. 2, in which Philosophy describes Boethius's process of being 'nourished' on her 'meats'. In his *Boece*, Chaucer translates the passage thus: '"Art nat thou he," quod sche, "that whilom, norissched with my melk and fostred with myne metes, were escaped and comyn to corage of a parfit man?"' (I. Pr. 2. 4–7). Usk's rendition also incorporates biblical allusion: Matthew 6:7's admonition not to throw pearls before swine; the term 'lyfelyche meate', which recalls the spiritual food (manna) that Moses and his brethren receive from heaven in I Corinthians 10:3; and the term 'chyldren of trouthe', which recalls Jesus's reference to his followers as 'children of light' (Lk. 16:8). Much as Chaucer strengthens his readers with 'bookes of his ornat endytyng', Usk claims that his text contains 'lyfelyche meate', to be used towards the reader's own spiritual strength. Usk returns to this idea (and to the word 'lyfelyche') at the end of his *Testament*:

> Also I praye that every man parfytly mowe knowe thorowe what intencion of herte this treatyse have I drawe. Howe was it that syghtful Manna in deserte to chyldren of Israel was spirytuel meate. Bodily also it was, for mennes bodies it norissheth. And yet neverthelater, Christ it signyfyed. Ryght so a jewel betokeneth a gemme and that is a stone vertuous or els a perle: Margarite a woman betokeneth grace, lernyng, or wisdom of God, or els holy church. If breed thorowe vertue is made holy flesshe, what is that our God saythe? It is the spyrite that yeveth lyfe; the flesshe of nothyng it profyteth. Flesshe is fleshly understandynge; flessh without grace and love naught is worth. The letter sleeth, the spyrit yeveth lyfelych understandyng.
>
> (3.1119–28)

Usk returns here to the notion of spiritual meat, connecting it explicitly to Christ's body. He then turns to the figure of Margarite to describe how he has developed her: as a symbol at once for grace, learning, the wisdom of God, and the Holy Church. The passage ends with Usk considering transubstantiation in the Eucharist, and the Spirit's ability to transform bread into 'holy flesshe'. Usk translates 2 Corinthians 3:6 – 'littera enim occidit, Spiritus autem vivificat'. He adapts the life-giving property of the Holy Spirit ['vivificat'] to emphasize the Spirit's role in proffering 'lyfelych

[54] Shoaf, *The Testament of Love*.

understandyng'. In doing so, he echoes the sense of Paul's epistle at 2 Corinthians 3:1–6: we understand not by ourselves, but by virtue of God, through the workings of the Holy Spirit.

It is fitting, given the sacramental context in which Usk uses the word 'lyfelych', that Hoccleve's only other use of the word 'lyfly' with 'vertu' occurs in a poetic invocation to the Holy Spirit. The words appear in 'Ad Spiritum Sanctum', which follows similar invocations to God and Christ in MS HM 744.[55] Hoccleve asks that the 'lyfly lemes' [vivifying beams] of the Spirit illuminate and invigorate our 'vertu bareyne':

> Kyndle eek and qwikne with thy lyfly lemes
> Our slouthly hertes / of vertu bareyne;
> Our soules perce with thy shynyng bemes.
> To thy godhede / thow vs knytte and cheyne.
> The ryuer of thy lust lat on vs reyne.
> Of worldly sweet venym souffre vs nat taaste,
> Ne our tyme in this world mis spende and waaste.
>
> (ll. 22–28)

Hoccleve uses 'lyfly' here to evoke a comparable quality to the power invested in Chaucerian 'vertu'. The Holy Spirit's 'lyfly lemes' serve to 'qwkne' (quicken) and 'kyndle' the 'slouthly hertes' of Hoccleve's readers. Chaucer's books, likewise, 'lyfly hertith' his readers – they invigorate, enliven, and hearten. In both presentations, such a process aligns with the spreading of light: the Holy Spirit pierces the reader's soul 'with … shynyng bemes'. Chaucer's 'vertu', on the other hand, illuminates the land ('is to al this land enlumynyng'). Hoccleve ends the stanza with a prayer that the Spirit might prevent him and his readers from misspending their time. Much as he positions translation in the *Regiment* as a means by which he awakens his spirit and avoids sloth, here the 'lyfly lemes' of the Spirit serve to inspire the reader away from sloth and towards virtuous activity.

The word 'lyueliche' is also used in Hoccleve's period to convey the living and life-giving properties of the Eucharist. For instance, in the Digby 102 poem 'Of the sacrament of the altere' (dated to the first quarter of the fifteenth century, making it contemporaneous with the *Regiment*), the poet writes: 'Lyueliche quyk bred is put forþ þis day'

55 This poem is printed in *Hoccleve's Works*, pp. 281–83. I quote from this edition here.

(l. 18).[56] The poem in question is a translation of 'Lauda Sion', which, as Helen Barr notes in her edition of the Digby poems, 'Pope Urban IV asked Thomas Aquinas to write in honour of Christ for the new feast of Corpus Christi'.[57] 'Lyueliche quyk bred' is a translation of the Latin phrase 'panis vivus et vitalis', where 'lyueliche' conveys the spirit of 'vivus'. The 'lyueliche quyk' quality of the Eucharistic bread stands in contrast to what the Digby poet calls the 'lamb al ded' – the roasted lamb that stands at the center of the Jewish Passover feast:

> In old lawe ȝe wyten how
> At estren þey eten a lamb al ded;
> Is ouer put in newe lawe now,
> At estre we eten quyk bred.
>
> (97–100)

The Digby poet's use of the word, in tandem with his use of the word 'quyk', cooperates with the purpose of the Corpus Christi feast, which is to centralize and heighten the Eucharist, and to emphasize the living quality of Christ's presence in the communal bread. In doing so, the feast positions the 'newe lawe' of Christianity against the 'old lawe' of Judaism by stressing the vital and vivifying nature of the Christian sacrament.

In endowing Chaucer with a 'lyfly' power, Hoccleve stresses the ability of Chaucer's books to strengthen and nourish their readers. Hoccleve later suggests that this 'lyfly' quality might prove not only energizing, but also transformative: in the portrait presentation stanzas, Hoccleve continues to refer to Chaucer in terms of 'lyflynesse', and he connects this quality to the image of Chaucer that he offers his readers:

> Althogh his lyf be qweynt, the resemblance
> Of him hath in me so fressh lyflynesse
> That to putte othir men in remembrance
> Of his persone, I have heere his liknesse
> Do make, to this ende, in soothfastnesse,
> That they that han of him lost thoght and mynde
> By this peynture may ageyn him fynde.
>
> (4992–98)

[56] Helen Barr suggests a date of 1413–14 for the Digby 102 poems. Barr, *Digby Poems*, 18.

[57] Ibid., 295.

Hoccleve puts himself forward as a vessel of 'lyflynesse' – a medium through whom Chaucer's own animating force reaches the reader.[58] As we saw in the last chapter, Hoccleve goes on to describe the process of engaging with images as a potentially transformative process: engaging with an image enables a change to take place within the viewer – 'Whan a thyng depeynt is / Or entaillid, if men take of it heede, / Thoght of the liknesse it wole in hem breede' (5003–05).[59] Communing with this image enables Chaucerian likeness to 'breede' in the given viewer. Shannon Gayk has discussed Hoccleve's presentation of the Chaucer image in terms of medieval optical theory, arguing that, in highlighting the reciprocity of reader and image – in which the reader gazes at the image and the image acts upon the reader – Hoccleve demonstrates a synthesis of medieval optical theories advocated by the philosopher Roger Bacon.[60] Furthermore, by comparing the process of viewing his image of Chaucer with the process of viewing an image of God (see ll. 4999–5003), and thereby having God's likeness 'breede' in the viewer, Hoccleve encourages his reader to compare these spiritual (as opposed to physical) transformations. As Gayk notes, the transformation that occurs when one internalizes an image of God and, thereby, 'breeds' a likeness of God, parallels the transformation enacted in the Eucharist: 'devotional images are powerful, Hoccleve implies, not primarily because of their mnemonic, exemplary, or pedagogical usefulness, but rather because they, like the Eucharist, enact a transformation in the willing recipient.'[61] The context for the word 'lyfly' that I have elaborated above emboldens Hoccleve's presentation: the word – used

[58] Hoccleve uses 'lyflynesse' on only one other occasion in the *Regiment*, and that use amplifies the sense of the word as 'animating force' or, in this case, 'soul': 'Evene as a soule is bodyes lyflynesse, / And whan that it is twynned from a wight / The herte is deed, so farith rightwisnesse' (2724–26).

[59] In the last chapter, we considered how these presentation stanzas – and their discussion of the role of images – contributed to the process of turning destructive thought into productive thought. In our present discussion, we focus rather on situating these lines with respect to the medieval theory of optics, and the *Regiment*'s concern with 'lyflynesse' and 'vertu'.

[60] In synthesizing the optical models of 'intromission' (in which the image enters the passive viewer) and 'extramission' (in which the viewer actively apprehends the image by sending out a visual beam), Bacon posited 'a reciprocal relationship between seer and seen' (Gayk, *Image, Text, and Religious Reform*, 52). For an overview of these concepts, see Michael Camille, 'Before the Gaze: The Internal Senses and Late Medieval Practices of Seeing', in *Visuality Before and Beyond the Renaissance: Seeing as Others Saw*, ed. Robert S. Nelson (Cambridge: Cambridge University Press, 2000), 197–223.

[61] Gayk, *Image, Text, and Religious Reform*, 52–53.

first to describe Chaucer's 'vertu', and then to describe the animating force that Hoccleve has internalized – is used elsewhere by Hoccleve to describe the actions of the Holy Spirit, and is used by the Digby poet and Usk to describe the living quality of the Eucharistic bread. The point is not to equate the Chaucer image with the Eucharist here, but rather to suggest the way in which it engages in a parallel process – a process whereby the reader actively takes in life by taking in the image; whereby this internalization enlivens the recipient; and whereby the recipient communes bodily with the image, sharing 'lyflynesse'.

The transformative element of this process is mutually constitutive, however, with the mnemonic element: engaging with the image, Hoccleve says, involves a process of bringing Chaucer back to 'thoght and mynde' (4997). The image serves here as a means to *memoria*, and in this respect too the image parallels the Eucharist: during the Last Supper, Christ offered the bread as consubstantial with his body and as a means to remembrance: 'Hoc est corpus meum, quod pro vobis datur: hoc facite in meam commemorationem' [This is my body, which is given for you. Do this in remembrance of me] (Lk. 22:19; cf. Mt. 26:26–29 & Mk. 14:22–25).[62] When the reader engages with the image he or she makes the 'likeness' of Chaucer within, and this process constitutes a bodying forth of Chaucer, a bringing of Chaucer – physically – to 'mynde'.[63]

As Mary Carruthers points out, however, the images involved in *memoria* need not be pictorial: 'the distinction we make between "verbal" and "visual" memory is not made by either ancient or medieval writers on memory; *memoria* is always a matter of images, both pictorial and graphic.'[64] We have already seen how Hoccleve brings the likeness of the crucified body to mind for Prince Henry within the *Regiment*: images of the wounded Christ resonated in the medieval period, as Michael Camille notes, not only because they appeared 'realistic', but rather because the 'emaciated body, the blood, the gaze of the suffering man/God carried

62 On the medieval use of *memoria*, see Mary Carruthers, *The Book of Memory: A Study of Memory in Medieval Culture*, 2nd ed. (Cambridge: Cambridge University Press, 2008).

63 Cf. Carruthers, *Book of Memory*, 68: 'memory, like thought and imagination, is also *vis*, an agent, a power, not just a receptacle'.

64 Mary J. Carruthers, 'Invention, Mnemonics, and Stylistic Ornament in *Psychomachia* and *Pearl*', in *The Endless Knot: Essays on Old and Middle English in Honor of Marie Borroff*, ed. M. Teresa Tavormina and R.F. Yeager (Woodbridge: Boydell and Brewer, 1995), 201–13 (202). Cf. Mary Carruthers, *The Craft of Thought: Meditation, Rhetoric, and the Making of Images, 400–1200* (Cambridge: Cambridge University Press, 1998), 122.

them physically into the mind'.[65] The visceral quality of wounds enables the process of internalization to take place; it provokes the process of embodiment, contemplation, and commemoration. Hoccleve illustrates this process in his invocations to God and Christ in MS HM 744. We have seen how Hoccleve describes the 'toren membres' and streaming blood of Christ in 'Inuocacio ad Patrem'. In the next poem, 'Ad filium', Hoccleve transitions from displaying these images of Christ to an internalization of such images.[66] The narrator absorbs Christ to the extent that he identifies with the wounds, and with the process of receiving the wounds:

> I am the wownde of al thy greuance;
> I am the cause of thyn occisioun,
> And of thy deeth / dessert / of thy vengeance
> I am also verray flagicioun;
> I causid thee thy greuous passioun;
> Of thy torment I am solicitour,
> Thow goddes sone / our Lord & Sauueour
>
> (ll. 8–14)

This allows the narrator to contemplate his own sinfulness, and then to transition, in the next poem, to a prayer for the Holy Spirit's guidance in enabling him to live a virtuous life. In the *Regiment*, by contrast, Hoccleve presents textual images of a wounded Christ and instructs his reader on how these images might be used – how they might effect their own spiritual transformations through demonstrations of peace, humility, and mercy. This also entails considering Christ's actions in the Gospels, where Christ acts out his exemplarity through his deeds.[67] In this sense, engagement with the image of Christ aligns with meditation on the texts that body Christ forth. With this in mind, we might consider what 'breeding' the 'likeness' of Chaucer means on a textual level – how the process of 'breeding' Chaucer interacts with actual Chaucerian texts.

---

65 Camille, 'Before the Gaze', 215. See also Suzannah Biernoff, *Sight and Embodiment in the Middle Ages* (Basingstoke: Palgrave, 2002), 144–49; Rubin, *Corpus Christi*, 308–10; Jeffrey F. Hamburger and Anne-Marie Bouche, eds., *The Mind's Eye: Art and Theological Argument in the Middle Ages* (Princeton, NJ: Princeton University Press, 2006).

66 This poem is included in *Hoccleve's Works*, pp. 279–81. I quote from this edition here.

67 See, for instance, *Regiment* ll. 3358–60: 'To mercy were hir hertes ay flexible; / Forwhy with mercy God shal qwyte hem wel, / Aftir the wordes write in the Gospel.'

In order to explore this question, we will return to the *Series*, and to that poem's opening stanza:

> Aftir þat heruest inned had hise sheues,
> And that the broun sesoun of Mihelmesse
> Was come, and gan the trees robbe of her leues,
> That grene had ben and in lusty freisshenesse,
> And hem into colour of ȝelownesse
> Had died and doun throwen vndirfoote,
> That chaunge sanke into myn herte roote.
>
> (1.1–7)

These lines have been read as a replaying of the opening lines of Chaucer's *Canterbury Tales*, albeit transposed into a minor key.[68] I have suggested that these lines indicate, given the broader context of the *Series*, a signal of remorse for the passing of a given period in the history of English *poesie*.[69] If we accept this as an allusion to the *Canterbury Tales*, then these lines indicate a textual transition from the spirited spring of Chaucer's rendition to the autumnal cast of Hoccleve's. This change manifests in the leaves themselves, which turn from green to yellow between lines 4 and 5; and which, in line 6, die and fall 'vndirfoote'. This change then moves from the external world to the internal body of the poet: 'That chaunge sanke into myn herte roote.' The narrator internalizes the very change he has just described – it 'sinks' into his heart. This change is simultaneously natural, emotional, and personal; and, insofar as it indicates a movement from the *Canterbury Tales* to the *Series*, it is also textual, located in the 'leues' of books. In this stanza, Hoccleve indicates a process of reading not unlike that of monastic *lectio divina*, wherein the words of the devotional text are internalized, chewed, digested, and then brought up in a new form.[70] These words transform in Hoccleve, and we experience them in this stanza *as* changed, but also as a meditation *on* change.

These twinned subjects – how a text can change a reader and how a text can change *in* a reader – recur repeatedly throughout the *Series*. We have

---

68 Knapp, *Bureaucratic Muse*, 164. I noted this description at the beginning of Chapter 1, where we first explored the stanza in question.

69 See Chapter 1.

70 On *lectio divina*, see Jean Leclercq, *The Love of Learning and the Desire for God: A Study of Monastic Culture*, trans. Catharine Misrahi (New York: Fordham University Press, 1982), especially Chapter 5.

noted how Thomas uses Isidore of Seville's *Synonyma* as a transformative text.[71] After having read it, he learns to treat his suffering as a blessing from God. The final lines of the 'Complaint' echo the final lines that Hoccleve quotes from the *Synonyma*: Isidore's 'Lorde, I me repente, and I the mercy crie' (1.371) infuses Hoccleve's final 'And vnto thi mercy and grace I calle' (1.414). The reader internalizes the text to the extent that he speaks through it, while also rendering it in a new form.[72] In the 'Dialogue', Hoccleve hopes that his translation of 'Lerne for to Die' will effect a specific transformation in his readers, too: 'Men may in þis tretiis hereaftirward, / If þat hym like rede and biholde, / Considre and see wel þat it is ful hard / Delaie acountis til liif begynne to colde' (2.225–27). Hoccleve positions the text to be used as a spur to penance. In inviting readers to 'rede and biholde' the translation, Hoccleve points up the dual nature of the text as a 'tretiis', and as an extended meditation on a textual image. Early in the narrative, Sapience (Eternal Wisdom) encourages the disciple to 'Beholde now the liknesse and figure / Of a man dyynge and talking with thee' (4.85–86). The disciple – and the reader, through him – 'beholds' this 'likeness' throughout the text, engaging with it as it despairs and as it becomes progressively more life-like. Steven Rozenski has shown how, in his translation, Hoccleve greatly amplifies and intensifies the imagery of Suso's Latin original, bringing this 'likeness' into sharper focus.[73] The dialogue between the disciple and 'th'ymage' escalates, until

[71] Given the context of our discussions of the *Roman de la Rose* in Chapter 2 and *Piers Plowman* in Chapter 4, it is important to note the variety of resonances that Hoccleve's 'dialogue with "Reason"' has in the 'Complaint': we might read Hoccleve's Reason in the light of the *Rose*'s character of Reason, as well as Langland's Reason – that character who (alongside Conscience) enables Will's self-description and self-defense in the C.5 *apologia*. Hoccleve's ability to change through 'reading Reason' here might be read, by extension, as an effect of wider poetic engagement.

[72] David Lawton has indicated the way in which Hoccleve uses Vulgate Psalm 30 (*Qui videbant me foras fugierunt a me*) to similar ends in his 'Complaint' – as a text that the reader/writer internalizes and revoices from his own standpoint, using the text to speak to his personal situation. In acting thus, Hoccleve embodies the text. See Lawton, 'Voice After Arundel', 144.

[73] Rozenski, 'Your Ensaumple'. On Hoccleve's treatment of the image, see also Christina von Nolcken, '"O, why ne had y lerned for to dye?": *Lerne for to Dye* and the Author's Death in Thomas Hoccleve's *Series*', *Essays in Medieval Studies* 10 (1993): 29–43; Simpson, *Reform and Cultural Revolution*, 429–34; Simpson, *Under the Hammer*, 78–83; Gayk, *Image, Text, and Religious Reform*, 74–82; Watt, *Making*, Chapter 5; Ashby Kinch, *Imago Mortis: Mediating Images of Death in Late Medieval Culture*, Visualising the Middle Ages (Leiden: Brill, 2013), Chapter 2.

at last the image dies, and the disciple is left unable to discern whether this death constitutes a death 'in deede' or 'in liknesse':[74]

> This sighte of deeth so sore me astoneth
> þat wite Y can vnnethe [scarcely], in soothfastnesse,
> But am in doute wher the soothe woneth –
> That is to meene, if this be in liknesse
> Or in deede, swich is my mazidnesse.
>
> (4.750–54)

This 'mazidnesse' proves ultimately transformative for the disciple: he reacts much as Thomas hopes his readers will react – by resolving not to postpone penance any longer (4.772), by realizing that he has been practicing willful blindness until this point (4.821–22), and by praying for help (4.799–800). The disciple's transformation results directly from the life-likeness of the image, and also from the intensity with which the image reveals his plight, and his 'mortel wownde', to the disciple (4.119).

To use Hoccleve's words, the disciple's engagement with the image provokes a 'chaunge' that sinks into his 'herte roote'. The transformative experience has an analogue in Hoccleve's reading of the *Synonyma*. It has a counterpoint, however, in Hoccleve's presentation of Prince Henry and John Badby in the *Regiment*:

> Also this noble prynce and worthy knyght –
> God qwyte him his charitable labour –
> Or any stikke kyndlid were or light,
> The sacrament, our blessid Sauveour,
> With reverence greet and hy honour,
> He fecche leet, this wrecche to converte,
> And make our feith to synken in his herte.
>
> (309–15)

The prince's failure in the *Regiment* stems from his inability to transform Badby – his inability to 'make our feith to synken in his herte'. The prince presents Badby with the sacrament, and he makes a display of acting as a 'mene' for his father, but Badby refuses to change. What is missing from this scene, in large part, is affective engagement: Badby is not being asked to invite Christ into his heart, to contemplate what virtues Christ

[74] As Simpson notes, 'the image is most fully alive as it's dying'. See Simpson, *Under the Hammer*, 82.

embodies, to meditate on the Passion, but rather to accept the church's specific definition of the sacrament. The *Series* and the *Regiment* proper, by contrast, are texts that illustrate the ability of vernacular poetry to enact change in the recipient. Hoccleve introduces his texts not as antidotes to heresy, but rather as ways of approaching spiritual wounds, and learning how to go about the process of healing such wounds. As such, these texts indicate how vernacular poetry might be used in a deeply divided, and deeply wounded, English church.

I suggested in Chapter 3 that Chaucer acts, on one level, as a figure for Hoccleve's read-knowledge in the *Regiment*. Chaucer's 'lyfly' aspect would then indicate the potential that *poesie* has to strengthen and enliven the individual Christian. Hoccleve positions himself as an intermediary for the 'lyfly' Chaucer image, much as Prince Henry acts as an intermediary in presenting the 'lyfly' Eucharist to Badby. Hoccleve 'do make' [causes to be made] the image of Chaucer, much as Henry 'fecche leet' [causes to be brought] the sacrament (314, 4996). The two presentations serve as bookends in the *Regiment* – one failed attempt at offering the 'lyfly' host to a recipient, and one more hopeful attempt to encourage the recipient to engage with a form of poetic 'lyflynesse'.

The *Regiment* and the *Series* feature a meditation on Hoccleve's limitations as a poet, and specifically on the subject matter that he feels comfortable approaching. But they also indicate ways around and *through* such subject matter. 'By commvnynge is the beste assay', Thomas says in the *Series* – 'I mene, to commvne of thingis mene' (1.217–18). Hoccleve's strength in the *Series*, as in the *Regiment*, lies in his ability to 'commvne of thingis mene' – both in his ability to focus on the details of everyday life, rather than heated and 'hy' subjects such as the nature of transubstantiation; and in his ability to entertain literary 'menes' – actual intermediaries such as Prince Henry, the Virgin, the old man, and Chaucer – as well as allusive discourses in which one can speak through 'menes', and can use 'menes' to create meaning. Such an approach indicates one path by which to engage with spiritual wounds both personal and communal – and it produces its own symbol, in 'Chaucer', around which to commune.

Conclusion: The Matter of Hocclevian Influence

In this study, I have put forward the idea that Hoccleve positions himself as a poetic mediator in his works – as an individual capable of mediating between otherwise disunited or contentious subjects, and also as the medium through which the figure of Chaucer is transformed and re-presented in the *Regiment*. Reading Hoccleve in this context allows us to see him as a middleman in the most virtuous sense: it presents a case not for Hoccleve attempting to 'usurp' Chaucer,[1] or betraying an anxiety of influence over his literary father,[2] but rather as a poet who toils to animate Chaucer as a moral authority. It is instructive, too, to read Hoccleve's late 'collected poems' manuscripts in this light: they might be seen as a compilation of poetic forms from which others might work, from the 'Cupid' poem to the *envoi*, from poems of Marian devotion to poems for political occasions, from rhyme royal to roundels.[3] This would put these manuscripts in the same category as Hoccleve's *Formulary*, which he was compiling in the same period, and in which Hoccleve compiled exemplary Privy Seal documents – or forms – from which future colleagues could work.[4] Hoccleve's *Regiment of Princes* and the *Series*, similarly, serve on one level as meditations on Hoccleve's poetic limits and as demonstrations of how Hoccleve transcends these limits: they teach

1 Knapp, *Bureaucratic Muse*, 14.

2 Spearing, *Medieval to Renaissance*; Lerer, *Chaucer and His Readers*. We examined Hoccleve in this context in the Introduction and Chapter 3 of the present study.

3 See San Marino, Huntington Library, MSS HM 111 and 744, reproduced in facsimile edition in Burrow and Doyle, *Facsimile*.

4 London, British Library, MS Additional 24062. On the dating of the autograph verse manuscripts, see Burrow and Doyle, *Facsimile*, xx–xxi. On the dating of Hoccleve's *Formulary*, see Burrow, *Thomas Hoccleve*, 26.

even as they preach. I have discussed both longer works in this context, and I have indicated how Hoccleve, in the *Regiment*, aligns his image of Chaucer with his more prudent, and more collegial, poetics – a poetics that warns its readers to practice prudence and discretion, and that uses careful and allusive language as a means to political and ecclesiastical commentary.

Among the first individuals to use Hocclevian poetry in his writing was George Ashby (d. 1475), who served for most of his career as a Signet clerk under Queen Margaret.[5] Ashby was imprisoned for his affiliation with the Lancastrians during the War of the Roses, and his *Complaint of a Prisoner in the Fleet 1463* – written during his imprisonment – echoes Hoccleve's *Series* on a number of levels.[6] It begins, for instance, with lines that rework the opening to Hoccleve's *Series* to speak to Ashby's specific situation:

> At the ende of somere, when wynter began,
> And trees, herbes, and flowres dyd fade,
> Blosteryng and blowyng, the gret wyndes than
> Threw doune the frutes with whyche they were lade,
> Levyng theym sone bare of that whyche they hade,
> Afore Myghelmas, that tyme of season,
> I was commyttyd geynst ryght and reason,
> Into a pryson …
>
> (1–8)[7]

---

5 On George Ashby's identity and career, see Josiah C. Wedgwood and Anne D. Holt, *History of Parliament, 1: Biographies of the Members of the Commons House, 1439–1509* (London: H.M. Stationery Office, 1936), 21–22; J. Otway-Ruthven, *The King's Secretary and the Signet Office in the XV Century* (Cambridge: Cambridge University Press, 1939); John Scattergood, 'The Date and Composition of George Ashby's Poems', *Leeds Studies in English* 21 (1990): 167–76; John Scattergood, 'George Ashby's Prisoner's Reflections and the Virtue of Patience', *Nottingham Medieval Studies* 37 (1993): 102–09; and Robert J. Meyer-Lee, 'Laureates and Beggars in Fifteenth-Century English Poetry: The Case of George Ashby', *Speculum* 79.3 (2004): 688–726.

6 Ethan Knapp mentions George Ashby in the context of Chaucer, Hoccleve, and Thomas Usk, as a civil servant with literary aspirations (*Bureaucratic Muse*, 6, 7, 30). However, he does not register Hoccleve's influence on Ashby's writing. He offers instead that 'unlike Lydgate, [Hoccleve] has no progeny' (11). Both David Lawton and Robert Meyer-Lee note Hoccleve's influence (see Lawton, 'Dullness and the Fifteenth Century', 772–73; Meyer-Lee, 'Laureates and Beggars', 702–06, 712–26). For Meyer-Lee, however, Hoccleve's influence on Ashby – paired with Ashby's failure to name Hoccleve as one of his poetic predecessors in *Active Policy of a Prince* – reflects ultimately on Hoccleve's failure to establish himself in English literary tradition. I present a much different reading of the Hoccleve–Ashby dynamic here.

7 George Ashby, 'Complaint of a Prisoner in the Fleet 1463', in *The Kingis Quair and*

Throughout the rest of the poem, Ashby echoes Hoccleve's concern that his fellows no longer acknowledge him (ll. 36–42);[8] and he uses the platform of complaint to state his name in full (l. 29)[9] and to describe his career in 'wrytyng', in a manner redolent of Hoccleve's self-presentation in the *Regiment* (ll. 57–70).[10] He echoes Hoccleve also in his message: he uses a Boethian framework to resituate his troubles as a blessing and, like Hoccleve, he frames his struggle in terms of gold being purged in a furnace (ll. 141–47).[11] This, it would seem, enables him to embrace his 'sharp persucicion':

> Wenest thow to have here perfeccion
> Of worldly joy, comfort, and delyces?
> Nay, bettyr ys sharp persecucion
> For thy synnes, offenses, and vyces,
> Kepyng pacience without malyces,
> Puttyng thy wyll to Goddes volunté,
> So thy spyryt may best in quyet be.
>
> (197–203)

As Hoccleve learns, through his reading of Isidore of Seville's *Synonyma*, to reinterpret his misfortune as a blessing from God, Ashby presents his imprisonment here as a means of aligning himself closer with God (in language, no less, that chimes with Hoccleve's personal motto (see l. 202)).[12] While Hoccleve's *Series* is not named within the poem, it would appear to have played a similar role for Ashby to Hoccleve's use of the *Synonyma*: the text presents Ashby with a means of reading, interpreting, and structuring his sufferings.

Ashby's discussion of having written the work for the spiritual benefit of others also bespeaks a characteristically Hocclevian *modus operandi*: in his

---

Other Prison Poems, ed. Linne R. Mooney and Mary-Jo Arn, TEAMS Middle English Texts (Kalamazoo, MI: Medieval Institute Publications, 2005). All quotations from Ashby's *Complaint* come from this edition.

8 Cf. *Series* 1.64–84.

9 Cf. *Series* 2.3, 2.10, 2.25, 2.199, 2.203, etc.

10 Cf. *Regiment* 988–1029.

11 Cf. the entirety of Hoccleve's 'Complaint'. For the metaphor of gold being purged in the furnace, see 1.358–59. As Roger Ellis notes, the image is a Biblical commonplace (cf. Prov. 17.3, 27.21, Ecclus. 2.5; see Ellis, *'My Compleinte'*, 130), but given the already established network of Hocclevian allusion in Ashby's piece, it is nevertheless instructive.

12 'Va ma voluntee [to God].' See Mooney, 'Some New Light', 317; Green and Knapp, 'Thomas Hoccleve's Seal', 319.

envoi, Ashby sends his poem in the direction of 'folk troubelyd and vexed grevously' to inspire them 'To kepe pacience thereyn joyously, / Redyng thys tretyse forth seryously …' (310, 312–13). In doing so, he takes a similar approach to Hoccleve in the *Series*, who positions his own 'Complaint' as a text through which others might learn to bear their sufferings proudly. Ashby clarifies that he undertakes the work not 'For worldly glory and thank to assume, / But vertu to encrese and lewdnes consume, / And namely to take trowble in suffraunce, / Paciently for deservyd penaunce' (318–22). Hoccleve positions himself similarly in the *Series* as a model for others, and as an individual through whom others might learn to re-examine their sufferings as blessings.[13] Ashby's poem suggests that at least one of Hoccleve's fifteenth-century readers experienced Hoccleve's poem in this way; indeed, in creating his own version of the poem, Ashby furthers the tradition of complaint and consolation that Hoccleve advanced with the *Series*.

Ashby's foregrounding of the virtue of patience in his poem comes hand in hand, as with Hoccleve, with a need for discretion. After inviting his reader to view life as a pilgrimage to Heaven, and to practice 'mekenes and werkes merytory',[14] Ashby redirects his reader towards the need to be 'wytty and dyscret':

> Thow canst nat be so pryvé ne secret
> But God ys there present and knoweth all thyng;
> Therfore be evyr wytty and dyscret,
> Nat for to do ne say Hym dysplesyng,
> But as thow woldest before Hym beyng.
> So by mekenes take all thyng for the best
> What that God sendeth, trouble or unrest.
>
> (211–17)

Ashby's exhortation to eschew secrecy and embrace instead wit and discretion chimes with Hoccleve's self-presentation as 'wys and waar' [wise and wary] in the *Regiment*, as well as his calls for prudence and

13 See *Series* 2.57–98.

14 The stanza in question recalls the prayer that Hoccleve attaches to the end of his Suso translation: 'the ixe lesson which is rad / In holy chirche vpon a[ll] halwen day' (4.925–6). See ll. 4.1007–12 in particular, which emphasize the necessity to practice good 'wirkes' in this life, and thereby 'cheese the bettre part'. For analogues to Ashby's description of life as a pilgrimage, see Chaucer's short poem 'Truth' (especially ll. 17–21); and 'The Knight's Tale', I.2848–49: 'This world nys but a thurghfare ful of wo, / And we been pilgrymes, passynge to and fro.'

discretion in the *Series*. The need to be 'wytty and dyscret' would seem to be less necessary before God, however, who 'knoweth all thyng', and more necessary before powerful secular men – those men before whom an individual such as Ashby might fear to say something 'dysplesyng'. We have seen how Hoccleve uses his 'Cupid' poem to comment allusively not on the pagan god, but rather on the deposition of Richard II and the accession of Henry IV.[15] And we have examined, in Chapter 5, the way in which Hoccleve aligns Prince Henry, if briefly, with God in the body of the *Regiment* – as a means of moving the prince to contemplate the ways in which he is not, in fact, a god. Here, Ashby would appear to use the conceit to direct his readers towards verbal prudence.

This passage has a parallel also in Hoccleve's *envoi* for Prince Henry in the *Regiment*. In the final stanza of the *envoi*, Hoccleve directs his book in how to approach Prince Henry. Here is the final stanza of the *envoi*, as it appears in London, British Library, MS Arundel 38 (c. 1411–12),[16] one of the earliest and most authoritative copies of the *Regiment*:

By seche hym of hys gracious noblesse
The holde excused of thyn innocence
Of endityng and wyþ hertes meeknesse
If any þyng the passe of negligence
By seche hym of mercy and indulgence
And that for thy good herte he be nouȝt foo
To the þat al seest of loues feruence
That knowyth he whom no þyng is hyd froo[17]

Hoccleve directs his book in how to keep from offending its intended recipient, and hopes that the prince will forgive any 'negligence' on the part of the book, seeing instead its 'good herte'. The final lines of the poem present an ambiguity, however: throughout the stanza 'he' and 'hym' refer only to Prince Henry – in lines 1 and 5 the book is told to 'by seche [beseech]' Henry and, in line 6, the 'he' that Hoccleve hopes will not become a 'foo' of the book is Henry. But the 'he' in the final line – 'whom no þyng is hyd froo' – is, in this rendition, uncertain. It opens up the question of whether this is He – i.e., God – or the 'he' that we have been referring to throughout – the prince. Hoccleve revises the *envoi* in

15 Chapter 2.

16 For the dating of MS Arundel 38 to 1411–12, see Blyth, *Regiment*, 15; Burrow, *Thomas Hoccleve*, 50.

17 MS Arundel 38, ff. 98r–98v.

MS HM 111 (c. 1422–26), remedying this ambiguity by replacing that final 'he' with 'God'.[18] In doing so, however, he admits the ambiguity with which he had initially imbued the pronoun.[19]

In Hoccleve's rendition, the alignment of 'Henry' with 'God' reflects back on the body of the *Regiment*, wherein Hoccleve has portrayed Henry using his secular power to exercise control in the ecclesiastical domain, and wherein Hoccleve had invited Henry, through Alexander, to question whether he is 'god, or man, or noght'. For Ashby, making God the focus of his stanza diverts attention from the fact that Ashby appears to be counseling discretion in a more general sense – or perhaps, more pointedly, counseling discretion as regards a specific individual. The focus on needing to talk as if one were 'before Hym beyng' indicates the need not to speak about the given individual, even in what would appear to be a discreet setting. It reflects back, for instance, on that 'lord' that Ashby refers to in the first lines of his poem, who had thrown him in prison with his 'gret myght' (ll. 9–10). Linne Mooney and Mary Jo-Arn suggest that this might have been the most powerful 'lord' of the period – the new Yorkist king, Edward of March.[20] The need to practice caution and patience would have been, in any case, a perennial concern for individuals such as Hoccleve and Ashby, and Ashby resounds Hoccleve's notes of caution here for a new audience, and in a new era.

Ashby's use of Hoccleve's poetry in his *Complaint of a Prisoner* indicates that poems such as the *Series* may have been intended, in part, for the benefit of peers in a similar situation to Hoccleve – men who made their

---

18 For the dating of MS HM 111 to the period between 1422 and 1426, see Burrow and Doyle, *Facsimile*, xx–xxi. This instance of Hoccleve including an *envoi*, on its own, in his 'collected poems' manuscript deserves further attention. (The piece in question is item 15 in MS HM 111.) On one level, Hoccleve may have wished to call attention to his most popular poem, the *Regiment of Princes*, and to forge a connection between these shorter poems and that longer poem. It may also indicate the extent to which Hoccleve considered such *envois* to be poems in their own right – with their own aspects of witty wordplay and useful ambiguity. In any case, it is telling that Hoccleve seized the opportunity to copy this particular *envoi*, and to remedy, therein, this particular ambiguity – replacing 'he' with 'God'. Hoccleve makes only two other changes to the *envoi*, and both also appear in the final stanza – he substitutes 'humblesse' for 'meeknesse' in the third line, and 'wil' for 'herte' in the sixth line. Charles Blyth notes these changes in *Regiment*, 252.

19 R.F. Yeager presents a similar reading of the end of Chaucer's 'Complaint to his Purse' in Yeager, 'Chaucer's "To His Purse"', 413. Indeed, Chaucer's poem may have influenced Hoccleve's presentation in his *envoi* for the *Regiment*.

20 See Mooney and Arn, 'Complaint of a Prisoner', note to line 9.

living by writing in service of the crown, who had to navigate factional politics, and who, by extension, needed consolation or advice in moments of particular political friction.[21] These men made a career writing letters in the service of the crown, and in one sense Hoccleve's poems might be seen as exemplars for a different type of writing – a discourse that enables consolation, and offers its readers a means of contemplating the virtues of discretion and patience, while also demonstrating the virtues of allusive and suggestive language. When Ashby writes his *speculum principis*, *Active Policy of a Prince*, he names Chaucer, Gower, and Lydgate as the 'Primier poetes of this nacion', and he does so using Hoccleve's 'first finder' terminology:

> Maisters Gower, Chauucer & Lydgate,
> Primier poetes of this nacion,
> Embelysshing oure englisshe tendure algate,
> Firste finders to oure consolacion
> Off fresshe, douce englisshe and formacion
> Of newe balades, not vsed before,
> By whome we all may haue lernyng and lore.
>
> (1–7)[22]

This stanza betrays Hocclevian influence not only in positioning these three poets as 'Firste finders' but, indeed, in the ability to position English poets – and Chaucer in particular – in such an exemplary and exalted way. As we have seen, in the *Regiment* Hoccleve recreates Chaucer so that he can serve as an unquestionable moral and intellectual authority. He then offers his version of Chaucer to the reader in the form of his 'peynture'. What Hoccleve offers, in part, is a form – an authorizing mechanism with which English vernacular writers can speak authoritatively. That Hoccleve is missing from Ashby's triumvirate should not necessarily be a mystery:[23] Hoccleve effaces his own identity in the *Regiment* even as he creates it; Chaucer's exemplarity is countered by the pained and wounded Hoccleve, who highlights his role

---

[21] Linne Mooney and Estelle Stubbs highlight the relationship between factional politics and the clerks they examine in *Scribes and the City*. See especially pp. 137–40.

[22] *Active Policy of a Prince* is collected in *George Ashby's Poems*, ed. Mary Bateson, EETS, E.S. 76 (London: Oxford University Press for the Early English Text Society, 1965).

[23] Meyer-Lee poses this question in 'Laureates and Beggars', and answers it by emphasizing Lydgate's success in establishing himself as 'unofficial poet laureate of the Lancastrian dynasty', whereas Hoccleve had failed to do so. See Meyer-Lee, 'Laureates and Beggars', 715. Hoccleve's exclusion from the triumvirate therefore serves to demonstrate, for Meyer-Lee, Lydgate's comparative success.

as an intermediary and a maker, rather than as a potential laureate. The poems of Hoccleve's Huntington manuscripts and the poems included in the *Series* do not bespeak an individual who uses the final years of his life to enhance his worldly fame, but rather one who focuses his energies on producing literature that might plausibly benefit others. 'Hoccleve' gives way to 'Thomas' in the *Series*, and the language of literary fame (Chaucer's fame) gives way to the language of consolation, virtue, and prayer (for use by Hoccleve's readers).[24] In Ashby, we see one reader who put to use the literary 'forms' that Hoccleve had created. That Hoccleve is not credited as a literary forefather might speak to his reputation as, foremost, a Privy Seal clerk and a maker of literary forms. His influence on the poetics of late medieval consolation and on the creation of Chaucer as a literary celebrity, though unattributed, proves no less evident to the close reader.

The version of Chaucer that Hoccleve renders in the *Regiment* enjoys, after all, a long-lasting existence of its own beyond the *Regiment*. As we have seen, Hoccleve's presentation stanzas in the *Regiment* suggest the way in which readers should use the image as a means of 'breeding' the likeness of Chaucer. One of the first individuals to 'breed' this version of

---

[24] The narrative of Hoccleve's life and career, as put forward by Bowers and Meyer-Lee, emphasizes the role that mental illness plays in the last decade of the author's life, and in his failure to achieve the status that Lydgate achieves (Bowers, 'Politics of Tradition', 359–60; Meyer-Lee, *Poets and Power*, 116–23, a section entitled 'The Selfhood of the Failed Laureate: "The Series"'). Meyer-Lee sees the *Series* as representing, on one level, 'a longing for public restoration following a failure as Lancastrian poet' (118). Bowers speaks of Hoccleve's self-presentation in the *Series* as if it were not self-conscious: he notes that Hoccleve might have just 'gloss[ed] over this episode of madness'. Because Hoccleve chose to dwell on the episode, however, his 'proclamations tended to have the … effect of fostering a public image in ways that were profoundly negative'. For Bowers, this offers 'one explanation why Hoccleve was quickly excluded from a literary genealogy that he himself had done so much to create' (360). We should keep in mind, however, that in the *Series* Hoccleve indicates (through the Friend) his self-awareness regarding the implications of his final poetic project: he acknowledges that publishing a poem that recounts personal trauma (2.52) will inevitably draw attention to such trauma. Having established this, he emphasizes the devotional focus of the poetic project and proceeds in this vein. As we have seen throughout this study, the status of Hoccleve's 'wildhede' as metonymic of the state of ecclesiastical division, and the attempt at reform 'in head and members', offers one means through which this episode could have afforded its readers wider meaning. This understanding of Hoccleve's persona falls in line with the Hoccleve we see in the *Regiment*, as well: as a writer who emphasizes his own bodily and mental sacrifice towards virtuous ends (in that case, so that Chaucer himself might enjoy a status of moral and intellectual exemplarity). He thereby cultivates his role as poetic mediator.

Chaucer within his own poetry appears to be John Lydgate, who presents Chaucer in very similar terms in his *Life of Our Lady*. Robert Meyer-Lee has recently suggested a date of 1421 for the composition of Lydgate's *Life of Our Lady*, which would make it contemporary with Hoccleve's *Series*.[25] Here is Lydgate's first mention of Chaucer in the poem:

> And eke my maister Chauser is ygrave,
> The noble Rethor, poete of Brytayne,
> That worthy was the laurer to haue
> Of poetrye, and the palme atteyne;
> That made firste to distille and rayne
> The golde dewe dropes of speche and eloquence
> Into our tunge thurgh his excellence,
>
> And fonde the floures firste of Retoryke,
> Our Rude speche only to enlumyne;
> That in our tunge, was neuere noon hym like.
>
> (2.1628–37)[26]

Like Hoccleve, Lydgate introduces Chaucer by way of an elegiac line (cf. 'But, weleaway … / That the honour of Englissh tonge is deed' (*RP* 1958–59)). Lydgate's phrase, 'found the floures firste of Retoryke', recalls Hoccleve's reference to Chaucer as both '*flour* of eloquence' and '*first fyndere* of our fair langage' in the *Regiment* (1962, 4978); and, furthermore, the language of illumination bridges the two presentations of Chaucer in the *Regiment* and *Life of Our Lady*: Chaucer 'enlumyne[s]' English in Lydgate's rendition, whereas, in the *Regiment*, Chaucer's books are 'enlumynyng' to 'al this land' (1974). Lydgate also stresses Chaucer's singularity ('was neuere noon hym like'), as Hoccleve does throughout the *Regiment* (e.g., 'this yle / May nevere man foorth brynge lyk to thee' (2103–04)).[27]

---

25 Robert J. Meyer-Lee, 'The Emergence of the Literary in John Lydgate's *Life of Our Lady*', *Journal of English and Germanic Philology* 109.3 (2010): 322–48 (340–41). Derek Pearsall suggests a date of c. 1415–22 for the poem (Pearsall, *Bio-Bibliography*, 50). In any case, the poem would have been written after Hoccleve's *Regiment*.

26 All *Life of Our Lady* quotations are from *A Critical Edition of John Lydgate's 'Life of Our Lady'*, ed. Joseph A. Lauritis, Ralph A. Klinefelter, and Vernon F. Gallagher (Pittsburgh, PA: Duquesne Univ. Press, 1961). I follow the amendments to the punctuation in this edition carried out in Meyer-Lee, 'Emergence of the Literary'.

27 Meyer-Lee notes in passing that one aspect of Lydgate's presentation of Chaucer in *Life of Our Lady* might have been inspired by Hoccleve, but does not dwell on this point. See Meyer-Lee, 'Emergence of the Literary', 329. Mary Flannery discusses

Lydgate also recalls Hoccleve's presentation of Chaucer, however, in endowing Chaucer with an animating force that the given writer internalizes. As we saw in Chapter 5, Hoccleve describes Chaucerian 'vertu' as having a 'lyfly' effect on its readers; likewise, when presenting his Chaucer image, Hoccleve depicts himself as having internalized Chaucer's 'lyflynesse' and, therefore, as being capable of producing the likeness of Chaucer for his readers. Hoccleve's presentation, as we have seen, is para-religious, insofar as Hoccleve compares his image of Chaucer to the images of 'God and … his seintes' that exist in churches, and insofar as Hoccleve presents his image of Chaucer by way of an invocation to the Virgin Mary. Lydgate's contribution in the *Life of Our Lady* is to make this religious connotation not implicit, but explicit, and to insinuate himself – as a Benedictine monk – into this matrix of divine animation and inspiration.[28] Lydgate aligns his ability to write with the Virgin Mary's production of the 'golde dewe of … grace' early in the poem:[29]

So late the golde dewe of thy grace fall
Into my breste, like skales fayre and white,
Me to enspyre of that I wolde endyte,
With thylke bame, sent downe by miracle,
Whan the hooly goost the made his habitacle;

And the licour of thy grace shede
Into my penne, t'enlumyne this dite

(1.52–58)

Lydgate positions himself here as a medium of divine inspiration, receiving the Virgin's 'golde dewe' and then using it to write his poem. Chaucer figures, by extension, as Lydgate's predecessor in this respect, insofar as he produces the 'golde dewe' of eloquence through which English becomes a language worthy of laureate poetics.[30]

Lydgate's approach to fame, in conversation with Chaucer's approach, in her recent monograph on Lydgate. She does not, however, entertain the question of whether Lydgate was influenced by Hoccleve on his attitudes towards fame. See Mary Flannery, *John Lydgate and the Poetics of Fame* (Cambridge: D.S. Brewer, 2012).

28 For an overview of Lydgate's career as a Benedictine monk, see Pearsall, *Bio-Bibliography*. See also Derek Pearsall, *John Lydgate*, Poets of the Later Middle Ages (London: Routledge and Kegan Paul, 1970).

29 Note also the 'daring parallel' established between Lydgate and the Virgin in Book II. See Philippa Hardman, 'Lydgate's *Life of Our Lady*: A Text in Transition', *MÆ* 65 (1996): 248–68 (250–51).

30 Meyer-Lee reads the Virgin's 'golde dewe' of grace in the context of Chaucer's 'golde

Whereas Hoccleve repositions Chaucer in order to proceed with the writing of the *Regiment* under the auspices of a credible and singular moral authority, Lydgate positions Chaucer here within a conspicuously Christian context in order to highlight his own ability to bridge the gap between the church and *poesie*. In Lydgate's rendition, however, Chaucer connects to divine inspiration by extension, whereas Lydgate positions himself to receive the 'golde dewe of [the Virgin's] grace' directly. In doing so, he emphasizes his specific role as a professional religious. Lydgate can claim divine inspiration for himself by virtue of the fact that he belongs to a monastic house, and he derives his authority from his position in that house.[31] This becomes apparent in John Shirley's colophons, in which Shirley positions Lydgate as a conspicuously moral poet:

His rymyng is so moralysed
That hym aught wel be solempneysed
Of all oure engelishe nacion
For his famus translacyon
Of this booke and of other mo[32]

Shirley recommends Lydgate on the basis that his poetry is 'moralysed'. Lydgate also proves conspicuously religious in his appearance, however, and Shirley's colophons dwell on this aspect of Lydgate's presentation:

Whos complaynt is al in balade
Þat daun Johan of Bury made
Lydegate þe Munk cloþed in blacke
In his makyng þer is no lacke
And thankeþe daun Johan for his peyne
Þat to plese gentyles is right feyne
Boþe with his laboure and his goode
God wolde of nobles he hade ful his hoode[33]

dewe dropes' of eloquence in 'Emergence of the Literary', 328–29.

31 Lydgate's self-presentation is also deeply informed by his processing of Italian humanists such as Boccaccio. 'Indebted to humanist thinking on poetic identity', he proves 'less uneasy with the idea of the "poet as theologian" topos'. See Gillespie, 'Authorship', 146–48. See also Flannery, *Lydgate and the Poetics of Fame*.

32 Margaret Connolly, *John Shirley: Book Production and the Noble Household in Fifteenth-Century England* (Aldershot: Ashgate, 1998), 209, ll. 31–35.

33 Ibid., 208, ll. 79–86.

The exemplary nature of Lydgate's 'makyng' is reflected in his status as 'Munk'; and Shirley emphasizes the physical accoutrements that render his exemplarity visible: he is 'cloþed in blacke' and has a 'hoode'. These aspects combine to create an authoritative picture of Lydgate, much as the rosary and black cloak with which Hoccleve ornaments Chaucer in his image reflect the poet's literary authority as proceeding from religious devotion.[34] Indeed, Shirley's description here points up the similarity between Lydgate's self-presentation and Hoccleve's presentation of Chaucer in the *Regiment*. It raises the question of whether Hoccleve's Chaucer not only inspired Lydgate to present Chaucer in a more reverent form in his *Life of Our Lady*, but also offered a model for Lydgate as he considered his own self-presentation. In contrast to John Walton's presentation of Chaucer in the prologue to his *Consolation of Philosophy* (which we explored in Chapter 3), Hoccleve harmonizes the figure of Chaucer with the concept of orthodox religious devotion.[35] Lydgate's *Life of Our Lady* indicates the next step in this progression – the step beyond the *Regiment* – wherein a professional religious accepts a 'moral' Chaucer, but also enters him more conspicuously into the orthodox framework of the church, and indicates his own official position, as a monk, within this religious framework.[36]

---

34 As W.H.E. Sweet notes, in the Cambridge University Library, MS Kk. 5.30 copy of the *Troy Book*, Lydgate is known throughout not by his proper name but simply as 'the monk'. In some respects, Lydgate was known to his contemporaries as much through his identity as a monk as by his name. See W.H.E. Sweet, 'Lydgate's Retraction and "his resorte to his religyoun"', in Gillespie and Ghosh, *After Arundel*, 343–59 (344). Sweet argues in this piece that, in his later years, Lydgate undergoes a reawakening of religious purpose and implicitly rejects his earlier 'secular and laureate poems' (359). If we read Lydgate's self-presentation as religious laureate as inspired by Hoccleve's presentation of Chaucer in the *Regiment*, Hoccleve's poem might be seen as 'dangerous' for Lydgate, to the extent that it provides the means for Lydgate to initially access this hybrid authority.

35 Stephen Hawes's *Pastime of Pleasure* (c. 1509) figures a moral Chaucer in terms that bear a striking resemblance to Hoccleve's presentation – particularly as we explored it in Chapter 5, in the context of Hoccleve's religious verse: 'Kyndlynge our hertes with the fyry leames / Of morall vertue' (1321–22), 'Our vyces to clense' (1320). (Stephen Hawes, *The Pastime of Pleasure*, ed. William Edward Mead, EETS, O.S. 173 (London: Oxford University Press for the Early English Text Society, 1928).)

36 This should raise anew the question of Hoccleve's role in implementing the figure of 'moral Chaucer' that finds a variety of expressions throughout English literary history. Jennifer Summit argues that the inclusion of Christine de Pizan's *Morall Prouerbes* (*Proverbes moraulx*) in Richard Pynson's 1526 edition of *The Boke of Fame, made by Geffray Chaucer: with Dyuers other of his Workes* denotes an appropriation of Christinian identity in the interest of enabling Chaucer's identity as a moralist

As I stated in Chapter 3, one notable aspect of Hoccleve's presentation of Chaucer is the poet's ability to create a setting in which Chaucerian authority is unquestioned and unquestionable – and in which the version of Chaucer that Hoccleve puts forth appears as if he has always enjoyed this eminent reputation. The extent to which this Chaucer becomes linked to a historical Chaucer becomes evident when Nicholas Brigham, a royal servant, uses a rendition of Hoccleve's Chaucer to adorn Chaucer's tomb during the poet's reburial in 1556.[37] Derek Pearsall argues persuasively that Brigham designed the new tomb as 'part of [a] larger programme of counter-reformation, a move to reappropriate England's greatest poet to the traditional faith' during the reign of – and likely under the encouragement of – Queen Mary.[38] The reburial falls in the middle of Queen Mary's short reign (1553–58) and reflects an initiative to reinstate Catholic Christianity in the face of reformist pressures. Like Hoccleve (and Ashby), Brigham was a civil servant with literary ambitions: he served as an Exchequer official and was also known as a Latin scholar and antiquarian. Brigham owned an extensive collection of manuscripts containing some seventy medieval authors, including, notably, Hoccleve's *Regiment of Princes*.[39] Hoccleve would have set the precedent for Brigham as a royal servant who undertook the task of presenting a sober and devout iteration of Chaucer. In perpetuating Hoccleve's image of Chaucer, Brigham can

(*Lost Property*, 81–93). We should note Hoccleve's precedent in blending Christinian and Chaucerian authority in the *Epistle* and his role in constructing a 'moral' Chaucer in the *Regiment*. See also Theresa Coletti, '"Paths of Long Study": Reading Chaucer and Christine de Pizan in Tandem', *SAC* 28 (2006): 1–40 on the Chaucer–Christine dynamic (Coletti notes that the inclusion of Lydgate's *Consulo Quisquis Eris* ('Prouerbes by Lydgate') in Pynson's *Boke* plays a similar role to Christine's *Morall Prouerbes* (30)). On Pynson's *Boke of Fame*, see also Julia Boffey, 'Richard Pynson's *Book of Fame* and the *Letter of Dido*', *Viator* 19 (1988): 339–53. We should also note the more direct role that Hoccleve's own Christinian and religious poetry plays in shaping Chaucer's corpus: Hoccleve's 'Miracle of the Virgin' is included, as 'The Ploughman's Tale', in the version of the *Canterbury Tales* in Oxford, Christ Church, MS 152; and Hoccleve's *Epistle* was collected in Thynne's 1532 edition of Chaucer's works (Burrow, *Thomas Hoccleve*, 53–54). For a case study in Chaucerian misattribution and evidence of the 'general tendency to regard Chaucer as a source of wisdom', see also Julia Boffey, 'Proverbial Chaucer and the Chaucer Canon', in *Reading from the Margins: Textual Studies, Chaucer, and Medieval Literature*, ed. Seth Lerer (San Marino, CA: Huntington Library, 1996), 37–47 (46).

37 For a comprehensive account of the reburial, see Derek Pearsall, 'Chaucer's Tomb: The Politics of Reburial', *MÆ* 64 (1995): 51–73.

38 Ibid., 62.

39 Ibid., 62–63.

Figure 7. Chaucer's tomb in Westminster Abbey, as engraved in Elias Ashmole, *Theatrum Chemicum Britannicarum* (1652).

be seen to use the image as Hoccleve suggests it be used in the *Regiment*: as a means to *memoria* and as a way of bodying the poet forth.[40]

[40] Pearsall notes in his study of Brigham's reburial that 'Brigham uses the Chaucer portrait derived from the Hoccleve *Regement of Princes* tradition', and argues that Brigham uses the portrait in much the same way that Hoccleve does, insofar as both individuals assert 'religious orthodoxy' in their positioning of England's literary father. See Pearsall, 'Politics of Reburial', 66. Pearsall points out that 'the presence of the rosary in Chaucer's left hand in the Hoccleve picture would obviously lend itself well to Brigham's purpose of re-Catholicizing Chaucer' (72). While the existing engravings of Brigham's version of the image do not show Chaucer holding the rosary, Pearsall suggests that the rosary may have been part of the original painting.

As with Hoccleve's *Regiment*, Brigham's presentation of Chaucer allows him to inscribe his own name, and thereby to record his own role in undertaking the labor of 'making' Chaucer. Here is a transcription of Brigham's dedication, as rendered in Elias Ashmole's engraving of the tomb:

M.S.
Qui fuit Anglorum vates ter maximus olim
Galfridus Chaucer conditur hoc tumulo
Annum si quaeras Domini, si tempora vitae
Ecce notae subsunt quae tibi cuncta notant.
25 Octobris 1400
Aerumnarum requies mors.
N.Brigham hos fecit Musarum nomine sumptus
1556

[Sacred to the Shades/Memory [M(anibus)/M(emoriae) S(acrum)]. He who was once the thrice greatest English poet, Geoffrey Chaucer, is buried in this grave; if you ask the year of the Lord, the period of his life, look at what is written below, which tells you all. / 25 October 1400 / Death is rest from afflictions. / N. Brigham undertook these costs in the name of the Muses / 1556][41]

Brigham's presentation recalls Hoccleve's in the *Regiment*: the image of Chaucer, clad in his black robe, gestures towards the text and, in doing so, presides over his own dedication.[42] Brigham's text draws attention to Chaucer's body, buried in the grave before the viewer, and the image of Chaucer presented here allows the viewer to remember the poet in living form. The appearance of Brigham's own name in the dedication – as with Hoccleve's self-naming in the *Regiment* – records his role as a virtuous intermediary, and as the means through which this virtuous labor was accomplished.

Brigham's use of the Chaucer image also highlights one of Hoccleve's main contributions to the perpetuation of Chaucer and, indeed, to the advancement of English portraiture: accurate embodiment. As Derek Pearsall points out, Hoccleve's life-like depiction of Chaucer – his ability to portray Chaucer three-dimensionally and accurately – played against the artistic

41 Ibid., 59, 71.

42 On the variations in transcriptions of the original inscriptions, see Joseph A. Dane and Alexandra Gillespie, 'Back at Chaucer's Tomb – Inscriptions in Two Early Copies of Chaucer's *Workes*', *Studies in Bibliography* 52 (1999): 89–96.

conventions of his age: 'it must be emphasized what an early date this is for a portrait to be and to be claimed as an accurate likeness.' Pearsall goes on to say that Hoccleve '"invented" English portraiture' with his image of Chaucer.[43] R.F. Yeager notes how stunning this accurate portrayal would have appeared for readers of Hoccleve's period – 'its physical immediacy, its embodied presence' would have been 'a startling discovery, as one of the first – if not *the* first – portraits from life that they were likely to have encountered in a manuscript'.[44] Yeager compares the experience of viewing the image to experiencing a 'revenant' Chaucer.[45] Brigham's use of the portrait can be seen to descend from this presentation: it offers a living, three-dimensional Chaucer in the wake of Chaucer's death. It invites the viewer to engage in Chaucer's 'lyflynesse' as the given viewer engages with the image.[46]

Hoccleve's focus on three-dimensional embodiment is not incidental to his portrayal of Chaucer, however, but rather a recurring feature in his poetry. As we saw in Chapters 4 and 5, Hoccleve's self-presentation proves exceptionally specific for the period – from the biographical details he offers to his description of wounds that are both mental and physical. In Chapter 5, we explored Hoccleve's comparison of his Chaucer image to devotional images of 'God and ... his seintes'; I suggested that Hoccleve's inclusion of textual images that foreground his own suffering as a writer compare, likewise, to textual images of Christ's suffering throughout the *Regiment*. Michael Camille has noted that images of the wounded Christ proved effective for the medieval viewer in large part because the 'emaciated body, the blood, the gaze of the suffering man/God carried them physically into the mind'.[47] Hoccleve's depiction of his own wounds, likewise, enables him to be carried physically into his readers' minds. (This proves equally true today, as attested by the continuing focus on the nature of Hoccleve's mental illness in the *Series*, and the concomitant interest in Hoccleve's description of the pains of being a writer in the *Regiment*.[48]) As we have

---

43 Pearsall, *Life of Geoffrey Chaucer*, 287–88.

44 Yeager, 'Death Is a Lady', 177.

45 Ibid., 162.

46 Hoccleve's image of Chaucer enjoys a long afterlife in manuscript illumination and individual portraiture in the centuries after the *Regiment* – Brigham's use of the image is but one example. For a survey of images that descend from Hoccleve's Chaucer image, see 'Appendix I' in Pearsall, *Life of Geoffrey Chaucer*.

47 Camille, 'Before the Gaze', 215.

48 The criticism dealing with the nature and context of the Thomas-narrator's 'wildhede' is vast. See, for example, Stephen Medcalf, 'Inner and Outer', in *The Later Middle Ages, The Context of English Literature*, ed. Medcalf (London: Methuen, 1981), 108–71; Stephan Kohl, 'More than Virtues and Vices: Self-Analysis in Hoccleve's

seen, Hoccleve's religious verse focuses in large part on the humanity of Christ and on the meaning and function of Christ's wounds. Hoccleve's self-presentation in the *Regiment* and the *Series* may plausibly derive from such a devotional focus, and from Hoccleve's desire to use his own body – and his own life – as a 'mirror' for Christian devotion.

The centrality of embodiment to Hocclevian poetics appears to have been evident to one early reader of Hoccleve's poetry in particular – the maker of the earliest and most authoritative scribal copy of the *Series*: Oxford, Bodleian Library, MS Selden supra 53.[49] This manuscript includes both the *Regiment* and the *Series*, and includes a three-dimensional image not of Chaucer but of the disciple and the dying man featured in Hoccleve's 'Lerne for to Die' (Figure 8). The flowing fuchsia gown, the prominent ribs of the bedridden man, the three-dimensionality of legs shifting beneath the bed covers, the bed jutting beyond the frame and into the text – all of these features give the image a life-likeness that surpasses even the Chaucer portrait. This manuscript has been dated by John Burrow to early in the second quarter of the fifteenth century.[50] Hoccleve was alive until 1426, so while it is possible that he had a role in the production of the manuscript, it is equally possible that the manuscript was undertaken after his death.[51] Whether this image was produced at the author's instigation or at the instigation of the manuscript's non-authorial overseer, it serves as a fitting complement to Hoccleve's poem: the poem depicts the process through which a disciple engages with a life-like 'image' of a dying man and is thereby moved to self-reflection and penance. This three-dimensional miniature affords the reader first-hand experience with such a life-like

"Autobiographies"', *Fifteenth-Century Studies* 14 (1988): 115–27; Gordon Claridge, Ruth Pryor, and Gwen Watkins, *Sounds from the Bell Jar: Ten Psychotic Authors* (London: Macmillan, 1990), 62–67, 69–70; James Simpson, 'Madness and Texts: Hoccleve's *Series*', in *Chaucer and Fifteenth-Century Poetry*, ed. Julia Boffey and Janet Cowen (King's College London: Centre for Late Antique and Medieval Studies, 1991), 15–29; Richard Lawes, 'Psychological Disorder and the Autobiographical Impulse in Julian of Norwich, Margery Kempe and Thomas Hoccleve', in *Writing Religious Women: Female Spiritual and Textual Practices in Late Medieval England*, ed. Denis Renevey and Christiania Whitehead (Cardiff: University of Wales Press, 2000), 217–43. For criticism that considers the physicality of Hoccleve's self-presentation as 'wryter' in the *Regiment*, see especially Hasler, 'Unregimented Body'; Perkins, *Hoccleve's Regiment*, 143–50; Knapp, *Bureaucratic Muse*, 83–93.

49 On MS Selden supra 53, see Burrow, *Complaint and Dialogue*, xi–xii; Watt, *Making*, Chapter 5.

50 Burrow, *Complaint and Dialogue*, xii.

51 Burrow, *Thomas Hoccleve*, 29–30.

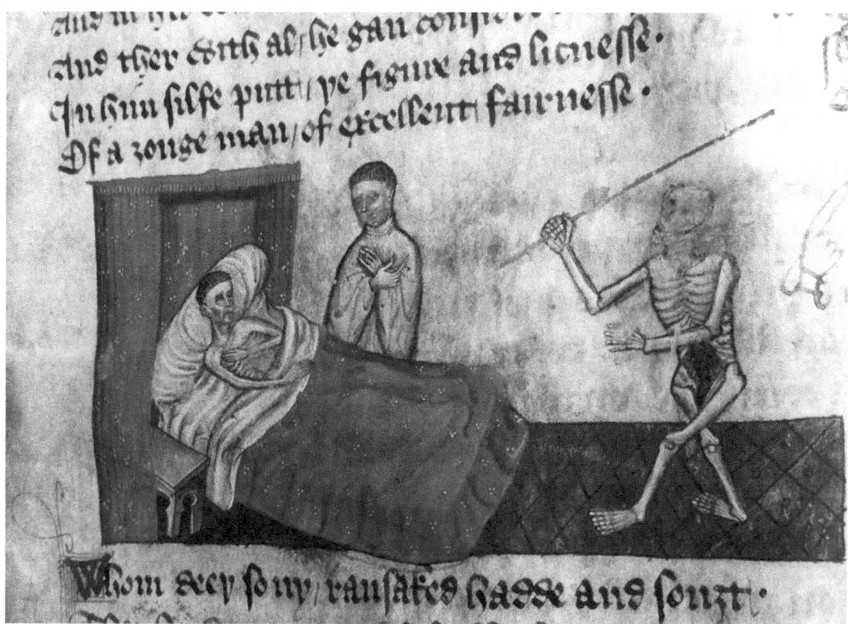

Figure 8. Miniature from Oxford, Bodleian Library, MS Selden supra 53, f. 118r.

image. It mirrors the text as a spur to reflection and contemplation. It serves as a metonym, too, for the character of Thomas in the 'Complaint' and 'Dialogue', who presents his own suffering as a mirror through which others might turn to devotion, penance, and prayer.[52]

In assessing Hoccleve's relationship to Prince Henry in the *Regiment*, Nicholas Perkins compares the poet to 'the long-standing veteran in the *Regiment*, who displays his wounds to Caesar in order to get him to listen and act for him by speaking "On heighte wel that al the peple it herde" (3278).'[53] I would extend this characterization of Hoccleve beyond the *Regiment* to the *Series*, and would underscore the strong religious connotations in the Caesar exemplum to which Perkins refers, and in Hoccleve's own act of baring his wounds. The exemplum in question, in which a soldier strips himself naked in order to bare his wounds before Caesar, bears a strong resemblance to the interaction between Doubting Thomas and Christ in the Gospels.[54] The soldier illustrates the power that wounds have to speak louder than words:

[52] Christina von Nolcken discusses connections between the Suso treatise and Hoccleve's 'Complaint' and 'Dialogue' in, 'O, why ne had y lerned for to die?'

[53] Perkins, *Hoccleve's Regiment*, 193. See also pp. 149–50.

[54] For Doubting Thomas, see John 20:26–30. For an insightful survey of the rendering

'My wowndes beren good witnesse ynow
That I sooth seye, and lest yee leeve it naght,
I shal yow shewe what harm have I caght,
The doute out of your herte for to dryve.'
He nakid him and shewid him as blyve.

Of which Cesar ful sore was ashamed,
And in his herte sorwe made and mone;
He heeld himselven worthy to be blamed.
'My freend,' he seide, 'let me now allone;
Advocat wole I be in my persone
For thee; I am wel holden to do so.'

(3286–96)

The scene recalls Christ allowing Thomas to touch his wounds, and to the same ends: 'the doute out of your herte for to dryve' (cf. 'noli esse incredulus, sed fidelis' (Jn. 20:27)).[55] But the concentration on baring wounds also resonates with Hoccleve's focus on confession throughout the *Regiment* and the *Series*: on the exposing and healing of wounds. I have argued that Hoccleve uses his poetry to magnify specific ecclesiastical wounds: the effects of heresy on the treatment of laypeople and on the unity of the church (in the *Regiment*), and the wounded church's attempt at reform after heresy (in the *Series*). In Chapter 5, we explored these issues in terms of confession and communion, and in the context of the priest's intended role as a spiritual physician, who searches wounds and treats them with the 'ointments' of oil and wine. Hoccleve's self-assigned role is, on one level, as a writer capable of drawing attention to – and dwelling on – given personal, political, and ecclesiastical wounds. In the *Regiment* in particular, we witness the transition from the Eucharist as a relatively 'un-touchable'

of Doubting Thomas throughout the medieval period, see Alexander Murray, *Doubting Thomas in Medieval Exegesis and Art* (Roma: Unione internazionale degli istituti di archeologia, storia e storia dell'Arte in Roma, 2006). See also the popular medieval devotional image of the Man of Sorrows, in which Christ bares his wounds for the viewer: Rubin, *Corpus Christi*, 308–10.

55 These parallels raise the question of whether Hoccleve, like Langland, uses his first name in part as a means of signaling broader Christian connotations: as Langland foregrounds the role of free will in his 'Will', Hoccleve foregrounds the Thomas-like ability to draw attention to, and examine, personal, political, and ecclesiastical wounds. When this aspect of his self-presentation is emphasized in the *Series*, Hoccleve noticeably draws attention to his Christian name, Thomas. On first and last names connoting, respectively, one's spiritual and civil identity, see Middleton, 'Kynde Name', 62–64.

Figure 9. Cover (detail), Derek Pearsall, *The Life of Geoffrey Chaucer* (Oxford: Blackwell, 1992).

matter, to the image of Chaucer – as poet (and *poesie*) incarnate – who invites communion.

Hoccleve's Chaucer remains in use in our contemporary scholarly circles as a means of both evoking Chaucer's life and inviting Chaucerian community – and both functions resonate with Hoccleve's original use of the likeness in the *Regiment*. Hoccleve's image appears on the cover of Derek Pearsall's biography of Chaucer, for instance, evoking the 'life' of the poet (Figure 9). And, for a time, the image presided over the website of the New Chaucer Society, a present-day center of intellectual activity based around the writings of Chaucer (Figure 10). In both instances, the image reflects Chaucerian authority, and – as with its use in MS Harley 4866 – the pointed finger ties the image to the respective context. In the case of the New Chaucer Society website, Chaucer calls attention to – and oversees – the text that describes the society's goals and invites scholars to become members. The image enables the poet to be bodily present – a feat that proves much less revolutionary today than it might have proved to Hoccleve's contemporary readers, but nevertheless patently useful.

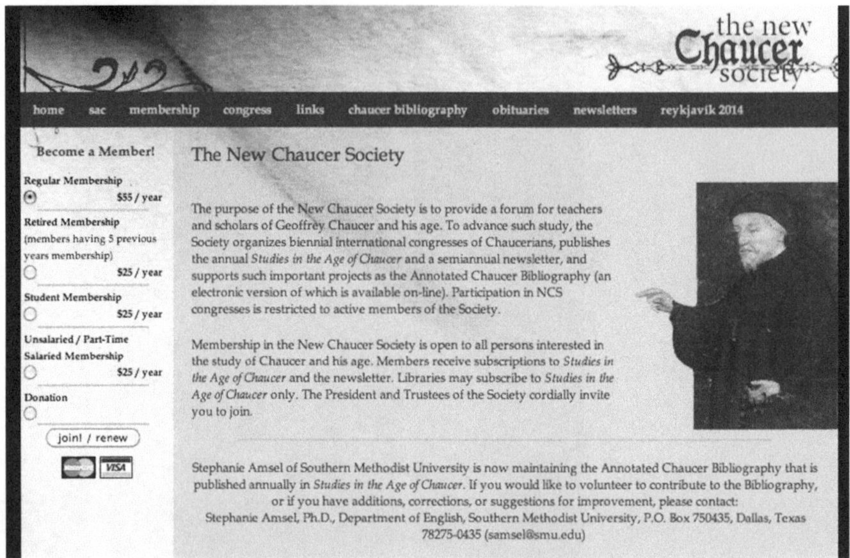

Figure 10. Homepage, New Chaucer Society website. July 2013.

The endurance of this image, and its role as a Chaucerian rather than a Hocclevian artifact, speaks to Hoccleve's unique poetic approach – a mode that mixes intricate and inventive presentation with relative self-effacement, to the extent that Hoccleve's own hand in the production is easily overlooked. It also speaks to the critical reception of Hoccleve: as a poet seen, on one hand, as a minor follower of Chaucer's; and, on the other, as an innovator responsible for what would appear to be major advancements. Since the 1980s Hoccleve's particular feats have been unraveled by critics: John Bowers credited Hoccleve with creating the 'first collected poems in English';[56] Ethan Knapp finds in Hoccleve 'the dramatic first stirrings of vernacular autobiography';[57] Bernard O'Donoghue sees 'the earliest and inchoate exponent of a mixed kind of writing that is found up to the early Elizabethans … drawing on conventional frameworks and apparently real experiences at the same time';[58] and, as we have seen, Derek Pearsall credits Hoccleve with nothing less than the 'invention' of English portraiture. In this study, I have aimed to highlight the ecclesiastical and transnational

[56] Bowers, 'Hoccleve's Huntington Holographs', 27.

[57] Ethan Knapp, 'Bureaucratic Identity and the Construction of the Self in Hoccleve's *Formulary* and *La male regle*', *Speculum* 74.2 (1999): 357–76 (357).

[58] Thomas Hoccleve, *Selected Poems*, ed. Bernard O'Donoghue (Manchester: Fyfield Books, 1982), 15–16.

literary contexts behind these aspects of Hoccleve's work – from the influence of French poetics on Hoccleve, to the religious contexts that align in Hoccleve's self-presentation and in his presentation of Chaucer. Recent Hoccleve criticism has shifted the focus from a Hoccleve who serves as a passive recipient of Chaucerian literary tradition, to one who serves as a more agential actor. The present study aims to advance this critical conversation still further by expanding on the religious and transnational contexts within which we position Hoccleve.

In this study, I have also suggested that we, as scholars, need to adjust the lens through which we see Hoccleve: not as a failed laureate or as a Chaucerian imitator, but rather, on one level, as a religious poet, and as an individual with an evident and enduring interest in ecclesiastical commentary and the devotional applications of vernacular poetry. I have put Hoccleve forward as a virtuous intermediary, as an intercessor, and even as a peacemaker. The political and religious contexts of Hoccleve's poetry are inextricably linked, as are the Chaucerian and devotional aspects of his corpus. Much work remains to be done in exploring these features of Hoccleve's life and work: from the understudied religious verse compiled in the 'collected poems' manuscripts, to the way in which Hoccleve's ostensibly 'secular' and 'religious' poems speak to each other (and through each other), to Hoccleve's position in relation not only to Chaucer, but also to Langland, the Digby poet, the author of *Richard the Redeless* and *Mum and the Sothsegger*, and John the Blind Audelay. Exploring these aspects of Hoccleve's corpus and his self-presentation affords us not only a clearer picture of how Hoccleve operates in English literary tradition, but also a more nuanced understanding of the fifteenth century, its place in the development of English literature, and its role in the grounding of English authorship.

Bibliography

I. Unprinted Primary Sources

Aberyswyth, National Library of Wales, MS Peniarth 392D ('Hengwrt')
Cambridge, Trinity College, MS B.15.17
— Trinity College, MS R.3.2
— University Library, MS Kk. 1.6
— University Library, MS Kk. 5.30
Coventry, City Record Office, MS Accession 325/1
Durham, University Library, MS Cosin V.iii.9
London, British Library, MS Additional 5141
— MS Additional 24062
— MS Arundel 38
— MS Harley 219
— MS Harley 4431
— MS Harley 4605
— MS Harley 4866
— MS Harley 7026
— MS Harley 7334
— MS Royal 15 E VI
— MS Royal 14 E II
— MS Royal 17 D.vi
— MS Royal 17 D.xviii
London, University Library, MS SL V.88 ('Ilchester')
New Haven, Yale University, Beinecke Library, MS 493
Oxford, Bodleian Library, MS Ashmole 59
— MS Bodley 221
— MS Bodley 649
— MS Digby 102
— MS Fairfax 16
— MS Laud misc. 570

— MS Laud misc. 735
— MS Selden supra 53
— MS Tanner 346
Oxford, Christ Church, MS 152
Oxford, Corpus Christi College, MS 198
San Marino, Huntington Library, MS EL 26 C 9 ('Ellesmere')
— MS HM 111
— MS HM 135
— MS HM 744

II. Printed Primary Sources

Andrew, Malcolm, and Ronald Waldron, eds. *The Poems of the Pearl Manuscript: Pearl, Cleanness, Patience, Sir Gawain and the Green Knight*. Exeter Medieval Texts and Studies. Exeter: University of Exeter Press, 2011.

Ashby, George. 'Complaint of a Prisoner in the Fleet 1463'. In *The Kingis Quair and Other Prison Poems*, edited by Linne R. Mooney and Mary-Jo Arn. TEAMS Middle English Texts. Kalamazoo, MI: Medieval Institute Publications, 2005.

—. *George Ashby's Poems*. Edited by Mary Bateson. EETS, E.S. 76. London: Oxford University Press for the Early English Text Society, 1965.

Barr, Helen, ed. *The Digby Poems: A New Edition of the Lyrics*. Exeter Medieval Texts and Studies. Exeter: University of Exeter Press, 2009.

—. *The Piers Plowman Tradition: A Critical Edition of Pierce the Ploughman's Crede, Richard the Redeless, Mum and the Sothsegger, and The Crowned King*. London: Everyman's Library, 1993.

Boethius. *Anicii Manlii Severini Boethii: Philosophiae Consolatio*. Edited by Ludwig Bieler. Turnhout: Brepols, 1957.

—. *Consolation of Philosophy*. Translated by V. Watts. Rev. ed. London: Penguin, 1999.

Boffey, Julia, ed. *Fifteenth-Century English Dream Visions: An Anthology*. Oxford: Oxford University Press, 2003.

Chaucer, Geoffrey. *The Ellesmere Manuscript of Chaucer's Canterbury Tales: A Working Facsimile*. Introduction by Ralph Hanna III. Woodbridge: D.S. Brewer, 1989.

—. *The Riverside Chaucer*. Edited by Larry D. Benson. 3rd ed. Oxford: Oxford University Press, 1987.

—. *Troilus and Criseyde*. Edited by Barry Windeatt. London: Penguin Books, 2003.

Christine de Pizan. *Epistre Othea*. Edited by Gabriella Parussa. Geneva: Librarie Droz, 1999.

—. *Lavision-Christine*. Edited by Sister Mary Louis Towner. Washington, D.C.: Catholic University of America, 1932.

—. *Le Livre du Chemin de Long Estude*. Edited by Robert Püschel. Paris: H. le Soudier, 1887.

—. *The Selected Writings of Christine de Pizan: New Translations, Criticism*. Translated by Renate Blumenfeld-Kosinski and Kevin Brownlee. London: Norton, 1999.

—. *The Vision of Christine de Pizan*. Translated by Glenda McLeod and Charity Cannon Willard. Cambridge: D.S. Brewer, 2012.

Crow, Martin M., and Clair C. Olson, eds. *Chaucer Life Records*. Oxford: Clarendon Press, 1966.

Dante Alighieri. *The Divine Comedy of Dante Alighieri: A Verse Translation*. Translated by Allen Mandelbaum. 3 vols. Berkeley: University of California Press, 1980.

Deschamps, Eustache. *Œuvres complètes de Eustache Deschamps*. Edited by Auguste Queux de Saint-Hilaire and Gaston Raynaud. 11 vols. Paris: Firmin Didot, 1878–1903.

Fenster, Thelma S., and Mary Carpenter Erler, eds. *Poems of Cupid, God of Love: Christine de Pizan's Epistre au dieu d'amours and Dit de la rose, Thomas Hoccleve's The Letter of Cupid: Editions and Translations with George Sewell's Proclamation of Cupid*. Leiden: Brill, 1990.

Forni, Kathleen, ed. *The Chaucerian Apocrypha: A Selection*. TEAMS Middle English Texts Series. Kalamazoo, MI: Medieval Institute Publications, 2005.

Gower, John. *Confessio Amantis*. Edited by Russell A. Peck, and translated by Andrew Galloway. 3 vols. TEAMS Middle English Texts. Kalamazoo, MI: Medieval Institute Publications, 2000–04.

—. *The English Works of John Gower*. Edited by G.C. Macaulay. 2 vols. EETS, E.S. 81–82. London: Oxford University Press for the Early English Text Society, 1957.

—. 'In Praise of Peace'. In Forni, *Chaucerian Apocrypha*.

Hartung, Albert E. *A Manual of the Writings in Middle English 1050–1500*. Vol. 3. Hamden, CT: Connecticut Academy of Arts and Sciences, 1972.

Hawes, Stephen. *The Pastime of Pleasure*. Edited by William Edward Mead. EETS, O.S. 173. London: Oxford University Press for the Early English Text Society, 1928.

Herrtage, Sidney J.H., ed. *The Early English Versions of the Gesta Romanorum*. EETS, E.S. 33. London: Oxford University Press for the Early English Text Society, 1879.

Hilton, Walter. *The Mixed Life*. Edited by S.J. Ogilvie-Thomson. Salzburg: Institut für Anglistik und Amerikanstik, Universität Salzburg, 1986.

Hoccleve, Thomas. *A Facsimile of the Autograph Verse Manuscripts: Henry E. Huntington Library, San Marino (California), MSS HM 111 and*

HM 744, University Library, Durham (England), MS Cosin V. III.9. Edited by J.A. Burrow and A.I. Doyle. EETS, S.S. 19. Oxford: Oxford University Press for the Early English Text Society, 2002.

—. 'The Formulary of Thomas Hoccleve'. Edited by E.J.Y. Bentley. Ph.D. diss., Emory University, 1965.

—. *Hoccleve's Works: The Minor Poems.* Edited by Frederick J. Furnivall and I. Gollancz. EETS, E.S. 61 & 73. London: Oxford University Press for the Early English Text Society, 1892. Revised by J. Mitchell and A.I. Doyle, 1970.

—. *'My Compleinte' and Other Poems.* Edited by Roger Ellis. Exeter Medieval Texts and Studies. Exeter: University of Exeter Press, 2001.

—. *The Regiment of Princes.* Edited by Charles R. Blyth. TEAMS Middle English Texts. Kalamazoo, MI: Medieval Institute Publications, 1999.

—. *Selected Poems.* Edited by Bernard O'Donoghue. Manchester: Fyfield Books, 1982.

—. *Selections from Hoccleve.* Edited by M.C. Seymour. Oxford: Clarendon Press, 1981.

—. *Thomas Hoccleve's Complaint and Dialogue.* Edited by J.A. Burrow. EETS, O.S. 313. Oxford: Oxford University Press for the Early English Text Society, 1999.

Holmstedt, Gustaf, ed. *Speculum Christiani: A Middle English Religious Treatise of the 14th Century.* EETS, O.S. 182. London: Oxford University Press for the Early English Text Society, 1933.

Horner, Patrick J., ed. *A Macaronic Sermon Collection from Late Medieval England: Oxford, MS Bodley 649.* Toronto: Pontifical Institute of Mediaeval Studies, 2006.

John the Blind Audelay. *Poems and Carols, Oxford, Bodleian Library, MS Douce 302.* Edited by Susanna Fein. TEAMS Middle English Texts. Kalamazoo, MI: Medieval Institute Publications, 2009.

Kempe, Margery. *The Book of Margery Kempe.* Edited by Barry Windeatt. Harlow: Longman, 2000.

Langland, William. *Piers Plowman: A New Annotated Edition of the C-text.* Edited by Derek Pearsall. Exeter Medieval Texts and Studies. Exeter: University of Exeter Press, 2008.

—. *The Vision of Piers Plowman: A Complete Edition of the B-Text.* Edited by A.V.C. Schmidt. London: Everyman's Library, 1987.

Lee, Sidney, ed. *Dictionary of National Biography.* London: Smith, Elder, and Co., 1903.

Love, Nicholas. *The Mirror of the Blessed Life of Jesus Christ: A Full Critical Edition, Based on Cambridge University Library Additional MSS 6578 and 6686 with Introduction, Notes, and Glossary.* Edited by Michael G. Sargent. Exeter Medieval Texts and Studies. Exeter: University of Exeter Press, 2005.

Lydgate, John. *A Critical Edition of John Lydgate's 'Life of Our Lady.'* Edited by Joseph A. Lauritis, Ralph A. Klinefelter, and Vernon F. Gallagher. Pittsburgh, PA: Duquesne University Press, 1961.

—. *Fall of Princes*. Edited by Henry Bergen. 4 vols. EETS, E.S. 121–24. London: Oxford University Press for the Early English Text Society, 1924–27.

—. *The Minor Poems of John Lydgate*. Edited by Henry Noble MacCracken. EETS, E.S. 107. Oxford: Oxford University Press for the Early English Text Society, 1967.

McCarthy, Adrian James, ed. *'Book to a Mother': An Edition with Commentary*. Salzburg: Institut fur Anglistik und Amerikanistik, 1981.

McWebb, Christine, ed. *Debating the Roman de la Rose: A Critical Anthology*. London: Routledge, 2007.

Moon, Helen, ed. *Þe Life of Soule: An Edition with Commentary*. Salzburg: Institut für Englische Sprache und Literatur, Universität Salzburg, 1978.

Novotný, Václav. 'Historické spisy Petra z Mladoňovic a jiné zprávy a paměti o M. Janovi Husovi a M. Jeronymovi z Prahy'. In *Fontes rerum Bohemicarum*, vol. 8, 25–120. Prague: Nákl. N.F. Palackého, 1932.

Oesterley, Hermann, ed. *Gesta Romanorum*. 1872. Reprint, Hildesheim: G. Olms, 1963.

O'Mara, Veronica, and Suzanne Paul, eds. *A Repertorium of Middle English Prose Sermons*. Turnhout: Brepols, 2007.

Paston, John. *The Paston Letters and Papers of the Fifteenth Century*. Edited by Norman Davis. 3 vols. EETS, S.S. 22. Oxford: Oxford University Press for the Early English Text Society, 2004.

Porter, S., and I. Roy, eds. *Handbook of British Chronology*. 3rd ed. London: Offices of the Royal Historical Society, 1986.

Schroeder, H.J. *Disciplinary Decrees of the General Councils: Text, Translation and Commentary*. St. Louis: B. Herder, 1937.

Scrope, Stephen. *The Epistle of Othea*. Edited by Curt F. Buhler. EETS, O.S. 264. Oxford: Oxford University Press for the Early English Text Society, 1970.

Spalding, Mary Caroline, ed. *The Middle English Charters of Christ*. Bryn Mawr: Bryn Mawr College, 1914.

Spinka, Matthew, trans. *John Hus at the Council of Constance*. New York: Columbia University Press, 1965.

Statius. *Thebaid; Achilleid*. Edited by D.R. Shackleton Bailey. 2 vols. Cambridge, MA: Harvard University Press, 2003.

Tanner, Norman P., ed. *Decrees of the Ecumenical Councils*. 2 vols. Washington, D.C.: Georgetown University Press, 1990.

Trevisa, John. *On the Properties of Things: John Trevisa's Translation of Bartholomaeus Anglicus De Proprietatibus Rerum: A Critical Text*. Oxford: Clarendon Press, 1975.

Usk, Thomas. *The Testament of Love*. Edited by R. Allen Shoaf. TEAMS Middle English Texts. Kalamazoo, MI: Medieval Institute Publications, 1998.

The Vernon Manuscript: A Facsimile of Bodleian Library, Oxford, MS. Eng. poet. A.1. Introduction by A.I. Doyle. Cambridge: Brewer, 1987.

Walsingham, Thomas. *The Chronica Maiora of Thomas Walsingham, 1376–1422*. Translated by David Preest. Woodbridge: Boydell Press, 2005.

Walton, John. *Boethius: De Consolatione Philosophiae*. Edited by Mark Science. EETS, O.S. 170. London: Oxford University Press for the Early English Text Society, 1927.

Wogan-Browne, Jocelyn, Nicholas Watson, Andrew Taylor, and Ruth Evans, eds. *The Idea of the Vernacular: An Anthology of Middle English Literary Theory, 1280–1520*. Exeter: University of Exeter Press, 1999.

III. Secondary Sources

Adams, Jenny. 'Pawn Takes Knight's Queen: Playing Chess in the *Book of the Duchess*'. *Chaucer Review* 34.2 (1999): 125–38.

—. *Power Play: The Literature and Politics of Chess in the Late Middle Ages*. Philadelphia: University of Pennsylvania Press, 2006.

Adams, Noël, John Cherry, and James Robinson, eds. *Good Impressions: Image and Authority in Medieval Seals*. London: The British Musuem, 2008.

Aers, David, ed. *Culture and History, 1350–1600: Essays on English Communities, Identities and Writing*. London: Harvester Wheatsheaf, 1992.

—. 'The Sacrament of the Altar in *Piers Plowman* and the Late Medieval Church in England'. In Dimmick, Simpson, and Zeeman, *Images, Idolatry, and Iconoclasm*, 63–80.

Akbari, Suzanne Conklin. *Seeing through the Veil: Optical Theory and Medieval Allegory*. London: University of Toronto Press, 2004.

Alsop, James. 'Nicolas Brigham († 1558), scholar, antiquary, and crown servant'. *Sixteenth-Century Journal* 12 (1981): 49–67.

Appleford, Amy. *Learning to Die in London, 1380–1540*. Philadelphia: University of Pennsylvania Press, 2015.

—. 'The Sea Ground and the London Street: The Ascetic Self in Julian of Norwich and Thomas Hoccleve'. *Chaucer Review* 51.1 (2016): 49–67.

Aston, Margaret. 'Lollardy and Sedition, 1381–1431'. *Past and Present* 17 (1960): 1–44.

Aungier, George James. *The History and Antiquities of Syon Monastery, the Parish of Isleworth, and the Chapelry of Hounslow, Compiled from Public Records, Ancient Manuscripts, Etc.* London: Nichols, 1840.

Bagley, J.J. *Margaret of Anjou, Queen of England*. London: H. Jenkins, 1948.

Barr, Helen. *Signes and Sothe: Language in the Piers Plowman Tradition*. Piers Plowman Studies, vol. 10. Cambridge: D.S. Brewer, 1994.
—. *Socioliterary Practice in Late Medieval England*. Oxford: Oxford University Press, 2001.
Beckett, Neil. 'St Bridget, Henry V and Syon Abbey'. In *Studies in St Birgitta and the Brigittine Order*, edited by James Hogg, *Analecta Cartusiana* 35.19 (1993): 125–50.
Beckwith, Sarah. *Christ's Body: Identity, Culture and Society in Late Medieval Writings*. London: Routledge, 1993.
—. 'Ritual, Church and Theatre: Medieval Dramas of the Sacramental Body'. In Aers, *Culture and History*, 65–89.
—. *Signifying God: Social Relation and Symbolic Act in the York Corpus Christi Plays*. Chicago, IL: University of Chicago Press, 2001.
Bedos-Rezak, Brigitte Miriam. 'In Search of a Semiotic Paradigm: The Matter of Sealing in Medieval Thought and Praxis (1050–1400)'. In Adams, Cherry, and Robinson, *Good Impressions*, 1–7.
Bennett, Michael. *Richard II and the Revolution of 1399*. Stroud: Sutton, 1999.
Benson, C. David. *The History of Troy in Middle English Literature: Guido delle Colonne's 'Historia Destructionis Troiae' in Medieval England*. Woodbridge: D.S. Brewer, 1980.
—. 'Prudence, Othea and Lydgate's Death of Hector'. *The American Benedictine Review* 26 (1975): 115–23.
Biernoff, Suzannah. *Sight and Embodiment in the Middle Ages*. Basingstoke: Palgrave, 2002.
Biller, Peter, and Alastair Minnis, eds. *Handling Sin: Confession in the Middle Ages*. York: York Medieval Press, 1998.
Bloom, Harold. *The Anxiety of Influence: A Theory of Poetry*. Oxford: Oxford University Press, 1975.
Boffey, Julia. 'Chaucerian Prisoners: The Context of the *Kingis Quair*'. In *Chaucer and Fifteenth-Century Poetry*, edited by Julia Boffey and Janet Cowen, 84–102. King's College London Medieval Studies 5. London: King's College, Centre for Late Antique and Medieval Studies, 1991.
—. 'Proverbial Chaucer and the Chaucer Canon'. In *Reading from the Margins: Textual Studies, Chaucer, and Medieval Literature*, edited by Seth Lerer, 37–47. San Marino, CA: Huntington Library, 1996.
—. 'Richard Pynson's *Book of Fame* and the *Letter of Dido*'. *Viator* 19 (1988): 339–53.
Boitani, Piero. *Chaucer and the Imaginary World of Fame*. Cambridge: D.S. Brewer, 1984.
—. 'What Dante Meant to Chaucer'. In *Chaucer and the Italian Trecento*, edited by Piero Boitani, 73–90. Cambridge: Cambridge University Press, 1983.

Bolens, Guillemette. 'The Game of Chess in Chaucer's *Book of the Duchess*'. *Chaucer Review* 32.4 (1998): 325–34.

Bornstein, Diane. 'Anti-Feminism in Thomas Hoccleve's Translation of Christine de Pizan's *Epistre au dieu d'amours*'. *ELN* 19 (1982): 7–14.

Bose, Mishtooni. 'Intellectual Life in Fifteenth-Century England'. *NML* 12 (2010): 333–70.

—. 'Reginald Pecock's Vernacular Voice'. In Somerset, Havens, and Pitard, *Lollards and Their Influence*, 217–36.

Bose, Mishtooni, and J. Patrick Hornbeck, eds. *Wycliffite Controversies*. Turnhout: Brepols, 2011.

Bowers, John. *Chaucer and Langland: The Antagonistic Tradition*. Notre Dame: University of Notre Dame Press, 2007.

—. 'Hoccleve's Huntington Holographs: The First "Collected Poems" in English'. *Fifteenth-Century Studies* 15 (1989): 27–51.

—. 'Thomas Hoccleve and the Politics of Tradition'. *Chaucer Review* 36.4 (2002): 352–69.

Brandmüller, Walter. *Das Konzil von Konstanz, 1414–1418*. 2 vols. Paderborn: Schöningh, 1991.

Brown, A.L. 'The Privy Seal Clerks in the Early Fifteenth Century'. In *The Study of Medieval Records: Essays in Honour of Kathleen Major*, edited by D.A. Bullough and R.L. Storey, 260–81. Oxford: Oxford University Press, 1971.

Brownlee, Kevin. 'Literary Genealogy and the Problem of the Father: Christine de Pizan and Dante'. *Journal of Medieval and Renaissance Studies* 23.3 (1993): 365–87.

Bryan, Jennifer. *Looking Inward: Devotional Reading and the Private Self in Late Medieval England*. Philadelphia: University of Pennsylvania Press, 2008.

Burnley, J.D. *Chaucer's Language and the Philosopher's Tradition*. Cambridge: D.S. Brewer, 1979.

Burns, J.H., and Thomas M. Izbicki, eds. *Conciliarism and Papalism*. Cambridge: Cambridge University Press, 1997.

Burrow, John. 'The Audience of *Piers Plowman*'. *Anglia* 75 (1957): 373–84. Reprinted in J.A. Burrow, *Essays on Medieval Literature*. Oxford: Clarendon Press, 1984.

—. *Autobiographical Poetry in the Middle Ages: The Case of Thomas Hoccleve*. Proceedings of the British Academy 68. London: Oxford University Press, 1982.

—. 'Hoccleve and Chaucer'. In *Chaucer Traditions: Studies in Honour of Derek Brewer*, edited by Ruth Morse and Barry Windeatt, 54–61. Cambridge: Cambridge University Press, 1990.

—. 'Hoccleve and the Middle French Poets'. In *The Long Fifteenth Century:*

Essays for Douglas Gray, edited by Helen Cooper and Sally Mapstone, 35–49. Oxford: Clarendon Press, 1997.

—. 'Hoccleve's Complaint and Isidore of Seville Again'. *Speculum* 73 (1998): 424–28.

—. *Langland's Fictions*. Oxford: Clarendon Press, 1993.

—. *Thomas Hoccleve*. Authors of the Middle Ages. Aldershot: Variorum, 1994.

Burrows, Mark S. *Jean Gerson and 'De consolatione theologie' (1418): The Consolation of a Biblical and Reforming Theology for a Disordered Age*. Beiträge zur historischen Theologie 78. Tübingen: Mohr, 1991.

Busby, Keith, and Christopher Kleinhenz, eds. *Medieval Multilingualism: The Francophone World and Its Neighbours*. Medieval Texts and Cultures of Northern Europe 20. Turnhout: Brepols, 2010.

Butterfield, Ardis. *The Familiar Enemy: Chaucer, Language, and Nation in the Hundred Years War*. Oxford: Oxford University Press, 2009.

Calder, Natalie. '"The puple is godes, and not ȝoures": Lancastrian Orthodoxy in the Digby Lyrics'. *RES* (2013): 1–18.

Calin, William. *The French Tradition and the Literature of Medieval England*. Toronto: University of Toronto Press, 1994.

Camille, Michael. 'Before the Gaze: The Internal Senses and Late Medieval Practices of Seeing'. In *Visuality Before and Beyond the Renaissance: Seeing as Others Saw*, edited by Robert S. Nelson, 197–223. Cambridge: Cambridge University Press, 2000.

Campbell, P.G.C. 'Christine de Pisan en Angleterre'. *Revue de littérature comparée* 5 (1925): 659–70.

Carlson, David R. 'Chaucer's Boethius and Thomas Usk's *Testament of Love*: Politics and Love in the Chaucerian Tradition'. In *The Centre and Its Compass: Studies in Medieval Literature in Honor of Professor John Leyerle*, edited by Robert A. Taylor, James F. Burke, Patricia J. Eberle, Ian Lancashire, and Brian S. Merrilees, 29–70. Kalamazoo, MI: Medieval Institute Publications, 1993.

—. 'The Chronology of Lydgate's Chaucer References'. *Chaucer Review* 38.3 (2004): 246–54.

—. 'Thomas Hoccleve and the Chaucer Portrait'. *Huntington Library Quarterly* 54 (1991): 283–300.

Carruthers, Mary. *The Book of Memory: A Study of Memory in Medieval Culture*. 2nd ed. Cambridge: Cambridge University Press, 2008.

—. *The Craft of Thought: Meditation, Rhetoric, and the Making of Images, 400–1200*. Cambridge: Cambridge University Press, 1998.

—. 'Invention, Mnemonics, and Stylistic Ornament in *Psychomachia* and *Pearl*'. In *The Endless Knot: Essays on Old and Middle English in Honor of Marie Borroff*, edited by M. Teresa Tavormina and R.F. Yeager, 201–13. Woodbridge: Boydell and Brewer, 1995.

Carruthers, Mary, and Jan M. Ziolkowski, eds. *The Medieval Craft of Memory: An Anthology of Texts and Pictures*. Philadelphia: University of Pennsylvania Press, 2003.

Catto, Jeremy. 'After Arundel: The Closing or the Opening of the English Mind?' In Gillespie and Ghosh, *After Arundel*, 43–54.

—. 'Religious Change Under Henry V'. In *Henry V: The Practice of Kingship*, edited by G.L. Harriss, 97–115. Stroud: Alan Sutton Publishing, 1993.

Catto, J.I., and Ralph Evans, eds. *The History of the University of Oxford Volume II: Late Medieval Oxford*. Oxford: Clarendon Press, 1984.

Cerquiglini, Jacqueline. 'Le clerc et l'écriture: le *voir dit* de Guillaume de Machaut et la définition du *dit*'. In *Literatur in der Gesellschaft des Spätmittelalters*, edited by Hans Ulrich Gumbrecht, 151–68. Heidelberg: C. Winter, 1980.

Cherry, John. 'Medieval and Post-Medieval Seals'. In *7000 Years of Seals*, edited by Dominique Collon, 124–42. London: British Museum Press, 1997.

Claridge, Gordon, Ruth Pryor, and Gwen Watkins. *Sounds from the Bell Jar: Ten Psychotic Authors*. London: Macmillan, 1990.

Clarke, K.P. *Chaucer and Italian Textuality*. Oxford English Monographs. Oxford: Oxford University Press, 2011.

Cole, Andrew. *Literature and Heresy in the Age of Chaucer*. Cambridge Studies in Medieval Literature 71. Cambridge: Cambridge University Press, 2008.

Coleman, Janet. *Ancient and Medieval Memories: Studies in the Reconstruction of the Past*. Cambridge: Cambridge University Press, 1992.

Coletti, Theresa. '"Paths of Long Study": Reading Chaucer and Christine de Pizan in Tandem'. *SAC* 28 (2006): 1–40.

Connolly, Margaret. *John Shirley: Book Production and the Noble Household in Fifteenth-Century England*. Aldershot: Ashgate, 1998.

Cooper, Helen. 'The Four Last Things in Dante and Chaucer: Ugolino in the House of Rumour'. *NML* 3 (1999): 39–66.

—. *The Structure of the Canterbury Tales*. London: Duckworth, 1983.

Copeland, Rita. *Pedagogy, Intellectuals, and Dissent in the Later Middle Ages: Lollardy and Ideas of Learning*. Cambridge Studies in Medieval Literature 44. Cambridge: Cambridge University Press, 2001.

Critten, Rory G. '"Her Heed They Caste Awry": The Transmission and Reception of Thomas Hoccleve's Personal Poetry'. *RES* 64 (2012): 386–409.

Crowder, C.M.D. 'Constance *Acta* in English Libraries'. In *Das Konzil von Konstanz; Beiträge zu seiner Geschichte und Theologie*, edited by A. Franzen and W. Müller, 477–517. Freiburg: Herder, 1964.

—. *Unity, Heresy, and Reform 1378–1460: The Conciliar Response to the Great Schism*. London: Edward Arnold, 1977.

Dane, Joseph A., and Alexandra Gillespie. 'Back at Chaucer's Tomb – Inscriptions in Two Early Copies of Chaucer's *Workes*'. *Studies in Bibliography* 52 (1999): 89–96.
Denery, Dallas G. *Seeing and Being Seen in the Later Medieval World: Optics, Theology and Religious Life*. Cambridge: Cambridge University Press, 2005.
Dimmick, Jeremy, James Simpson, and Nicolette Zeeman, eds. *Images, Idolatry, and Iconoclasm in Late Medieval England: Textuality and the Visual Image*. Oxford: Oxford University Press, 2002.
Donaldson, E. Talbot. *Piers Plowman: The C-Text and Its Poet*. New Haven, CT: Yale University Press, 1949.
Downes, Stephanie. 'A "Frenche booke called the Pistill of Othea": Christine de Pizan's French in England'. In Wogan-Browne, et al., *Language and Culture in Medieval Britain*, 457–68.
Doyle, A.I. 'Remarks on Surviving Manuscripts of *Piers Plowman*'. In *Medieval English Religious and Ethical Literature: Essays in Honour of G.H. Russell*, edited by Gregory Kratzmann and James Simpson, 35–48. Cambridge: D.S. Brewer, 1986.
Doyle, A.I., and M.B. Parkes, 'Paleographical Introduction'. In *The Canterbury Tales: A Facsimile and Transcription of the Hengwrt Manuscript, with Variants from the Ellesmere Manuscript*, edited by Paul Ruggiers, xix–xlix. Norman, OK: University of Oklahoma Press, 1979.
—. 'The Production of Copies of the *Canterbury Tales* and the *Confessio Amantis* in the Early Fifteenth Century'. In M.B. Parkes, *Scribes, Scripts, and Readers: Studies in the Communication, Presentation and Dissemination of Medieval Texts*, 201–48. London: Hambledon Press, 1991. Originally published in *Medieval Scribes, Manuscripts, and Libraries: Essays Presented to N.R. Ker*, edited by M.B. Parkes and Andrew G. Watson, 163–210. London: Scolar, 1978.
Duffy, Eamon. *The Stripping of the Altars: Traditional Religion in England c.1400–c.1580*. New Haven, CT: Yale University Press, 1992.
Ebin, Lois. *Illuminator, Makar, Vates: Visions of Poetry in the Fifteenth Century*. Lincoln: University of Nebraska Press, 1988.
Ellis, Roger. 'Chaucer, Christine de Pisan, and Hoccleve: The "Letter of Cupid"'. In *Essays on Thomas Hoccleve*, edited by Catherine Batt, 29–54. Westfield Publications in Medieval Studies 10. London: Centre for Medieval and Renaissance Studies, Queen Mary and Westfield College/Brepols, 1996.
Ellis, Steve. 'Chaucer, Dante, and Damnation'. *Chaucer Review* 22.4 (1988): 282–94.
Epstein, Robert. 'Prisoners of Reflection: The Fifteenth-Century Poetry of Exile and Imprisonment'. *Exemplaria* 15 (2003): 159–98.
Fein, Susanna, ed. *My Wyl and My Wrytyng: Essays on John the Blind Audelay*. Kalamazoo, MI: Medieval Institute Publications, 2009.

Fisher, John H. *John Gower: Moral Philosopher and Friend of Chaucer*. London: Methuen, 1965.
Flannery, Mary. *John Lydgate and the Poetics of Fame*. Cambridge: D.S. Brewer, 2012.
Fleming, John V. 'Hoccleve's "Letter of Cupid" and the "Quarrel" over the *Roman de la Rose*'. *MÆ* 40 (1971): 21–40.
Ganim, John M. 'Lydgate, Location, and the Poetics of Exemption'. In *Lydgate Matters: Poetry and Material Culture in the Fifteenth Century*, edited by Lisa H. Cooper and Andrea Denny-Brown, 165–83. New York: Palgrave Macmillan, 2008.
Garrison, Jennifer. 'Failed Signification: *Corpus Christi* and *Corpus Mysticum* in *Piers Plowman*'. *YLS* 23 (2009): 97–123.
Gayk, Shannon. *Image, Text, and Religious Reform in Fifteenth-Century England*. Cambridge Studies in Medieval Literature 81. Cambridge: Cambridge University Press, 2010.
Ghosh, Kantik. 'Bishop Reginald Pecock and the Idea of "Lollardy"'. In *Text and Controversy from Wyclif to Bale: Essays in Honour of Anne Hudson*, edited by Helen Barr and Ann M. Hutchison, 251–65. Turnhout: Brepols, 2005.
—. 'Wyclif, Arundel, and the Long Fifteenth Century'. In Gillespie and Ghosh, *After Arundel*, 545–62.
—. *The Wycliffite Heresy: Authority and the Interpretation of Texts*. Cambridge Studies in Medieval Literature 45. Cambridge: Cambridge University Press, 2002.
Giancarlo, Matthew. *Parliament and Literature in Late Medieval England*. Cambridge, Cambridge University Press, 2007.
Gillespie, Alexandra. *Print Culture and the Medieval Author: Chaucer, Lydgate, and Their Books 1473–1557*. Oxford: Oxford University Press, 2006.
Gillespie, Vincent. 'Authorship'. In Turner, *Handbook of Middle English Studies*, 137–54.
—. 'Chichele's Church: Vernacular Theology in England After Thomas Arundel'. In Gillespie and Ghosh, *After Arundel*, 3–42.
—. '"lukinge in haly bukes": *Lectio* in some Late Medieval Spiritual Miscellanies'. *Analecta Cartusiana* 106 (1984): 1–27.
—. 'Lunatics, Lovers, and Poets: Compact Imaginations in Chaucer and Medieval Literary Theory'. In *Shakespeare: Between the Middle Ages and Modernism: From Translator's Art to Academic Discourse*, edited by Martin Procházka and Jan Cermák, 11–39. Prague: Charles University, 2008.
—. 'Thy Will Be Done: *Piers Plowman* and the *Paternoster*'. In *Late-Medieval Religious Texts and Their Transmission: Essays in Honour of A.I. Doyle*, edited by A.J. Minnis, 95–119. Cambridge: D.S. Brewer, 1994.
—. 'Vernacular Theology'. In *Middle English*, edited by Paul Strohm, 401–20. Oxford: Oxford University Press, 2007.

Gillespie, Vincent, and Kantik Ghosh, eds. *After Arundel: Religious Writing in Fifteenth-Century England.* Medieval Church Studies, vol. 21. Turnhout: Brepols, 2011.

Given-Wilson, Chris. *Chronicles of the Revolution, 1397–1400: The Reign of Richard II.* Manchester: Manchester University Press, 1993.

Green, R.F. *Poets and Princepleasers: Literature and the English Court in the Late Middle Ages.* Toronto: University of Toronto Press, 1980.

Green, R.F., and Ethan Knapp. 'Thomas Hoccleve's Seal'. *MÆ* 77 (2008): 319–21.

Greenwood, Ormerod. *Sir Gawain and the Green Knight.* London: Lion and Unicorn Press, 1956.

Greetham, D.C. 'Self-Referential Artifacts: Hoccleve's Persona as a Literary Device'. *Modern Philology* 86.3 (1989): 242–51.

Gross, Karen Elizabeth. 'Chaucer, Mary Magdalene, and the Consolation of Love'. *Chaucer Review* 41.1 (2006): 1–37.

Hamburger, Jeffrey F., and Anne-Marie Bouche, eds. *The Mind's Eye: Art and Theological Argument in the Middle Ages.* Princeton, NJ: Princeton University Press, 2006.

Hanna III, Ralph. 'Sir Thomas Berkeley and His Patronage'. *Speculum* 64 (1989): 878–916.

—. *William Langland.* Authors of the Middle Ages. Aldershot: Variorum, 1993.

Hardman, Philippa. 'Lydgate's *Life of Our Lady*: A Text in Transition'. *MÆ* 65 (1996): 248–68.

Harvey, Margaret. *England, Rome and the Papacy 1417–1464: The Study of a Relationship.* Manchester: Manchester University Press, 1993.

Harvey, P.D.A., and Andrew McGuinness. *A Guide to British Medieval Seals.* London: The British Library and Public Record Office, 1996.

Hasler, Antony. 'Hoccleve's Unregimented Body'. *Paragraph* 13 (1990): 164–83.

Havely, Nicholas. 'Tearing or Breathing? Dante's Influence on *Filostrato* and *Troilus*'. In *Studies in the Age of Chaucer Proceedings*, no. 1, edited by Paul Strohm and Thomas J. Heffernan, 51–59. Knoxville: New Chaucer Society, 1985.

Hobbins, Daniel. *Authorship and Publicity Before Print: Jean Gerson and the Transformation of Late Medieval Learning.* Philadelphia: University of Pennsylvania Press, 2009.

Hoche, Dominique T. *The Reception of Christine de Pizan's Fais d'Armes in Fifteenth-Century England: Chivalric Self-Fashioning.* New York: Edwin Mellen Press, 2007.

Holsinger, Bruce, ed. *Literary History and the Religious Turn*, *ELN* 44.1 (2006).

Horobin, Simon. 'Adam Pinkhurst and the Copying of British Library, MS Additional 35287 of the B Version of *Piers Plowman*'. *YLS* 23 (2009): 61–83.

—. 'Thomas Hoccleve: Chaucer's First Editor?' *The Chaucer Review* 50.3–4 (2015): 228–50.

Hudson, Anne. 'Epilogue: The Legacy of *Piers Plowman*'. In *A Companion to Piers Plowman*, edited by John A. Alford, 251–66. Los Angeles: University of California Press, 1988.

—. *The Premature Reformation: Wycliffite Texts and Lollard History*. Oxford: Clarendon Press, 1988.

Huot, Sylvia. *From Song to Book: The Poetics of Writing in Old French Lyrics and Lyrical Narrative Poetry* (Ithaca, NY: Cornell University Press, 1987).

—. 'Seduction and Sublimation: Christine de Pizan, Jean de Meun, and Dante'. *Romance Notes* 25.3 (1985): 361–73.

James, Mervyn. 'Ritual, Drama, and Social Body in the Late Medieval English Town'. *Past and Present* 98 (1983): 3–29.

Johnson, Eleanor. *Practicing Literary Theory in the Middle Ages: Ethics and the Mixed Form in Chaucer, Gower, Usk, and Hoccleve*. Chicago, IL: University of Chicago Press, 2013.

Johnson, James D. 'Identifying Chaucer Allusions, 1953–1980: An Annotated Bibliography'. *Chaucer Review* 19 (1984): 62–86.

Justice, Steven, and Kathryn Kerby-Fulton, eds. *Written Work: Langland, Labor, and Authorship*. Philadelphia: University of Pennsylvania Press, 1997.

Kane, George. *Chaucer and Langland: Historical and Textual Approaches*. Los Angeles: University of California Press, 1989.

Kay, Sarah. *Subjectivity in Troubadour Poetry*. Cambridge Studies in French. Cambridge: Cambridge University Press, 1990.

Kerby-Fulton, Kathryn. *Books Under Suspicion: Censorship and Tolerance of Religious Writing in Late Medieval England*. Notre Dame: University of Notre Dame Press, 2006.

—. 'Langland and the Bibliographic Ego'. In Justice and Kerby-Fulton, *Written Work*, 67–143.

Kerby-Fulton, Kathryn, and Steven Justice. 'Langlandian Reading Circles and the Civil Service in London and Dublin, 1380–1427'. *NML* 1 (1997): 59–83.

Killick, Helen. 'Thomas Hoccleve as Poet and Clerk'. Ph.D. diss., University of York, 2010.

Kinch, Ashby. *Imago Mortis: Mediating Images of Death in Late Medieval Culture*. Visualising the Middle Ages. Leiden: Brill, 2013.

Kirk, Elizabeth. 'Langland's Plowman and the Recreation of Fourteenth-Century Religious Metaphor'. *YLS* 2 (1988): 1–21.

Knapp, Ethan. 'Bureaucratic Identity and the Construction of the Self in Hoccleve's *Formulary* and *La male regle*'. *Speculum* 74.2 (1999): 357–76.

—. *The Bureaucratic Muse: Thomas Hoccleve and the Literature of Late Medieval England*. University Park, PA: Pennsylvania State University Press, 2001.

—. 'Poetic Work and Scribal Labor in Hoccleve and Langland'. In *The Middle Ages at Work: Practicing Labor in Late Medieval England*, edited by Kellie Robertson and Michael Uebel, 209–28. New York: Palgrave, 2004.

Kohl, Stephan. 'More than Virtues and Vices: Self-Analysis in Hoccleve's "Autobiographies"'. *Fifteenth-Century Studies* 14 (1988): 115–27.

Kolve, V.A. *The Play Called Corpus Christi*. Stanford, CA: Stanford University Press, 1966.

Krochalis, Jeanne E. 'Hoccleve's Chaucer Portrait'. *Chaucer Review* 21.2 (1986): 234–45.

Kuczynski, Michael. *Prophetic Song: The Psalms as Moral Discourse in Late Medieval England*. Philadelphia: University of Pennsylvania Press, 1995.

Laidlaw, J.C. 'Christine de Pizan, the Earl of Salisbury, and Henry IV'. *French Studies* 36.2 (1982): 129–43.

Langdell, Sebastian J. 'A Study of Speech-Markers in the Early- to Mid-Fifteenth-Century Hocclevian Manuscript Tradition'. *Notes & Queries* 59.3 (2012): 323–31.

—. '"What shal I calle thee? What is thy name?": Thomas Hoccleve and the Making of "Chaucer"'. *New Medieval Literatures* 16 (2016): 250–76.

—. '"What World Is This? How Vndirstande Am I?": A Reappraisal of Poetic Authority in Thomas Hoccleve's *Series*'. *MÆ* 78.2 (2009): 281–99.

Lawes, Richard. 'Psychological Disorder and the Autobiographical Impulse in Julian of Norwich, Margery Kempe and Thomas Hoccleve'. In *Writing Religious Women: Female Spiritual and Textual Practices in Late Medieval England*, edited by Denis Renevey and Christiania Whitehead, 217–43. Cardiff: University of Wales Press, 2000.

Lawton, David. 'Dullness and the Fifteenth Century'. *ELH* 54.5 (1987): 761–99.

—. 'English Literary Voices, 1350–1500'. In *The Cambridge Companion to Medieval England*, edited by Andrew Galloway, 237–58. Cambridge: Cambridge University Press, 2011.

—. 'Lollardy and the "Piers Plowman" Tradition'. *The Modern Language Review* 76.4 (1981): 780–93.

—. 'Public Interiorities'. In Turner, *Handbook of Middle English Studies*, 93–107.

—. 'The Subject of *Piers Plowman*'. *YLS* 1 (1987): 1–30.

—. 'Voice After Arundel'. In Gillespie and Ghosh, *After Arundel*, 133–51.

Leclercq, Jean. *The Love of Learning and the Desire for God: A Study of Monastic Culture*. Translated by Catharine Misrahi. New York: Fordham University Press, 1982.

Lerer, Seth. *Chaucer and His Readers: Imagining the Author in Late-Medieval England*. Princeton, NJ: Princeton University Press, 1993.

Lewis, C.S. *The Allegory of Love*. Oxford: Oxford University Press, 1936.

Lindberg, David C. *Theories of Vision from Al-Kindi to Kepler*. Chicago, IL: University of Chicago Press, 1976.

Little, Katherine C. *Confession and Resistance: Defining the Self in Late Medieval England*. Notre Dame: University of Notre Dame Press, 2006.

Lowes, J.L. 'Chaucer and the *Ovid Moralisé*'. *PMLA* 33 (1918): 302–25.

McDermott, Ryan. '"Beatus qui verba vertit in opera": Langland's Ethical Invention and the Tropological Sense'. *YLS* 24 (2010): 169–204.

McFarlane, K.B. *John Wycliffe and the Beginnings of English Noncomformity*. London: English Universities Press, 1952.

—. *Lancastrian Kings and Lollard Knights*. Oxford: Clarendon Press, 1972.

McGregor, James H. 'The Iconography of Chaucer in Hoccleve's *De Regimine Principum* and in the *Troilus* Frontispiece'. *Chaucer Review* 11.4 (1977): 338–50.

McGuire, Brian Patrick, ed. *A Companion to Jean Gerson*. Leiden: Brill, 2006.

— (as author), *Jean Gerson and the Last Medieval Reformation*. University Park, PA: Pennsylvania State University Press, 2005.

McNiven, Peter. *Heresy and Politics in the Reign of Henry IV: The Burning of John Badby*. Woodbridge: Boydell Press, 1987.

—. 'Prince Henry and the English Political Crisis of 1412'. *History* 65 (1980): 1–16.

Malo, Robyn. 'Penitential Discourse in Thomas Hoccleve's *Series*'. *SAC* 34 (2012): 277–305.

Manly, John M., and Edith Rickert. *The Text of the 'Canterbury Tales'*. 8 vols. Chicago, IL: University of Chicago Press, 1940.

Margolis, Nadia. 'The Human Prison: The Metamorphosis of Misery in the Poetry of Christine de Pizan, Charles d'Orléans, and Francois Villon'. *Fifteenth Century Studies* 1 (1978): 185–92.

Mathew, Gervase. *The Court of Richard II*. London: John Murray, 1968.

Meale, Carol M. '"... alle the bokes that I haue of latyn, englisch, and frensch": Laywomen and Their Books in Late Medieval England'. In *Women and Literature in Britain, 1150–1500*, edited by Carol M. Meale, 128–58. 2nd ed. Cambridge: Cambridge University Press, 1997.

Medcalf, Stephen. 'Inner and Outer'. In *The Later Middle Ages*, edited by Stephen Medcalf, 108–71. The Context of English Literature 4. London: Methuen, 1981.

Meech, S.B. 'Chaucer and the *Ovid Moralisé*: A Further Study'. *PMLA* 45 (1931): 182–204.

Meyer-Lee, Robert. 'The Emergence of the Literary in John Lydgate's *Life of Our Lady*'. *Journal of English and Germanic Philology* 109.3 (2010): 322–48.

—. 'Laureates and Beggars in Fifteenth-Century English Poetry: The Case of George Ashby'. *Speculum* 79.3 (2004): 688–726.

—. *Poets and Power from Chaucer to Wyatt*. Cambridge Studies in Medieval Literature 61. Cambridge: Cambridge University Press, 2007.

Middleton, Anne. 'Acts of Vagrancy: The C Version "Autobiography" and the Statute of 1388'. In Justice and Kerby-Fulton, *Written Work*, 208–317.

—. 'The Audience and Public of *Piers Plowman*'. In *Middle English Poetry and Its Literary Background*, edited by David Lawton, 101–23. Cambridge: D.S. Brewer, 1982.

—. 'Chaucer's "New Men" and the Good of Literature in the *Canterbury Tales*'. In *Chaucer, Langland, and Fourteenth-Century Literary History*, edited by Steven Justice, 27–60. Farnham: Ashgate Variorum, 2013. Originally published in *Literature and Society*, edited by Edward W. Said, 15–56. Baltimore, MD: Johns Hopkins University Press, 1980.

—. 'William Langland's "Kynde Name": Authorial Signature and Social Identity in Late Fourteenth-Century England'. In Patterson, *Literary Practice and Social Change*, 15–82.

Minnis, Alastair J. *Magister Amoris: The Roman de la Rose and Vernacular Hermeneutics*. Oxford: Oxford University Press, 2001.

—. 'A Note on Chaucer and the *Ovid Moralisé*'. *MÆ* 48 (1979): 254–57.

Mitchell, Jerome. *Thomas Hoccleve: A Study in Early Fifteenth-Century English Poetic*. Urbana: University of Illinois Press, 1968.

Mooney, Linne R. 'Chaucer's Scribe'. *Speculum* 81 (2006): 97–138.

—. 'A Holograph Copy of Thomas Hoccleve's *Regiment of Princes*'. *SAC* 33 (2011): 263–96.

—. 'Some New Light on Thomas Hoccleve'. *SAC* 29 (2007): 293–340.

Mooney, Linne R., and Estelle Stubbs. *Scribes and the City: London Guildhall Clerks and the Dissemination of Middle English Literature, 1375–1425*. Woodbridge: York Medieval Press; Boydell Press, 2013.

Mundy, John Hine, and Kennerly M. Woody, eds. *The Council of Constance: The Unification of the Church*. Translated by Louise R. Loomis. Records of Civilization: Sources and Studies 63. New York: Columbia University Press, 1961.

Murray, Alexander. *Doubting Thomas in Medieval Exegesis and Art*. Rome: Unione internazionale degli istituti di archeologia, storia e storia dell'Arte in Roma, 2006.

Nissé, Ruth. '"Our fadres olde and modres": Gender, Heresy, and Hoccleve's Literary Politics'. *SAC* 21 (1999): 275–99.

Nolan, Barbara, and David Farley-Hills. 'The Authorship of *Pearl*: Two Notes'. *RES* 22 (1971): 295–302.

Nuttall, Jenni. *The Creation of Lancastrian Kingship: Literature, Language and Politics in Late Medieval England*. Cambridge Studies in Medieval Literature 67. Cambridge: Cambridge University Press, 2007.

—. 'Thomas Hoccleve's Poems for Henry V: Anti-Occasional Verse and Ecclesiastical Reform'. In *Oxford Handbooks Online*. Oxford: Oxford University Press, 2015. 1–23.

—. *Troilus and Criseyde: A Reader's Guide*. Cambridge: Cambridge University Press, 2012.

O'Donoghue, J.B. 'Medieval Moralizations and Literary Virtues'. In *Sentences for Alan Ward*, edited by D.M. Reeks, 3–20. Southampton: Bosphoros Books, 1988.

Otway-Ruthven, J. *The King's Secretary and the Signet Office in the XV Century*. Cambridge: Cambridge University Press, 1939.

Parkes, Malcolm. 'Patterns of Scribal Activity and Revisions of the Text in Early Copies of Works by John Gower'. In *New Science Out of Old Books: Studies in Manuscripts and Early Printed Books in Honour of A.I. Doyle*, edited by Richard Beadle and A.J. Piper, 81–121. Aldershot: Scolar Press, 1995.

Patterson, Lee. 'Beinecke MS 493 and the Survival of Hoccleve's *Series*'. In *Old Books, New Learning: Essays on Medieval and Renaissance Books at Yale*, edited by Robert G. Babcock and Lee Patterson, 80–92. New Haven, CT: Beinecke Rare Book and Manuscript Library, 2001.

—. 'Court Politics and the Invention of Literature: The Case of Sir John Clanvowe'. In Aers, *Culture and History*, 7–41.

—. ed. *Literary Practice and Social Change in Britain, 1380–1530*. Berkeley: University of California Press, 1990.

—. '"What Is Me?": Self and Society in the Poetry of Thomas Hoccleve'. *SAC* 23 (2001): 437–70.

—. '"What Man Artow?": Authorial Self-Definition in *The Tale of Sir Thopas* and *The Tale of Melibee*'. *SAC* 11 (1989): 117–75.

Pearsall, Derek. 'Chaucer's Tomb: The Politics of Reburial'. *MÆ* 64 (1995): 51–73.

—. '*Crowned King*: War and Peace in 1415'. In *The Lancastrian Court: Proceedings of the 2001 Harlaxton Symposium*, edited by Jenny Stratford, 163–72. Harlaxton Medieval Studies 13. Donington: Tyas, 2003.

—. 'The English Chaucerians'. In *Chaucer and Chaucerians: Critical Studies in Middle English Literature*, edited by D.S. Brewer, 201–39. London: Nelson, 1966.

—. 'Hoccleve's *Regement of Princes*: The Poetics of Royal Self-Representation'. *Speculum* 69.2 (1994): 386–410.

—. *John Lydgate*. Poets of the Later Middle Ages. London: Routledge and Kegan Paul, 1970.

—. *John Lydgate (1371–1449): A Bio-Bibliography*. Victoria, B.C.: University of Victoria, 1997.

—. *The Life of Geoffrey Chaucer: A Critical Biography*. Oxford: Blackwell, 1992.

Peck, Russell A. *Kingship and Common Profit in Gower's Confessio Amantis*. Carbondale: Southern Illinois University Press, 1978.

Perkins, Nicholas. 'Haunted Hoccleve? *The Regiment of Princes*, the Troilean Intertext, and Conversations with the Dead'. *Chaucer Review* 43.2 (2008): 103–39.

—. *Hoccleve's Regiment of Princes: Counsel and Constraint*. Cambridge: D.S. Brewer, 2001.

Peterson, Clifford, and Edward Wilson, 'Hoccleve, the Old Hall Manuscript, Cotton Nero A.x., and the Pearl-poet'. *RES* 28 (1977): 49–56.

Pollard, A.J. *The Wars of the Roses*. 2nd ed. British History in Perspective. Basingstoke: Palgrave, 2001.

Reeves, A. Compton, 'The World of Thomas Hoccleve'. *Fifteenth Century Studies* 2 (1979): 187–99.

Rice, Nicole R. *Lay Piety and Religious Discipline in Middle English Literature*. Cambridge Studies in Medieval Literature 73. Cambridge: Cambridge University Press, 2008.

Richards, Earl Jeffrey. 'Christine de Pizan and Dante: A Reexamination'. *Archiv für das Studium der neueren Sprachen und Literaturen* 222 (1985): 100–11.

Richardson, Malcolm. 'The Earliest Known Owners of *Canterbury Tales* MSS and Chaucer's Secondary Audience'. *Chaucer Review* 25 (1990): 17–32.

Rigg, A.G. 'Hoccleve's Complaint and Isidore of Seville'. *Speculum* 45 (1970): 564–74.

Ringbom, Sixten. *Icon to Narrative: The Rise of the Dramatic Close-Up in Fifteenth-Century Devotional Painting*. Doornspijk: Davaco, 1984.

Roberts, Jane. 'On giving Scribe B a name and a clutch of London manuscripts from *c.*1400'. *MÆ* 80 (2011): 247–70.

Rowland, Beryl. 'Chaucer's Duchess and Chess'. *Florilegium* 16 (1999): 41–59.

Rozenski, Steven. '"Your Ensaumple and Your Mirour": Hoccleve's Amplification of the Imagery and Intimacy of Henry Suso's *Ars Moriendi*'. *Parergon* 25.2 (2008): 1–16.

Rubin, Miri. *Corpus Christi: The Eucharist in Late Medieval Culture*. Cambridge: Cambridge University Press, 1991.

—. 'The Eucharist and the Construction of Medieval Identities'. In Aers, *Culture and History*, 43–63.

Russell, Alexander. 'Conciliarism and Heresy in England'. In Gillespie and Ghosh, *After Arundel*, 155–65.

Russell, Frederick H. *The Just War in the Middle Ages*. Cambridge: Cambridge University Press, 1975.

Salter, Elisabeth. 'Chaucer and Internationalism'. *SAC* 2 (1980): 71–79.

Sanok, Catherine. 'Saints' Lives and the Literary After Arundel'. In Gillespie and Ghosh, *After Arundel*, 469–86.

Scanlon, Larry. 'The King's Two Voices: Narrative and Power in Hoccleve's *Regement of Princes*'. In Patterson, *Literary Practice and Social Change*, 216–47.

Scase, Wendy. 'Reginald Pecock'. In *Authors of the Middle Ages: English Writers of the Late Middle Ages, Volume III*, edited by M.C. Seymour. Aldershot: Variorum, 1996.

Scattergood, John. 'The Date and Composition of George Ashby's Poems'. *Leeds Studies in English* 21 (1990): 167–76.

—. 'George Ashby's Prisoner's Reflections and the Virtue of Patience'. *Nottingham Medieval Studies* 37 (1993): 102–09.

Schlauch, Margaret. 'Chaucer's Doctrine of Kings and Tyrants'. *Speculum* 20.2 (1945): 133–56.

Schless, Howard. *Chaucer and Dante: A Revaluation*. Norman, OK: Pilgrim Books, 1984.

Scott, Kathleen. 'An Hours and Psalter by Two Ellesmere Illuminators'. In *The Ellesmere Chaucer: Essays in Interpretation*, edited by Martin Stevens and Daniel Woodward, 87–119. San Marino, CA: Huntington Library, 1997.

—. *Later Gothic Manuscripts, 1390–1490*. 2 vols. London: H. Miller, 1996.

Shoaf, R. Allen. 'Dante's *Commedia* and Chaucer's Theory of Mediation: A Preliminary Sketch'. In *New Perspectives in Chaucer Criticism*, edited by Donald M. Rose, 83–103. Norman, OK: Pilgrims Books, 1981.

Simpson, James. 'Chaucer's Presence and Absence 1400–1550'. In *A Chaucer Companion*, edited by Jill Mann and Piero Boitani, 251–69. 2nd ed. Cambridge: Cambridge University Press, 2003.

—. 'The Constraints of Satire in "Piers Plowman" and "Mum and the Sothsegger"'. In *Langland, The Mystics, and the Medieval English Religious Tradition: Essays in Honour of S.S. Hussey*, edited by Helen Phillips, 11–30. Cambridge: D.S. Brewer, 1990.

—. 'Madness and Texts: Hoccleve's *Series*'. In *Chaucer and Fifteenth-Century Poetry*, edited by Julia Boffey and Janet Cowen, 15–29. King's College London: Centre for Late Antique and Medieval Studies, 1991.

—. 'Orthodoxy's Image Trouble in and after Arundel's Constitutions'. In Gillespie and Ghosh, *After Arundel*, 91–113.

—. *Piers Plowman: An Introduction*. 2nd rev. ed. Exeter Medieval Texts and Studies. Exeter: University of Exeter Press, 2007.

—. *Reform and Cultural Revolution: The Oxford English Literary History*, II: *1350–1547*. Oxford: Oxford University Press, 2002.

—. 'Saving Satire After Arundel's *Constitutions*: John Audelay's "Marcol and Solomon"'. In *Text and Controversy from Wyclif to Bale: Essays in Honour of Anne Hudson*, edited by Helen Barr and Ann M. Hutchison, 387–404. Turnhout: Brepols, 2005.

—. *Under the Hammer: Iconoclasm in the Anglo-American Tradition*. Clarendon Lectures in English. Oxford: Oxford University Press, 2010.

Somerset, Fiona. 'Censorship'. In *The Production of Books in England 1350–1500*, edited by Alexandra Gillespie and Daniel Wakelin, 239–58. Cambridge: Cambridge University Press, 2011.

Somerset, Fiona, Jill C. Havens, and Derrick Pitard, eds. *Lollards and Their Influence in Late Medieval England*. Woodbridge: The Boydell Press, 2003.

Spearing, A.C. *Medieval Autographies: The 'I' of the Text*. Notre Dame: University of Notre Dame Press, 2012.

—. *Medieval to Renaissance in English Poetry*. Cambridge: Cambridge University Press, 1985.

—. 'Renaissance Chaucer and Father Chaucer'. *English: The Journal of the English Association* 34 (1985): 1–38.

Spencer, Helen Leith. *English Preaching in the Late Middle Ages*. Oxford: Clarendon Press, 1993.

Spurgeon, Caroline. *Five Hundred Years of Chaucer Criticism and Allusion, 1357–1900*. 3 vols. Cambridge: Cambridge University Press, 1925.

Staley, Lynn. 'Gower, Richard II, Henry of Derby, and the Business of Making Culture'. *Speculum* 75 (2000): 68–96.

Steinberg, Glenn A. 'Chaucer in the Field of Cultural Production: Humanism, Dante, and the "House of Fame"'. *Chaucer Review* 35.2 (2000): 182–203.

Steiner, Emily. *Documentary Culture and the Making of Medieval English Literature*. Cambridge Studies in Medieval Literature 50. Cambridge: Cambridge University Press, 2003.

Stokes, Charity Scott. 'Sir John Oldcastle, the Office of the Privy Seal, and Thomas Hoccleve's "Remonstrance Against Oldcastle" of 1415'. *Anglia* 118.4 (2001): 556–70.

Strohm, Paul. *England's Empty Throne: Usurpation and the Language of Legitimation, 1399–1422*. New Haven, CT: Yale University Press, 1998.

—. *Hochon's Arrow: The Social Imagination of Fourteenth-Century Texts*. Princeton, NJ: Princeton University Press, 1992.

—. 'Politics and Poetics: Usk and Chaucer in the 1380s'. In Patterson, *Literary Practice and Social Change*, 83–112.

—. *Social Chaucer*. Cambridge, MA: Harvard University Press, 1994.

Summit, Jennifer. *Lost Property: The Woman Writer and English Literary History, 1380–1589*. Chicago, IL: University of Chicago Press, 2000.

Sumption, Jonathan. *The Hundred Years War*. 3 vols. 2nd rev. ed. Philadelphia: University of Pennsylvania Press, 1999.

Swanson, Robert N. *Church and Society in Late Medieval England*. Oxford: Blackwell, 1989.

Sweet, W.H.E. 'Lydgate's Retraction and "his resorte to his religyoun"'. In Gillespie and Ghosh, *After Arundel*, 343–59.

Tachau, Katherine H. *Vision and Certitude in the Age of Ockham: Optics, Epistemology and the Foundations of Semantics 1250–1345*. Leiden: Brill, 1988.

Tarantino, Elisabetta. 'The Dante Anecdote in Gower's *Confessio Amantis*, Book VII'. *Chaucer Review* 39.4 (2005): 420–35.

Taylor, Karla. 'A Text and Its Afterlife: Dante and Chaucer'. *Comparative Literature* 35.1 (1983): 1–20.

Tolmie, Sarah. 'The *Priue Scilence* of Thomas Hoccleve'. *SAC* 22 (2000): 281–309.

—. 'The Professional: Thomas Hoccleve'. *SAC* 29 (2007): 341–73.

Torti, Anna. 'Hoccleve's Attitude Towards Women: "I shoop me do my peyne and diligence / To wynne hir loue by obedience"'. In *A Wyf Ther Was: Essays in Honour of Paule Mertens-Fonck*, edited by Juliette Dor, 264–74. Liège: Université de Liège, 1992.

Tout, T.F. 'The English Civil Service in the Fourteenth Century'. In *Collected Papers*, vol. 3, 191–221. Manchester: Manchester University Press, 1934.

Turner, Marion. '"Certaynly His Noble Sayenges Can I Not Amende": Thomas Usk and *Troilus and Criseyde*'. *Chaucer Review* 37 (2002): 26–39.

—. ed. *A Handbook of Middle English Studies*. Chichester: Wiley-Blackwell, 2013.

Turville-Petre, Thorlac, and Edward Wilson. 'Hoccleve, "Maistir Massy" and the Pearl Poet: Two Notes'. *RES* 26 (1975): 129–43.

Tuve, Rosemond. *Allegorical Imagery: Some Mediaeval Books and Their Posterity*. Princeton, NJ: Princeton University Press, 1966.

Van Dussen, Michael. *From England to Bohemia: Heresy and Communication in the Later Middle Ages*. Cambridge: Cambridge University Press, 2012.

Vickers, K.H. *Humphrey Duke of Gloucester*. London: Archibald Constable, 1907.

Von Nolcken, Christina. '"O, why ne had y lerned for to dye?": *Lerne for to Dye* and the Author's Death in Thomas Hoccleve's *Series*'. *Essays in Medieval Studies* 10 (1993): 29–43.

Wallace, David. *Chaucer and the Early Writings of Boccaccio*. Chaucer Studies 12. Cambridge: D.S. Brewer, 1985.

—. *Chaucerian Polity: Absolutist Lineages and Associational Forms in England and Italy*. Stanford, CA: Stanford University Press, 1997.

—. *Premodern Places: Calais to Surinam, Chaucer to Aphra Behn*. Oxford: Wiley-Blackwell, 2006.

Wathey, A.B. 'Music in the Royal and Noble Households in Late Medieval England: Studies of Source and Patronage'. Ph.D. diss., University of Oxford, 1987.

Watson, Nicholas. 'Censorship and Cultural Change in Late Medieval England: Vernacular Theology, the Oxford Translation Debate and Arundel's Constitutions of 1409'. *Speculum* 70 (1995): 822–64.

—. 'Chaucer's Public Christianity'. *Religion and Literature* 37.2 (2005): 99–114.

—. 'Cultural Changes'. *ELH* 44.1 (2006): 127–37.

—. '*Piers Plowman*, Pastoral Theology, and Spiritual Perfectionism: Hawkyn's Coat and Patience's *Pater Noster*'. *YLS* 21 (2007): 83–118.

Watt, David. *The Making of Thomas Hoccleve's Series*. Exeter Medieval Texts and Studies. Liverpool: University of Liverpool Press, 2013.

—. 'The Thoughtful Maladie: Melancholy and Society in Thomas Hoccleve's *Series*'. Ph.D. diss., University of Oxford, 2004.

Watt, Diane. 'Literary Genealogy, Virile Rhetoric, and John Gower's *Confessio Amantis*'. *Philological Quarterly* 78.4 (1999): 389–415.

Wedgwood, Josiah C., and Anne D. Holt. *History of Parliament, 1: Biographies of the Members of the Commons House, 1439–1509*. London: H.M. Stationery Office, 1936.

Weiske, Brigitte. *Gesta Romanorum*. 2 vols. Tübingen: M. Niemeyer, 1992.

Wenzel, Siegfried. *Latin Sermon Collections from Later Medieval England: Orthodox Preaching in the Age of Wyclif.* Cambridge: Cambridge University Press, 2005.

Wetherbee, Winthrop. *Chaucer and the Poets: An Essay on Troilus and Criseyde*. Ithaca, NY: Cornell University Press, 1984.

—. 'The Descent from Bliss: *Troilus*, III, 1310–1582'. In *Chaucer's 'Troilus': Essays in Criticism*, edited by Stephen A. Barney, 297–317. London: Scolar Press, 1980.

Wheeler, Bonnie. 'Dante, Chaucer, and the Ending of *Troilus and Criseyde*'. *Philological Quarterly* 61 (1982): 105–23.

Willard, Charity Cannon. *Christine de Pizan: Her Life and Works*. New York: Persea Books, 1984.

Wimsatt, James I. *Chaucer and His French Contemporaries: Natural Music in the Fourteenth Century*. Toronto: University of Toronto Press, 1991.

—. *Chaucer and the French Love Poets*. Chapel Hill: University of North Carolina Press, 1968.

Windeatt, Barry. *Oxford Guides to Chaucer: Troilus and Criseyde*. Oxford: Clarendon Press, 1992.

Winstead, Karen A. '"I Am Al Othir to Yow Than Yee Weene": Hoccleve, Women, and the *Series*'. *Philological Quarterly* 72.2 (1993): 143–55.

Wogan-Browne, Jocelyn, Carolyn Colette, Maryanne Kowaleski, Linne Mooney, Ad Putter, and David Trotter, eds. *Language and Culture in Medieval Britain: The French of England c. 1100–c.1500*. York: York Medieval Press, 2009.

Yeager, R.F. 'Chaucer's "To His Purse": Begging, of Begging Off?' *Viator* 36 (2005): 373–414.

—. 'Death Is a Lady: *The Regiment of Princes* as Gendered Political Commentary'. *SAC* 26 (2004): 147–93.

—. '*Pax Poetica*: On the Pacifism of Chaucer and Gower'. *SAC* 9 (1987): 97–121.

Yeager, Stephen. 'Lollardy in *Mum and the Sothsegger*: A Reconsideration'. *YLS* 25 (2011): 161–88.

Zink, Michael. *The Invention of Literary Subjectivity*. Translated by David Sices. Baltimore, MD: Johns Hopkins University Press, 1999.

Index